The Milltown Boys Revisited

The Milltown Boys Revisited

Howard Williamson

Oxford • New York

English edition
First published in 2004 by
Berg
Editorial offices:
First Floor, Angel Court, 81 St Clements Street, Oxford OX4 1AW, UK
175 Fifth Avenue, New York, NY 10010, USA

Berg is the imprint of Oxford International Publishers Ltd.

Library of Congress Cataloging-in-Publication Data
A catalogue record for this book is available from the Library of Congress.

British Library Cataloguing-in-Publication Data
A catalogue record for this book is available from the British Library.

ISBN 1 85973 819 2 (hardback)
          1 85973 824 9 (paperback)

Typeset by Avocet Typeset, Chilton, Aylesbury, Bucks
Printed in the United Kingdom by Biddles Ltd, King's Lynn

www.bergpublishers.com

Contents

List of Figures and Tables

Figures

Tables

Acknowledgements

It has been more than five years since I first thought about undertaking this follow-up study of the Milltown Boys. That is about the same length of time I 'hung around' with them when I first knew them. Since the year (2000) when I grittily pursued the fieldwork I have worked on the interview data in a myriad of ways. Rarely have I got bored with it; in fact, I remain excited by the rich vein of data that can be mined in so many ways.

My core and lasting debt is to the Boys themselves. I hope I have treated them with a sympathetic, though critical, eye. Life has not dealt many of them a fair hand, but they have handled it with the best efforts they can give, even though these have sometimes been inconsiderate and self-centred. I hope the Boys will feel I have conveyed their essential humanity, although I have necessarily had to consider their faults and frailties, for they may be classified by a wider world as delinquents, druggies and dropouts, but I have also known them as friends, fathers and family men. I want the wider world to see them in that light too.

Thanks also to my colleagues in the School of Social Sciences at Cardiff University who, in many different ways, gave me support and feedback when I was doing the fieldwork and starting to write it up. The Institute for Psychology at the University of Copenhagen gave me a critical space to get on with my first sift of the interview data; without those six months in Denmark, I would probably never have completed even my first trawl of the material. A special thanks to my friend and colleague Tom Hall for his willingness to read through everything and give me a valued critique. Tom and I have collaborated a great deal in teaching and research. His support has been both psychological and academic, although I doubt he is aware of how much it has meant to me.

Finally I would like to thank my publisher Berg and in particular Kathryn Earle for showing confidence in the draft material I sent – sufficient confidence to provide me with a book contract. This was the catalyst I needed to whittle down the huge volume of material I had produced into a manageable and, I hope, readable text. I am reasonably optimistic that this book will persuade its readers that those on the margins of society must be considered not only by the public issues they present but also, simultaneously, through the private troubles that they seek to tackle and, perhaps surprisingly, often manage to overcome.

Howard Williamson

Scattered Biographies, Developing Themes – Reading the Text

Right now the Milltown Boys are strangers to you. In contrast, I know them well. I have known them for three decades. During that period they were the subjects of two moments of intensive study – the first between 1975 and 1978 when I conducted a participant observation with them, the second in the year 2000 when I carried out extended interviews with thirty of them. Prior to the first study I had lived close by them for a couple of years and had become informally acquainted with them. After the completion of that first study I gradually lost contact with most of them; indeed, with all but Danny and, to a lesser extent, Marty. They were my first port of call when I thought about 'revisiting' the Boys some twenty-five years after I had first studied them.

The individual biographies of the Boys are scattered through this book because the book is guided by the public and private themes of human lives: employment, crime, relationships, health, housing and so on. As a result, it will take some time for the character of individuals to come through. Some will emerge more rapidly and forcefully than others but even with the most prominent among them, patience is required if you are to get to know them. One way of doing so, I suggest, is to give specific attention to three or four of the Boys, one from each of the columns in the list below. It will, in time, become apparent why the Boys have been grouped in this way. The characters you have picked to 'pursue' in more depth will, through their own accounts and explanations of the pathways they have taken in their lives, provide you with a strong feel for the divergence of those pathways.

The Boys could easily appear to be a disparate group of men, spread across the socio-economic spectrum and differing dramatically in their approaches to family life and the raising of their children. But what must not be forgotten are their common roots and the bonds cemented in their youth that have often persisted to the present day. Indeed, the divergence of many aspects of their lives can be contrasted with their continuing social and spatial proximity, though there have been many twists and turns along the way. The development and divergence of various themes within the collective life course of the Boys is informed by the increasing convergence of what starts initially as the fragmented and piecemeal biographies of individual lives. But, by the end of this book, you too will have become acquainted with the Milltown Boys and the ways in which their different public and private experiences have given shape to the particular directions their lives have taken.

Ted	Richard	Gary	Spaceman
Danny	Denny	Tony	Marty
Matt	Ryan	Shaun	Eddie
Paul	Alex	Jamie	Pete
Mack	Mark	Gordon	Nutter
Nathan	Jerry	Kelvin	
Vic	Derek		
	Colin		
	Nick		
	Trevor		
	Tommy		
	Mal		

Dedication

Geoff Mungham and Geoff Pearson

To the memory of Geoff Mungham, who died suddenly and unexpectedly in November 2003 while teaching in the Netherlands. Geoff taught me as an undergraduate and was the joint supervisor for my PhD. He and another Geoff, Professor Geoff Pearson – through their teaching and encouragement – influenced my own life-course trajectory, for they inspired my interest in youth culture, and in crime and delinquency. They were the editors of *Working Class Youth Culture* (Routledge & Kegan Paul 1976).

I remember sitting in the university coffee bar with Geoff Pearson in 1976, when he drew my attention to *Cultural Studies 7/8*, published initially by the Centre for Contemporary Cultural Studies, and later, as *Resistance through Rituals*, by Hutchinson (1978). Geoff Mungham encouraged me to do postgraduate work on the Milltown Boys, though I will also remember him for his great parties and for a sharp left foot in our kickarounds most Sundays in Roath Park.

Introduction

In 1977 some of the Boys were on a job creation programme, and as part of their 'social and life skills' training, they produced a tourist guide for the estate, *Scammy Tours* – Scam being one of the Boys (though he is not included in this study). Before computers and desktop printing, they collated a range of black and white photographs they had taken of the exotic wildlife (stray dogs), night-time eating houses (chip shops) and unusual attractions (ripped-open bin bags and burnt-out cars). Crudely stapled together, those few badly photocopied pages captured some of the contemporary realities of Milltown.

At the turn of the nineteenth century, the area comprised a couple of farms and a hamlet with a popuation of 183. It rose to 360 by 1861 following the building of a railway and the establishment of a station in Milltown. In the 1870s, the first resident police constable was appointed. Following the First World War and in a climate of building 'homes fit for heroes', the neighbouring city expanded its boundaries and, in February 1920, purchased two farms for the princely sum of £72,000. By 1924, some roads had been completed, though they had yet to be named.

Milltown is now routinely depicted as one of the largest council estates in Europe. With a population of over 30,000, it has all the characteristics of a 'worst estate' or 'poor neighbourhood': high unemployment, high rates of teenage pregnancy, high take-up of free school meals, high numbers of lone-parent families, low proportion of car-ownership, low levels of owner-occupation, and so on. It is regularly vilified in the media for the prevalence of delinquency, antisocial behaviour and drug misuse. The local comprehensive school has been judged a 'failing school' uniquely in Wales on two occasions. Community facilities are scarce and run-down, shops are boarded up, and litter abounds.

Yet, on a sunny day, it doesn't look so bad, for Milltown is a monument to early municipal housing. The top half of the estate still conveys the ideal of the 'garden suburb' with its 'half-hearted attempts at axial layouts, crescents galore and above all the central avenue, a dual carriageway running down the middle of the whole development like a useless spine'.[1] By 1929, a further 3,412 houses had been provided to meet the needs of the city, and more development took place during the 1930s, though little more in the post-war period, except for some newer houses built on former allotment sites. There is still a lot of open space and, since rioting in the early 1990s, some of the more delapidated housing and shopping blocks have been razed and replaced with grassy knolls.

During the inter-war and post-war periods, inner-city residents steadily relocated to this expanding estate on the edge of the city, which is still surrounded by farmland, woods and fields. As one local commentator recorded:

> The surplus population of the older, crowded areas took to the hills and remained there, busily spinning its own web of relationships on the unbreakable framework of birth, maturity and death. Here was hammered out during the grey days of the Depression, the war years, and the times of relative plenty, a pattern of life, an identity and a folklore.

Milltown attracted a substantial Catholic population, who were immediately seen to bring problems to the district:

> They were not 'Chapel' or 'Church' and attended 'Catholic' schools. They had strange names that all began with O or 'Mac', they belonged to large families, they tended to be poorly dressed, and were dangerous if provoked. Their homes were often a rent collector's nightmare, and occasionally poverty would drive them to bizarre behaviour.

Newspaper reports during the pre-war period referred to minor 'gang' warfare, and to a general lack of care for the environment on the part of the population in general. In 1929, 127 trees planted on the estate were 'wilfully' destroyed, and in response to this 'disgraceful state of affairs', the council agreed to defer repairing the damage done for twelve months 'to let older people know that it is their duty to look after the trees'! Throughout its history Milltown, more than any other area of the city, has had a tendency to ignore less serious offending, especially if it is directed at public targets (Herbert and Evans 1973).

The people of Milltown have typically worked at the bottom end of the labour market, for the estate was planned and designed for 'working people', and characteristic jobs of residents in the 1920s and 1930s were 'labourers, boilermen, mates in various trades, and railway workers'. Over the years, Milltown increasingly acquired a reputation in the city as an area where large numbers of 'problem' families lived, and certainly the poverty of the official economy produced a flourishing unofficial economy, including the 'fencing' of stolen goods and extensive 'fiddli~   upplementing state benefits by doing odd jobs, or doing casual labour
       s not involve paying tax). Herbert and Evans (1973) suggested that no
       ` per cent of the population could be considered middle class; of the
       ` per cent were skilled working class, 46 per cent were 'other working
       ` per cent were at the lowest level of subsistence.
            mstances that, arguably, have produced a culture of solidarity and
            reflected in its social infrastructure. The pubs and clubs are far

more than places just to have a drink: they offer an incessant round of leisure possibilities (darts, cards, skittles, sport, snooker and pigeons), arrange regular social
excursions and are invariably the location for birthday, anniversary and marriage
celebrations. There are, admittedly, some strict gender divisions concerning what
can and cannot be done, though age differentiation is virtually non-existent. Men
of all ages drink and mix together for sport and cards, while women across the generations (and, indeed, some of the men) congregate for bingo.

The 'privatization of leisure' appears to have had only a relatively marginal
effect on Milltown. Life, at most ages and stages, is lived in the public sphere, with
children playing in the street, teenagers hanging around the corners, and parents
and grandparents gathering in the pubs and clubs. In many respects, it is as if time
has stood still – a cautionary note to those who argue for the dramatic transformation of youth transitions and the decline of traditional 'working-class' community, for in places such as Milltown, there is as much continuity as change.

'Lend me a tenner', said the angel-faced boy in the smartly ironed Wrangler jacket
and 'spoon' loafers. It was the autumn of 1973, and I had just 'accidentally' moved
to Milltown, the outcome of a random choice from a list of housing association
flats available. I looked askance. 'What for?' I asked. Marty told me he had to pay
a fine for court, and he had to get the money somehow, for his mother was in no
position to help. His three mates were grinning. It was obviously a wind-up, I felt.
Court? I had never met anyone who had been to court, let alone kids so young, but
the sheer impertinence of the request literally paid off, for I lent Marty the tenner
and he paid it back at a pound a week, turning up diligently at the flat every
Thursday evening. Through this chance encounter, we discovered a shared love of
David Bowie, and I learned that most evenings Marty and his mates hung around
the 'club', an adventure playground on the top corner of the estate. Twelve years
later, as part of an evaluation of the Milltown Youth and Community Project, I
identified this corner, comprising a dozen streets and a couple of thousand people,
as the 'critical patch' – the area *within* Milltown with an *even greater* preponder-
ance of pathologies, social need and disadvantage. This was where the Boys grew
up. I became a volunteer at the 'club', and through that link, got to know the Boys,
who were my subjects for my PhD thesis (Williamson 1981), when I spent three
years 'hanging around' with them in the mid-1970s, before I left Milltown in 1979
to pursue my own career.

By the mid-1990s, youth research was reporting on the dramatically changed
nature of youth transitions. They had become prolonged and more complex. They
were inbued with greater opportunities – and more risk (Furlong and Cartmel
1997). Young people who succumbed to that risk were, apparently, destined for a
future at the margins. There was increasingly policy concern, ratcheted up with a

vengeance following the election of the Labour government in 1997, with young people dropping out of education, training and employment. These were 'status zer0' young people, first identified in 1994 in a study of South Glamorgan (Istance et al. 1994), and their prognosis was bleak, according to the Social Exclusion Unit (2000). While the Social Exclusion Unit was deliberating on the subject of neigh-bourhood renewal and the position of young people, I remembered the Milltown Boys.

Marty and his friends were not over-preoccupied with learning. Marty attended (from time to time) the Catholic school on the south side of the estate, though most of his mates went to the local comprehensive school. A few, however, were in the care of the local authority, 'banged up' in community homes with education on the premises or in approved schools. Marty himself was sent to Detention Centre for three months at the earliest possible age of 14, for by then he was already an incor-rigible burglar.

Notwithstanding their poor educational participation and involvement in crime, they all expected to get jobs – some kind of job. The typical occupational destina-tions for young people on the estate were, first, the local fruit market for a couple of years, then, when they turned 18, the unskilled labouring jobs in the local brewery, the paper mill or, if particularly lucky or with the necessary family con-nections, the steelworks. Formal educational qualifications were considered to be unnecessary and irrelevant, because through fathers, uncles and neighbours, they had alternative routes into the labour market. Or so they thought, but by 1978, these prospective destinations were rapidly diminishing, as these sources of employment closed down or stopped recruiting. The Boys found that their antici-pated avenues to work, following in the time-honoured footsteps of their fathers and older brothers, were now dead-ends.

The Milltown Boys were, with hindsight, the first generation of 'status zer0' young people, for they left school with no, or very few, formal qualifications, and had criminal records. So, of course, had cohorts of similar young people before them, but the labour market had changed, and according to both research and political analysis in the mid-1970s, individuals like the Boys had 'no future', for job oppor-tunities had declined and the risk of 'social exclusion' had dramatically increased. In 1999, I therefore wondered what had become of them.

In the acknowledgements page of my doctoral thesis, I paid special thanks to twelve of the Boys and mentioned another forty-one. Early in 1999 I racked my brain for any more I could remember and added a further fourteen names, pro-ducing a list of sixty-seven individuals. I sounded out the idea of a follow-up study with my university colleagues, who commended the idea, but felt it had little in the early 1990s, some of the more delapidated housing and shopping blocks have been razed and replaced with grassy knolls.

During the inter-war and post-war periods, inner-city residents steadily relocated to this expanding estate on the edge of the city, which is still surrounded by farmland, woods and fields. As one local commentator recorded:

> The surplus population of the older, crowded areas took to the hills and remained there, busily spinning its own web of relationships on the unbreakable framework of birth, maturity and death. Here was hammered out during the grey days of the Depression, the war years, and the times of relative plenty, a pattern of life, an identity and a folk-lore.

Milltown attracted a substantial Catholic population, who were immediately seen to bring problems to the district:

> They were not 'Chapel' or 'Church' and attended 'Catholic' schools. They had strange names that all began with O or 'Mac', they belonged to large families, they tended to be poorly dressed, and were dangerous if provoked. Their homes were often a rent collector's nightmare, and occasionally poverty would drive them to bizarre behaviour.

Newspaper reports during the pre-war period referred to minor 'gang' warfare, and to a general lack of care for the environment on the part of the population in general. In 1929, 127 trees planted on the estate were 'wilfully' destroyed, and in response to this 'disgraceful state of affairs', the council agreed to defer repairing the damage done for twelve months 'to let older people know that it is their duty to look after the trees'! Throughout its history Milltown, more than any other area of the city, has had a tendency to ignore less serious offending, especially if it is directed at public targets (Herbert and Evans 1973).

The people of Milltown have typically worked at the bottom end of the labour market, for the estate was planned and designed for 'working people', and characteristic jobs of residents in the 1920s and 1930s were 'labourers, boilermen, mates in various trades, and railway workers'. Over the years, Milltown increasingly acquired a reputation in the city as an area where large numbers of 'problem' families lived, and certainly the poverty of the official economy produced a flourishing unofficial economy, including the 'fencing' of stolen goods and extensive 'fiddling' (supplementing state benefits by doing odd jobs, or doing casual labour which does not involve paying tax). Herbert and Evans (1973) suggested that no more than 4 per cent of the population could be considered middle class; of the remainder, 19 per cent were skilled working class, 46 per cent were 'other working classes', and 31 per cent were at the lowest level of subsistence.

It is such circumstances that, arguably, have produced a culture of solidarity and loyalty to the area, reflected in its social infrastructure. The pubs and clubs are far

Introduction

In 1977 some of the Boys were on a job creation programme, and as part of their 'social and life skills' training, they produced a tourist guide for the estate, *Scammy Tours* – Scam being one of the Boys (though he is not included in this study). Before computers and desktop printing, they collated a range of black and white photographs they had taken of the exotic wildlife (stray dogs), night-time eating houses (chip shops) and unusual attractions (ripped-open bin bags and burnt-out cars). Crudely stapled together, those few badly photocopied pages captured some of the contemporary realities of Milltown.

At the turn of the nineteenth century, the area comprised a couple of farms and a hamlet with a popuation of 183. It rose to 360 by 1861 following the building of a railway and the establishment of a station in Milltown. In the 1870s, the first resident police constable was appointed. Following the First World War and in a climate of building 'homes fit for heroes', the neighbouring city expanded its boundaries and, in February 1920, purchased two farms for the princely sum of £72,000. By 1924, some roads had been completed, though they had yet to be named.

Milltown is now routinely depicted as one of the largest council estates in Europe. With a population of over 30,000, it has all the characteristics of a 'worst estate' or 'poor neighbourhood': high unemployment, high rates of teenage pregnancy, high take-up of free school meals, high numbers of lone-parent families, low proportion of car-ownership, low levels of owner-occupation, and so on. It is regularly vilified in the media for the prevalence of delinquency, antisocial behaviour and drug misuse. The local comprehensive school has been judged a 'failing school' uniquely in Wales on two occasions. Community facilities are scarce and run-down, shops are boarded up, and litter abounds.

Yet, on a sunny day, it doesn't look so bad, for Milltown is a monument to early municipal housing. The top half of the estate still conveys the ideal of the 'garden suburb' with its 'half-hearted attempts at axial layouts, crescents galore and above all the central avenue, a dual carriageway running down the middle of the whole development like a useless spine'.[1] By 1929, a further 3,412 houses had been provided to meet the needs of the city, and more development took place during the 1930s, though little more in the post-war period, except for some newer houses built on former allotment sites. There is still a lot of open space and, since rioting chance of success, for attrition rates in even short-term follow-up studies are considerable (see Johnston et al. 2000), and I was talking about a time-span of nearly twenty-five years. However, I decided to persevere, starting by dropping in on Danny, whom I had first met in 1974 when he was 'on the run' from approved school, and with whom I had stayed in touch over the years. I showed him my list of sixty-seven names, and immediately I was on the trail, for Danny was confident that I could find a fair number of them (he was still in regular contact with about a dozen) and felt that most would be willing to cooperate. Marty – who now suffers from paranoid schizophrenia – was my next port of call, and was not so sure, warning me to be careful: 'Just remember, How, they're not kids any more'.

Six of the Boys, Danny informed me, were dead, while another – Johnny Albright – died, kicked to death in a drunken fight with his friends in the middle of the year 2000, shortly before I was due to interview him. By the end of 2000, however, I had conducted extended interviews with thirty of the Boys and, at the time of writing, have set eyes on and spoken to forty-seven of them. Through a snowballing approach recounted later, I discovered the whereabouts of the Boys, made contact explaining what I wanted to do, and subsequently interviewed them. Not one of them refused and only one was in any way cautious about speaking to me. Of the 'core' twelve, I interviewed ten. Of the next forty-one, I interviewed sixteen, and the remaining four respondents were drawn from my supplementary list of fourteen.

The Boys grew up within a stone's throw of each other. All lived in social housing, most with both of their natural parents and a number of brothers and sisters, and many of their extended family often lived close by. From an early age, they spent their time in public space, away from their overcrowded houses and the gaze of their often precipitously punitive fathers and overworked mothers. Their corner of the estate backed on to woods and fields leading down to the river which separated Milltown from Fairfield, another rambling council estate on the edge of the city. This was the northern border, the site of rivalry and sometimes conflict with the boys from Fairfield, while the southern border was the main road dividing 'old' Milltown from the rest of the estate, which had been built in the post-war years on a racetrack.

The club – a run-down, graffiti-riven, semi-derelict building with threadbare furnishings and virtually no equipment – was rarely more than five minutes' walk for any of the Boys, and was where they congregated in their early teenage years, advancing from there to the nearby shops and off-licence, where they hung around, indulging in 'ostentatious smoking' to the reprimands of women alighting from the bus after their daily shop. Even when they had little money, the Boys could always get a cigarette from the general store, where the owner was 'kind' enough to sell them 'separates' – single cigarettes for two pence each.

It was by the off-licence, where Johnny was killed twenty-five years later, that the Boys planned their daily round. Sometimes they disappeared into the woods on the 'mitch' from school, sometimes they went into town to shoplift clothes and glue. In the evenings, after the club closed, they roamed the streets, often 'screwing' (burgling) houses, and even if they were not active burglars, they were usually close by, on the lookout and ready to run. By the time they were 15 or so, few were regularly attending school and most had acquired criminal records, with some having already been taken into local authority care or spent some time in custody.

As well as burglary and theft, the Boys became increasingly involved in motor vehicle crime, stealing motorbikes and cars to race and dump in the woods, and beyond their instrumental and expressive offending, many also did odd jobs, selling firewood and collecting pop bottles for return to the general store.

They were a large and loose-knit crowd, with affiliations overlapping and constantly shifting, although most could be reasonably firmly identified with a core cluster of mates. During their teenage years, these clusters consolidated distinctive, though never exclusive, social and cultural practices. The nature and severity of their offending differed. Musical affiliations evolved in different ways and this, in turn, affected their preferred youth cultural styles. Likewise, sporting interests guided the Boys in different directions in terms of both passive and active participation. By the age of 16, different clusters elected to drink in different pubs, and a year or so later, their city-centre weekend venues also varied according to the group with which they primarily associated.

Most left school with very little idea about what they wanted to do, and were generally willing to take 'anything going', which they usually heard about through word of mouth. Rates of pay and proximity to home were the main guiding force to any decisions they made. The Boys had no commitments, and any money they made was for their disposal alone, most being frittered away on cigarettes and drink. Drug use was limited, except for a period of glue-sniffing, which many of the Boys did for a short while, though a few persisted for considerably longer.

Girls were largely marginal to the Boys' teenage lives, and relationships were generally restricted to fleeting sexual contact with local 'slags', through which the Boys were responsible for some unplanned pregnancies, though they took no responsibility for them. Very few had more prolonged relationships, and most considered that future, more permanent relationships lay in the distant future, though many eventually 'settled down' sooner than they had anticipated with local girls.

The cohesion of the Boys dissipated as they approached their twenties and slowly went their relatively separate ways. Some moved away (to join the Merchant Navy or the army), while others were sent away – to Borstal and to prison. Some, predictably, settled down, fracturing though rarely completely severing their peer group relationships, for the overlapping friendship groups persisted, though in a diluted form. These bonds remain active today, despite many of

1975

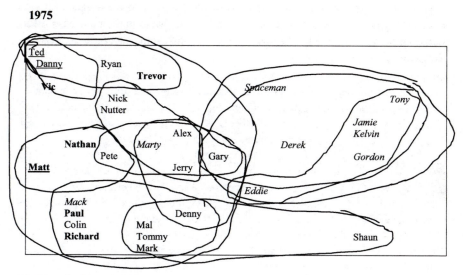

Black or mixed race: **bold**
Catholic school Boys: *italic*
Approved school: underlined
Position left = more persistent offenders; right = 'more Monty Python than Al Capone'

2000

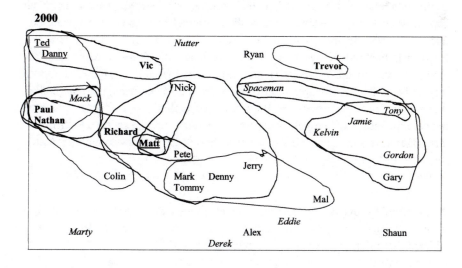

Figure 1.1 'Clusters' in the Networks of the Milltown Boys – 1975 and 2000

their teenage ties having disappeared (Figure 1.1). Some individuals, however, especially those who were never firmly attached to any particular cluster, rapidly lost touch with the Boys, largely through a processes of self-exclusion (through moving away, starting a family or trying to pursue a career).

All the Boys, however, recall their teenage years with fond nostalgia, for it was when they were *together*, and occasionally, when they were in their early twenties, they endeavoured to recreate the spirit of their youth, though the time had passed. As I wrote in 1981:

> The male peer group – the Boys – which had had considerable solidarity for a number of years, was increasingly being penetrated from many sides. Some of the more charismatic leaders had been 'stuck away'; other Boys no longer wanted to become involved in 'trouble' and girls applied pressure on yet others to 'settle down' . . .
>
> They turned to romanticising about the past and having the occasional fling reminded them of the good old days (which had not necessarily been that good!) . . .
>
> In this way, the 'golden years' were remembered and, even when they were into their 20s, a number of the Boys would still sneak off from their wives and girlfriends to go on a 'bender' and have a rampage in town. They would reminisce about their younger days and seek out those places which played their favourite music – the Electric Light Orchestra, Thin Lizzy, Sham 69 and David Bowie. Boys keep swinging. (Williamson and Williamson 1981, p. 64)

Such romantic celebration of their youthful freedoms conceals the deep disadvantages experienced and faced by the Boys as they approached adulthood, for in a contracting manual labour market, their prospects appeared gloomy. They had little to show for their education, and their criminal records created further obstacles to access and progression in the legitimate economy. In terms of all the contemporary thinking about 'risk' and 'transitions', the Boys were on thin ice. However, beyond the essential human interest of the Boys' story, what follows implicitly challenges (though, in other respects, it also confirms) the marginalization and exclusion theses advanced by youth researchers, for it is as much a testimony to the resilience of many of the Boys (against the odds) as it is an affirmation that youth disadvantage translates, *for ever*, into social and economic marginality.

Note

1. Some of the quotations in these opening pages cannot be fully referenced in order to preserve the anonymity of the estate; many are drawn from my PhD thesis (Williamson 1981). See also Williams (1973, 1977).

–2–

Renewing Contact with the Milltown Boys
– Access and Assent

Introduction

Paul was not hard to find, for Danny had told me he was always in the pub. After his parallel relationships with two different women collapsed, Paul's excuse to each of them that he had been down the pub became the reality. He 'lived' (or rather slept) in a maisonette, with no furniture. The best time for me to call for an interview was early in the morning; that was the only time he was sure he would be in. When I called, another of the Boys on my list was there. Richard lived over the road and Paul had told him I was coming.

We decamped to Richard's flat to do the interview, where we could at least make coffee and had chairs to sit on. Halfway through his interview, Paul remembered he had to sign on, saying he would be back in half an hour, though I was not surprised when he failed to return and, after interviewing Richard, I went to The Fountain. Paul put down his pint to offer profuse apologies: 'I thought I'd come by here for one'. It was obviously his fifth or sixth. We agreed to conclude the interview in the pub, though at some other time.

Jerry was reluctant about my request for an interview, for though he was happy to see me again, these days he had a family to consider. The father of two teenage girls, the elder of whom was profoundly disabled, Jerry had changed his life course quite significantly in order to provide for her. I accepted his refusal, but some months later he phoned, saying he had changed his mind after talking things through with his wife. He was the only one of the Boys who had prevaricated; the rest had all cooperated willingly, even enthusiastically.

The fieldwork took about a year. My first interview was with Ted on 11 October 1999, the last with Nutter on 23 November 2000. Once I had made contact with each of the Boys, the interviews were largely unproblematic, for I had the legacy of trust and respect from twenty (and more) years before.

The challenge had been to track them down. Some, like Paul, were easy to find, others, like Pete, who no one had seen since the early 1980s, remained elusive. Making contact was a hit and miss affair, dependent on snowballing, opportunism and chance. Once I had produced my list of sixty-seven names and discovered that six of these were dead, I felt that a target number of thirty (half) was a realistic if still demanding proposition. This proved to be the case, with the interviews eventually yielding over half a million words of transcript.

Building the Sample

As I noted, I had always remained in touch with Danny and, to a lesser extent, with Marty, both of whom were immediately able to help trace some of the other Boys. However, before many of the formal interviews had taken place, other casual encounters occurred even as the wheels for the formal moment were being oiled. (A flow chart of how I tracked down the Milltown Boys is provided in Figure 2.1.)

Danny set the ball rolling. We went to The Fountain, where I quickly made contact with Paul, Mack and Colin, and through Paul I met Richard (as described). In The Fountain, I asked after Ted and was told he was currently doing time, so I wrote to him at the local prison and within two days he phoned to say he would soon be released on an electronic tag. Some weeks later I interviewed him at home.

The Boys in the pub also linked me up with Nathan. He too was serving a prison sentence at the time, and on his release I went to his flat and got his mobile phone number. Some months later I met him at the pub and set a date for the interview. Vic also drank in the pub, though was never there when I showed up. Through Ted, however, I was invited to Vic's fortieth birthday party, where I made a date to interview him. This 'network' therefore provided me with contact with eight of the Fountain Boys, those who generally have continued to live their lives on the edge and 'on the street'.

Marty attached me to a different, though overlapping, group of the Boys. He told me that Gary still lived in the house where he had grown up and we walked round the corner to see him. Marty also gave me Matt's address and told me where Ryan now lived. In turn, Ryan told me of Trevor's whereabouts, while Matt described where Nick was now living. Marty also gave me a clue to where Alex had his business and I visited him there.

For very different reasons (mental illness, alcoholism, self-employment, drug addiction), these six of the Boys were partially or almost wholly 'dislocated' from any of their old friendship clusters, though personal friendships and loyalties remained. Gary and Marty, Ryan and Trevor, and Matt and Nick have each sustained close relationships since childhood, irrespective of the wider, different networks to which they had once been attached.

A cluster of the Boys now drank in the local working men's club, though none of those already mentioned could tell me where any of these particular individuals lived, or had a phone number for any one of them. I therefore bit the bullet, turning up one Tuesday evening at the social club, and mentioning a number of the Boys' names to the man on the door. Not surprisingly he was cautious, perhaps even suspicious, though he went through the motions of checking inside the club, returning

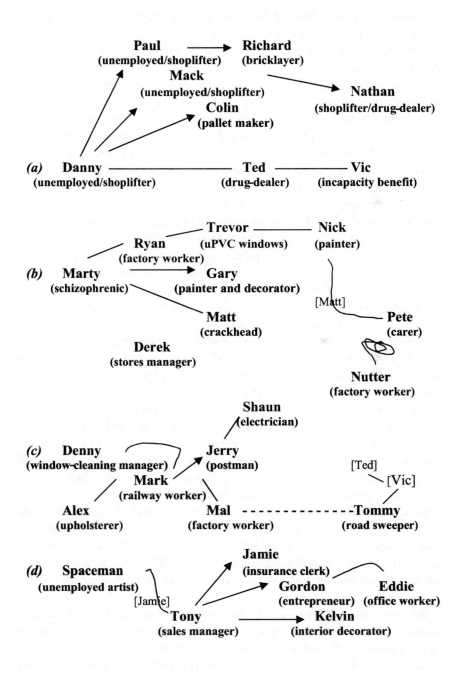

Figure 2.1 Making Contact after Twenty-five Years

eventually to say that none of those named was there that night. I persisted, however, and he told me that some of those I'd mentioned might be playing skittles that night 'down the Legion'. I thanked him, saying I would head down to the British Legion. This confidence seemed to relax the steward, who said that I might just catch Denny at home before he left, and directed me to Denny's house.

I parked my car, ran across the main road and rang the bell. A woman answered and I asked for Denny. 'Who are you?', she said, as Denny appeared behind her with his evening meal in his hand, inviting me in. As I sat down, the phone rang, and a look of amazement crossed Denny's face, for the call was for me! It was Mark, who had been on his way up to the club. He had seen me – at least he thought it was me – running across the main road, and when the steward described my appearance and accent, telling Mark I had been asking for him and that I had gone to Denny's, Mark had picked up the phone. After arranging to interview Denny, I went back to the club to have a drink with Mark. Mal, who was also in the club that evening, gave me his phone number, and told me Tommy was also a regular there, though he was currently banned for fighting. However, Tommy turned up at Vic's fortieth birthday party, where I took his phone number.

Although this 'network' of four of the Boys was rather more elastic, it largely comprised those who had (nearly) always been in regular employment, still lived in Milltown and, as adults, had desisted from active criminality.

Most of the Boys already mentioned had attended the local comprehensive school. The exceptions were Ted, Danny and Matt, who had been in approved schools and community homes, while Mack and Marty had gone to the Catholic school on the other side of the estate. These two had, however, severed links with the Catholic school Boys at a relatively early stage, and my challenge now was how to find the others for, according to those I had spoken to, they seemed to have become widely dispersed. Names were mentioned in passing conversations, though no one had any idea how I might find them. I had no addresses, no phone numbers and no idea of any meeting place they might frequent.

Then I had a stroke of luck. I was walking through a shopping precinct in the city centre when a thin, balding and rather haggard-looking man came towards me. Though I felt I knew him, I could not place him and he walked straight past me, but something clicked and I called out his teenage nickname. He turned round in surprise, recognized me immediately, and off I went with Spaceman for a cup of tea.

Spaceman, as a result of various addictions, had lost touch with all the Boys, except Jamie. Jamie, however, was still in touch with Tony, so Spaceman took my mobile phone number and some weeks later Tony phoned me, telling me he now lived in a quiet Cheshire village. At his fortieth birthday party, to which I was invited, a number of his old friends from Milltown were there. I took their details and later interviewed Gordon, Jamie and Kelvin. Two weeks later, this same group gathered to celebrate Spaceman's forthieth birthday (which few, including himself, thought he would ever reach) in a pub in the city, and there I bumped into Eddie.

With the exception of Eddie and Spaceman, these six Catholic Boys have done quite well, some very well. They have been geographically and occupationally mobile, are owner-occupiers and have desisted from crime. After all, as Tony put it, they had always been 'more Monty Python than Al Capone'.

The remaining five Boys were 'discovered' as a result of some special combinations of chance and persistence. Mark had told me where Jerry lived, though at first he had not wanted to be interviewed, which disappointed me, as he had been one of the central figures in the original research. I did not try to persuade him, but fortunately he changed his mind, as we have seen.

I had also wanted to interview Shaun because I vaguely recalled he was unique among the Boys from the comprehensive school for having secured a 'proper' apprenticeship. However, no one had seen him for years. I mentioned this to Jerry, and he too had no idea as to Shaun's whereabouts, but Jerry's wife heard us talking and recognized the name, though she had never met him. There and then she made a phone call to a friend who was, apparently, a friend of Shaun's second wife; and so I got a phone number!

Derek was one of the Catholic Boys but, like Shaun, he now lived away from the estate and no one had seen him for years but, quite by chance, I bumped into his mother and she gave me his address.

Pete appeared to be an irresolvable challenge. No one had seen him since the early 1980s, though a number of the Boys *thought* they had seen him in television footage of the nail bombing at the Atlanta Olympics in 1996. They had concluded, however, that it could not possibly be him, though in fact it was, as we learned in the autumn of 2000 when Pete came back to Milltown for the first time since 1982. He was visiting the site of the old club, with his partner Barry, when he ran into Matt. Matt told Nick. Nick called me. I called Matt to get Pete's phone number, rang Pete, who now lives in the east of England, who said he was planning another visit to Milltown in a couple of weeks' time.

I interviewed Pete on the Saturday afternoon, and in the evening a rather strange group of the Boys gathered in The Centurion, one of the pubs they frequented years earlier: Matt, Pete, Jerry, Mark, Nick and myself, together with partners and children. Pete, in his flamboyant camp style, was holding court. Nick, a recovering alcoholic, was drinking orange juice. Mark was downing pints at his usual frenetic pace. Matt, a black crackhead, was bringing a touch of the Caribbean to the proceedings in his bright tropical shirt, and Jerry's 18-year-old wheelchair-bound daughter Rachael was lapping up the occasion.

This was a powerful celebration of old friendships traversing current differences, when in walked Nutter, a racist, homophobic alcoholic! He was the last piece in my research jigsaw and he clearly could hardly believe his eyes as he took in the fact of this grouping together of the Boys for the first time in over two decades. I extracted a telephone number from his garbled speech and interviewed him a few days later.

The Final Sample – Some Vignettes

The final sample therefore produced a reasonable balance between three cross-cutting groupings of the Boys, though for a number of reasons some no longer fitted easily into any of the groups. Some had moved away, some had become cut off from the Boys for other reasons, such as illness or social mobility, while others had crossed between groups during the course of their teenage and adult lives. There are always different ways of classifying any group, but it is still possible to give some impression of the different 'positions' occupied by those Boys who were eventually interviewed (Table 2.1).

In Table 2.1 the Boys are grouped according to their current *social* networks, which both informs and is informed by other aspects of their lives, such as employment status and family responsibilities, as well as their criminal enterprise. Some are tightly bound to these networks, some are more loosely connected, while others are more dislocated, though some are more dislocated than others. The following vignettes convey the extent of dislocation or attachment to the different settings from which the final sample of the Milltown Boys was drawn.

Spaceman, who attended the Catholic school, increasingly became detached from the other Catholic Boys, though he has recently re-established contact.

Matt drifts in and out of various circles, but still sees Nick regularly and plays table tennis with him at the local leisure centre. Nick is a recovering alcoholic, so rarely socializes with the other Boys, though in the past he knocked around with the Fountain Boys but was equally 'at home' with some of the Boys at the club.

Alex lives and works some distance from the estate, keeping in touch with the Boys only through his occasional participation in sporting trips arranged from the social club.

Eddie lives on the estate, but suffers from mental health problems and now mixes in completely different social circles.

Derek now lives on the other side of the city and has seen none of the Catholic Boys, among whom he was once a pivotal figure, for many years.

Nutter always was a loner, though dipping in and out of each of the groupings when he was younger, and now spends most of his time drinking on his own.

Marty suffers from paranoid schizophrenia, and though he sees some of the Boys in the street, they have little to say to each other. However, his lifelong friend Gary continues to keep a watching eye on him.

Shaun no longer has anything to do with the estate or the Boys, and lives near the city centre on a private housing estate with his second wife.

Table 2.1 The Final Sample

The Fountain Boys	The social club Boys	The Catholic Boys
Danny	Denny	*Jamie*
Paul	Mark	*Gordon*
Mack	Mal	*Kelvin*
Nathan		Gary
Colin	Tommy	
Vic		*Tony*
	Jerry	
Ted		
	Trevor	
Richard		
	Ryan	
		Spaceman
Dislocated:		
Matt Nick		
	Alex	
		Eddie
	Pete	*Derek*
Nutter *Marty*	Shaun	

Black or mixed race: **bold**
Catholic school Boys: *italic*
Approved school: underlined

Pete, who had lost contact with the Boys for almost two decades (he left immediately he declared his homosexuality), has now returned to the estate on a few occasions, always making contact with Matt and Mark, and sometimes with Nick and Jerry.

Just as those portrayed as 'dislocated' have rarely lost all contact with the Boys, so those identified with particular settings are not always firmly located within them. Tony has lived a long way from Milltown for many years, meeting up with the Catholic Boys (notably Jamie, Kelvin and Gordon, and latterly Spaceman) only occasionally.

Gary, despite having gone to the comprehensive school, has long been associated with the Catholic Boys, though his work commitments mean he rarely gets much chance to socialize with them. Like Nick, however, he is also 'at home' with the Boys from the social club, joining them from time to time on coach trips to major sporting events.

Ted has strong links with the Fountain Boys but rarely goes to the pub, for he has not lived in Milltown since he was a teenager, and usually meets the Boys in other places away from Milltown.

Richard is also associated with the Fountain Boys but is equally at ease with those from the social club, particularly Mark, though he is not a regular in either place.

Tommy was once a stalwart (committee) member of the social club but now puts in only an occasional appearance, preferring to drink in a social club nearer his home on the other side of the estate.

Trevor is well known in the club, but goes only for some specific social function rather than routinely for an evening pint, unlike Mark, Denny and Mal.

Ryan, a non-smoker who cannot bear a smoky atmosphere, attends the social club even less frequently, though he does make it to special events. Generally, he stays at home and pursues more individualized leisure activities.

Conclusion

Renewing contact with the Milltown Boys was an exciting challenge to which I was totally committed, and which was rewarded by the welcome and cooperation I hoped for but did not necessarily expect. After all, my life course – in contrast to many of theirs – has been one of reasonable comfort and success, and as Denny likes to assert, I had achieved this 'on their backs'.

The Boys might, therefore, have been resentful about me reappearing in their lives after all this time in order to write another book. However, it seemed they felt as I did, for despite the gap of over twenty years, we had still known each other for almost three decades, and like it or not, we were now umbilically joined together through that shared past experience.

They dealt drugs, made pallets, installed windows or worked on the railways, while I wrote books, and so long as I was prepared to take the ridicule about being a 'pen-pusher' who had never done a proper day's work in my life, they accepted me. They were willing to help with my latest project as best they could, though they couldn't understand why anybody should be at all interested in their 'ordinary' lives.

Methodology

The Interview Process and Content

The interviews were conducted in very different settings. The second half of the interview with Paul, and the whole interview with Colin, took place in the pub (though admittedly in the quiet of the lounge, with no one else around). Most of the interviews were conducted at the Boys' homes, during the day or in the evening. My interview with Mark took virtually all day, with regular breaks for coffee and sandwiches provided by his wife Veronica. Sometimes interviews took place in the lounge, sometimes in the kitchen. On occasions we were alone, at other times I was conscious of the curious eyes of partners and children penetrating our space. With the exception of Jerry's initial caution, all of the other Boys said they would tell me whatever I wanted to know. On my part, my opening gambit was to put three simple requests:

1. I know we have not seen each other for at least twenty years, but please be as open and as honest with me as you can.
2. If there are things that you want to tell me but want me to treat with confidence, then tell me, and you will have to trust me.
3. If you do not trust me, you will not tell me.

Not one of the Boys objected to being tape-recorded, despite the sensitivity of some of the issues discussed. (Danny rolled a spliff to establish some concentration, commenting that the only 'interviews' he had ever done before were with the police or at the Job Centre, where he had always been a pathological liar; now he had to think hard because he wanted to tell the truth!) Most interviews lasted between two and four hours. Some of the territory covered demanded immense details, if for example individuals had regularly changed jobs or sustained a complex criminal career, while with others, this did not apply and the subject was covered swiftly.

It is apparent from the data that the Boys were reasonably relaxed in discussing their lives. Generally, they were certainly not guarded in what they said, though some were visibly uncomfortable in having to talk so profoundly about their lives, and were certainly unaccustomed to doing so. The Boys tend not to look back and reflect on what they have done, so being pressed to do so can be disconcerting. As a result, some of the questions asked clearly made little sense to them, for they had simply never thought about such issues.

Each interview was framed by a topic guide designed to cover all aspects of their lives, and intended to trigger their focused recollections:

- memories of schooling
- teenage aspirations and expectations
- employment (formal and informal) and training
- health (including drug and alcohol misuse)
- housing and mobility
- family and personal relationships; family formation and breakdown
- maintenance of peer groups (or otherwise)
- leisure and social activities
- contact with the criminal justice system
- political and religious engagement, affiliations, and rationale (if any) engagement with, and assessment of professional intervention
- experience of community opportunities and intervention
- community involvement and ideas about 'neighbourhood renewal'
- aspirations and expectations for their children (and grandchildren)
- expectations for the future
- regrets
- self-reflection

Data Management and Analysis

The interviews inevitably roamed around these themes, according to the ways in which the Boys chose to address them. Each interview was transcribed and coded according to the dominant themes outlined above, using Atlas Ti, with the interview data comprising over half a million words of transcript. Thematic printouts of the thirty interviews were then produced, and this provided the basis for an initial comprehensive thematic 'chapter'.

These 'chapters' themselves produced approaching half a million words and took two years to write – a terrifying volume of material! It was, however, my intention that few words should be lost at the first hurdle for, despite being rather unwieldy, each 'chapter' is a coherent account of a particular dimension of the Boys' lives. Each stands alone and now – through ruthless editing – is the basis of this book. It is certainly unnecessary to have repeated quotations by different individuals in support of the same contention, though on the other hand, had these been omitted prior to this stage, they would probably have been lost forever. The data therefore offered a rich seam of experience and perspective to be mined, and the first step – covering substantive themes in significant depth – provided the basis on which to develop this portrait of the Boys' lives in the round, across the many dimensions of their lives, and over time.

The Researcher's Position

On many topical issues for social research (such as unemployment, crime, health or housing), researchers cannot help noticing – and feeling – the striking contrasts between their own position and circumstances and those of their subjects. It can be an emotional experience (Carter and Delamont 1996), even during a first encounter, and it is self-delusionary to suggest that researchers can, somehow, dis-passionately stand above such feelings. When the respondents are individuals known to the researcher from the past, such feelings are inevitably magnified.

The fieldwork with the Milltown Boys was certainly an emotional roller coaster, though one which generally brought more feelings of elation than of despondency. Nevertheless, it was still tough going meeting the Boys again, for I remembered them as being spirited and often quite charismatic, if usually rather nasty, teenagers, while now they were all middle-aged men set in their particular ways. One can, of course, 'read' their current circumstances, which are very different, from a variety of perspectives, and some of the Boys have done remarkably well, considering their backgrounds and childhood origins. Others, however, have little to show for their lives and are unlikely to have much to show in the future. In com-parison to my own trajectory in adulthood, their lives seem to have been rather dull, parochial and limited, though I am sure the Boys themselves would argue otherwise. Indeed, they would wish to celebrate their achievements, not commis-erate with any 'failure'.

With very few exceptions, I had never met their current partners and none of their children. This was, of itself, an interesting and sometimes exciting experience. Some of the Boys had clearly talked about me from time to time. Mal's wife, on our first meeting, put her arms around me and kissed me, saying Mal thought the world of me (the reason was a humble one: I had accompanied him to Bristol juvenile court when he was 15, when his parents had washed their hands of his errant behav-iour). Their younger daughter, Bethan, was fascinated by me, for I was the man who had written 'the book' about her dad! Indeed, many of the children wanted to know more about what their fathers had been like when they were around the same age as they are now. The children may have wanted to expose their fathers' hypocrisy, though many of their fathers were forthright about their past and adopted the same attitude towards their children as Jerry: 'Do as I say, not as I done'.

On the day I interviewed Ryan, his wife, whom I had known when she was a girl, left work early just to meet me again, while Ted took me round the corner to see his sister once again. There was also some unexpected 'knowledge' about me across the generations, beyond some of the children knowing that I had written 'the book'. Unknown to me, Mark's daughter Eirlys had spent a weekend at my 'cottage project' in Snowdonia, for in her final year of schooling, she had been part of a Prince's Trust XL programme, and the youth worker connected to the programme had occasionally used my cottage for a residential weekend. I was delighted that some of the children of the Milltown Boys were making use of a resource I had developed for 'disadvantaged' young people, and somehow it seemed to square a circle.

It was also very satisfying to witness the comfortable, if far from luxurious, lifestyles many of the Boys had achieved. I was meeting them in *their* own homes, whereas, during the 1970s, it was very rare for anybody to be invited to someone's house (people met up in the pubs and clubs), and I had been in only a few of the Boys' parents' homes: those of Danny, Marty, Jerry, Pete and Gary. Even some of the Boys who still lived 'on the street' (through criminal enterprise) had the trappings of 'success', with modernized kitchens, wide-screen TVs and leather three-piece suites.

In contrast, though, it was quite traumatic to hear of various events and episodes which had affected and afflicted the Boys' lives. Being told by Danny that some were dead was a draining experience, and hearing of the breakdowns in their relationships, their imprisonment and their addictions saddened me enormously. There were occasions when, following the research interview, I drove the car away round the corner and sat there in a state of shock and disbelief for an hour or so, for I had been cut off from such experiences for many years, despite having worked as a youth worker throughout this time.

Yet I celebrated many of their forthieth birthdays with the Boys, and have subsequently been involved in a number of further social events, though funerals have been as commonplace as anything else. I have been reconnected with them and predict that the links now re-established are unlikely to be broken once again in the future.

Risk and Reciprocity

Without wanting to overstate the scenario, this research did involve venturing into an arena of 'hard men'. As Marty had forewarned, 'remember, they're not kids any more', and though I was not concerned for my personal safety, the simple association with some of the Boys carried certain risks. My interview with Ted took place over a huge block of cannabis. He had told people not to 'knock his door' that afternoon and told me, therefore, that if there was a knock on the door, it was likely to be the police, 'and, if it is, that's yours'! This was, no doubt, just another aspect of Ted's 'front' and image management, but nonetheless it was a risk. Researchers, as I wrote many years ago, do not have immunity from the law.

There was one individual I was very keen to interview, but a number of the Boys warned me off. They said he was a 'nasty piece of work' and could turn 'vicious' at any time, so perhaps I was fortunate not to have made contact with him.

What clearly stood me in good stead was that the Boys remembered me as an individual who had 'served' them well, and it had not all been one-way traffic. Small favours I had done for some of them had magnified in their memory and they seemed happy to 'return the favour' so many years later. Indeed, my routine introduction to others in The Fountain was 'This is How, he used to look after us when we were little', though the image of these scarred and burly men as ever being 'little' tested the imagination to its limits.

Furthermore, I was able to sustain such reciprocity in the context of the current research, particularly in relation to their children's education. I spent over an hour in the garden at Tommy's house talking to his youngest daughter, Vanessa, who was 13 at the time, about the 'trap' she was in between the environment of Milltown and the culture of her elite public school. Her parents, she said, did not really understand, and she had no local friends any more, while her school 'friends' never invited her to their houses and only rarely did any of them come home with her. She had nowhere to do her homework in peace and quiet, and she was regularly depressed. I could empathize to some extent with that experience from my own background and schooling, and Vanessa was clearly delighted to have found someone who 'understood', for her mother told me later that she appeared to be much happier following our conversation.

Jerry's wife asked me to talk with their younger daughter about possible options for A (Advanced) level, for she and Jerry simply had no idea what advice to dispense, while Denny asked me to have a word with his middle son, who was starting to get into a lot of trouble. Tony's daughter consulted me on a sociology assignment she had to do at school.

Even the Boys themselves sought various bits of advice and support from me, for, after all, I was a 'youth worker'. Shortly before he was due to graduate, Spaceman found himself desperately short of money and it was a case of buying materials for his final portfolio – or eating. He phoned me to see whether or not I knew of any grants that might be available. Nick sought advice about a situation which was appearing to drive a rift in his friendship with Matt, and Richard was keen to check with me whether or not he was 'doing the right thing' for his son.

Gone Native?

Such close association with the Boys has, therefore, cut both ways. At times they even introduce me to others as one of their own, though Tommy, like Denny, always revels in saying that all I have ever done is made money on their backs. Some might contend that I have got too close, and there is no doubt I am firmly attached to their personal, domestic and social lives, receiving invitations to parties, weddings and funerals.

Methodology textbooks point to the risks of 'going native', though I would counter this by saying that, when researchers remain too aloof, the essential element of *trust* also remains absent, for if we are seeking to illuminate what is really going on in the lives of those such as the Boys, trust is the necessary precursor of 'truth'. It may not be an absolute truth, but it is their truth. Unfortunately, they are so accustomed to lying that it takes considerable effort for them to think hard about their 'truth'. For most of their lives, they have driven forward with arguments of convenience and with humour. Throwaway lines are far easier than more profound self-reflection. The Boys were positively uncomfortable with some of the probing questions I asked, though they also transparently made the effort to deal with them. Had others interviewed them I am pretty sure they would not have done so. If that is a product of 'going native', then I make no apology for it, for it has uncovered a seam of understanding which is rarely made visible. As war photographers, among others, assert: if you want to get a good picture, you have to get close.

Conclusion

This is a unique study, built on relationships forged and formed when the Boys were teenagers. It suggests the need for caution over a range of policy assumptions which are routinely made. It also suggests that we need to temper the theoretical assertions advanced on the basis of both one-off ethnographic research projects on young people or relatively short-term cohort studies. Methodologically, the fact that I was able to find, and engage, almost every single individual I sought to re-contact is probably the best testimony to the quality of the evidence produced. There was no attrition. There were no refusals.

The data provide a basis for a number of departures. First and foremost, there is the academic potential for some detailed life-course analysis and, in particular, the ways in which more private experiences (in family, relationships and leisure) have both shaped, and been shaped by the public trajectories of the Boys (in employment, crime and housing). Far greater attention needs to be paid to these interrelationships if we are to develop a stronger understanding of the emphasis and direction of the life course.

Second, the data offer the opportunity to subject theories of 'risk', and especially theories of risk within youth transitions, to more robust interrogation. According to contemporary social theory, these individuals didn't stand a chance. The odds were firmly weighted against them. How and why the majority of them have 'come through', then, demands some careful reflection.

Third, the interrelationships alluded to present a critical challenge to public policy development, particularly in an age of rhetoric about 'joined-up thinking'.

Most of the Boys have managed to get by *somehow* and will continue to do so, by playing around (and 'working' hard) within a system which, to coin a wonderful phrase used by a colleague of mine, is too often 'hitting the targets, but missing the point'. The point is that, even in this postmodernist world, economic autonomy is paramount and, if it is not forthcoming by legitimate means, then it will be sought through other combinations of activity. The Boys, or at least some of them, may be shady operators at the margins of society and the economy, but they are also parents and partners and seek to do their best for their families and their friends.

This is an unashamedly empirical study, a wholehearted exercise in 'grounded theory'. The Milltown Boys should open our eyes to some of the social realities of contemporary Britain, and how individuals in particular circumstances have endeavoured to deal with them over the course of their lives.

–4–

Looking Back on Schooling

Introduction

The acquisition of formal qualifications, as a mechanism for occupational choice, had never been very high on the Boys' agenda, and most left school with few credentials, though some later gained degrees (Table 4.1). At school they had been quintessential 'lads' – celebrating machismo, manualism and anti-mentalism (Willis 1978). They had attended different secondary schools. Eighteen had gone to the local comprehensive, nine to the nearby Catholic school, and three to approved schools or community homes with education on the premises. Danny was one of the latter (along with Ted and Matt), never missing the opportunity to repeat the old cliché that it must have been a good school because it was 'approved'. None of these three Boys acquired any qualifications.

Table 4.1 Educational Qualifications Achieved at School and Beyond

	CSEs	CSE/O Level	A Level	Degree	Any formal qualification
Comprehensive (18)	1	—	—	1	1
Catholic (9)	2	4	1	2	6
Other (3)	—	—	—	—	—
All the Boys (30)	**3**	**4**	**1**	**3**	**7**

Most of the Boys had left school unofficially well before the official school leaving age. Their attendance dropped away around the age of 13 and, by the age of 15, few were attending regularly, preferring to 'doss about' in the woods or do casual work with their fathers or neighbours. Only two of the eighteen Boys who went to the comprehensive school took any examinations. Denny, however, never went back for his results:

> I absolutely hated school. I went to school but I didn't do a lot when I was there. If I could get out of it I would get out of it. I had no interest in school. I learnt more out of school than I did in there.

Shaun achieved three Certificates of Secondary Education (CSEs), which was sufficient for him to secure an apprenticeship as an electrician because, for once, the adverse reputation of the estate appeared to confer an advantage:

> My spelling was atrocious, but I answered all the questions right and that's what impressed them. Plus the fact it was a nationalized industry and I think there might have been a policy there of offering apprenticeships to what they considered to be underprivileged people. The fact I came from Milltown and my dad was there went some way to get me that apprenticeship. There was certainly better candidates than me from the point of view that they might have had six or seven O [Ordinary] levels.

Much later in his life Shaun went on to study electrical engineering at university, one of three of the Boys who now possesses a degree.

In some contrast to the abject educational failure of the Boys from the 'comp', six of the nine Boys who attended the Catholic school obtained some level of formal qualification. Spaceman and Gordon achieved an array of O levels and stayed on to do A (Advanced) levels. Gordon went on to university and graduated in his early twenties. Spaceman soon dropped out and descended into serious drug and alcohol addiction, though he returned to learning in his late thirties and graduated at the age of 41. Tony also got respectable O levels and CSEs and subsequently climbed the occupational ladder with one single company, which he joined on a temporary basis at the age of 18. Three others (Derek, Jamie and Eddie) achieved a handful of CSEs (Eddie at O level equivalents), and have had chequered histories since. Mack and Marty had, more or less, stopped going to school around the age of 14 and left with nothing, while Kelvin also left with no qualifications, though for very different reasons.

'It wasn't cool to be clever' (Ryan)

Threading through their retrospective thoughts on schooling was a clearly juxtaposed 'public' imperative to be uninterested in and dismissive of school and a more 'private' need to emphasize that they either were or wished they had been 'clever'. As a teenager, Ryan had established himself as the 'hard man' of the peer group:

> Tough man! Yeah, because there was nothing else to do. I never had no brains to do anything else. But you let yourself down, don't you, because I would like to be clever. I would have liked to be, but I wasn't. I remember in school I tried and tried and then I thought no, fuck this, I am not going no more. The other thing as well, it wasn't cool to be clever. But I wanted to be.

Interrupted Schooling

Beyond the three Boys who were taken into care, others had their schooling interrupted by spells in custody. Both Pete and Marty, for example, were sent to Detention Centre (DC) for three months at the age of 14, and Nick received the same sentence when he was 15:

> No I didn't do any qualifications, although I was set up for them. I was quite good educational wise as far as they were concerned. But I never, ever saw it – that was the problem. Only recently I dug out an old school report and they were saying this guy is O level material minimum. But then I started mitching [truanting] and then I went to DC. I always had to walk to school and it depended on who you bumped into. You might be thinking of going to school but then you'd go off to break into gas meters or whatever . . . instead.

Vocabularies of Motive – Disengaging from School

Much has been made, in recent years, of the problem of 'disaffection' from school. The Boys' accounts foreshadow much of this debate, identifying *institutional practice, individual 'choice'*, more desirable *alternatives* and specific *personal circumstances* as their reasons for non-attendance and underachievement.

Many of the Boys were quick to attribute their growing disengagement from school to the 'unfair' and inequitable practices of their schools towards them. Both Danny and Matt were placed on Care Orders and removed from home for non-school attendance and unruly behaviour when they were in school. (Ted was made subject to a Care Order for family reasons.) Danny observed,

> See if something kicked off in school . . . I mean, I was a bit of a lad and if something went wrong, nine times out of ten I would get the blame. Eight out of ten it was me! But you had the once when it wasn't me and that's the specific reason: why did I get blamed for something I didn't do? And I'd let off, I'd go mad and walk out of school, so that's why they put me away until I was 16.

Matt conceded he was also an 'uncontrollable kid' and probably deserved to be 'put away', while though Paul was not sent away, he was placed in 'lower level' classes, which he resented, 'so I started mitching and taking glue and all that'. Many of the Boys, like Paul, felt that they had been unjustly penalized, labelled and 'picked on' because of who they were and where they came from. Teachers had simply not given them a chance. Even Spaceman, indisputably the most intellectual of the Boys, was the victim of such processes and, having decided to stay on to do his A levels, dropped out within a few months:

I loved school. I was about the only one who did out of all my peer group. I never admitted it because I would lose face. But I stayed on because I wanted to do my A levels and go on to Art College . . . I never did my A levels because they threw me out, forced me out. I was never a troublemaker but I was always like one of the Boys, and when I stayed on I was like a fish out of water. All my mates had left and all these poncey little fuckers had stayed behind who I wasn't mates with.

And when you're in the sixth form they instantly make you a prefect. But not me. I was the only fucking person in the sixth form that wasn't a prefect. So I had to fucking sit in the playground with all the fifth formers. And I just got fed up of that after a while. I went to see the headmaster and he said there's too many prefects, we haven't got room for you as a prefect, which is a stupid excuse. So, in the end, he basically railroaded me, that's the way I look at it. I was shit hot at Art and English, but they didn't like it because I was always asking questions, too many fucking questions. And you mustn't do that in Catholic schools. I didn't toe the line and they didn't like my attitude and so they fucking railroaded me. I was all right. I wanted to see the world so I joined the Merchant Navy.

Before he reached his twenties, Spaceman had become entangled on the fringes of the informal economy and was rapidly establishing a lifestyle revolving around crime, drugs and drink, from which it took him fifteen years to extricate himself.

Institutional exclusionary practices dovetailed into individual self-exclusionary practices, some of which took place irrespective of individual attitudes to school. Gary left school 'with zilch, the big zero', pointing out that he didn't go to school for the last year and instead went to work for his father. Tommy, likewise, started serious 'mitching' at the age of 14 'and my old man said right you can come and work with me if you are going mitching all the time . . . so that's what I done'. Gary has followed in his father's footsteps as a painter and decorator and now runs his own successful business, while Tommy has moved erratically between jobs in the unskilled labour market, though he has rarely been out of work, and is currently a street cleaner.

For virtually all the Boys formal education lacked both meaning and relevance, for jobs were obtained through word of mouth and through personal contacts and their aspirations were low, though they 'matched' the occupational possibilities available to them at the time. The unskilled labour market was still relatively buoyant as they moved through their teenage years, but its collapse was dramatic towards the end of the 1970s. The Boys simply did not recognize that baseline qualifications were becoming important, as Richard (who had gone to the comprehensive school) acknowledged:

Yeah, I did a bit of mitching. I didn't even consider doing exams or even furthering my education at all because I didn't think it was necessary. You know, I thought you could just walk into a job. I was ignorant really. I thought there was plenty of jobs around. Well, at the time, there was a reasonable amount of work and I didn't think it was necessary to do exams and go to college and whatever.

Kelvin left the Catholic school with no qualifications, but asserted that he 'wasn't dull', though he could see no point in studying geography or French, subjects which had no purpose for him. He did attend more practical lessons such as metalwork:

> I could have done a lot better in school but I went the other way. I strayed. A lot of things in school I thought were unnecessary and I made a point of making sure they knew about it! I mean, for four or five months my geography teacher didn't know who the hell I was because I was going off doing metalwork which was something that I knew was going to be good for me. And geography was something totally irrelevant, I didn't need at all.

Kelvin clearly did not disengage from *school*, though he disengaged strategically from those aspects of schooling he considered to be unnecessary and meaningless. For him, it was a case of pick'n'mix, informed by his own perceived learning needs, not those dictated by the school curriculum. Throughout his life, he has continued to learn on a 'need to know' basis: domestically (such as rewiring a house he bought), personally (learning some Spanish when his in-laws were charged with murder in Spain), and occupationally (for many years he was a self-taught freelance photographer). He certainly is *not* 'dull'.

Jerry (who went to the comprehensive school) said he had had no need for qualifications, for he was going in the army. Later, he became a taxi driver and now works for the Post Office, acknowledging some weaknesses arising from his lack of education, but asserting these had not really affected him in any way:

> I left school at 14, no qualifications. Even today my spelling is atrocious. But I get by. I've got a good mind. If I've got to put something on paper, then I just ask someone to fill it in for me. Obviously as long as I can remember the details, I'm all right, like, you know.

The main catalyst for self-determined disengagement from school, however, was the competing alternatives to which the Boys were attracted. Casual work, opportunistic shoplifting and simply 'dossing around' in the woods – especially during the warmer months of the year – were eminently more appealing than buckling down to schoolwork, as Trevor testified:

> I left school early. I'd missed so many lessons so they told me I couldn't stay for exams. My parents wasn't too happy but I left at Easter and went straight to work on the

market. I never went to school that much. The only time I didn't go truant was cookery classes. You can't miss them, because you've got to bring the goods home! Some aspects of school were all right but towards the end, as I got older, I seemed to get more bored. I was bored. And then a lot of the Boys were going down the woods and you'd want to be down there with them. And as you got older all you could think about was money and how to earn money, not be in school. So that's what we ended up doing, just going on the mitch, finding ways to make money.

There were also some more deeply personal reasons for persistent absenteeism and lack of educational achievement. Pete came from a seriously dysfunctional family and estimates he missed about two-thirds of his junior schooling. His mother was taken to court, though Pete recalls this had no effect: 'I think they just gave up on us, it didn't make any difference, and I did what I wanted'. Eddie had his first mental breakdown the year before he was due to leave school. Instead of sitting O levels, as planned, he was entered for CSEs but still managed to get five grade 1s (O level equivalent).

Kelvin used his personal circumstances as a pretext for *not* staying on to do exams, for there seemed little point. Since the age of 13, his name had been 'down for' an apprenticeship with a local engineering company, and when his mother was taken ill, he took a part-time job there to support the family. This subsequently became full-time: 'it was great, you know, an escape for me to get out of school'.

Maintaining Engagement and Reflections on Schooling

Very few of the Boys had any strong personal motivation towards learning and education, and even fewer could resist the strong pulls of the social and cultural context in which they lived towards 'ducking and diving' and 'living for the present'. The long-term gains arising from investment in education were viewed with suspicion, while the short-term rewards of casual and manual work (both legal and more dubious) appeared to be immediately within their grasp. Stories abounded of 'people with degrees who were on the dole', juxtaposed with 'thick people who are millionaires'. (One of the most successful of the Boys, who was not interviewed for this study, made his fortune through the door-to-door sale of potatoes.) Such stories need to be firmly related to cultural imperatives to become embedded, at the earliest opportunity, in the macho culture of the market, the building site and the pub, and the cultural denigration of pen-pushers and those who 'work' behind desks all day. Indeed, the two Boys who have studied for a degree later in life have done so through cutting themselves off from the daily round of ridicule they would have encountered had they remained living on the estate. Gordon, who did continue in learning as a teenager, tells a salutary tale about the pressures and challenges of doing so:

Yeah, I got seven O levels and three A levels. It was really difficult for me, because I didn't do any work, because all my friends . . . I don't really have an answer for why I did it. My mother worked nights and my father was in the Merchant Navy, so he was away a lot. No, I have no idea why . . . But my mother was brilliant, she was strong. She nearly killed herself working so hard for me . . . she wanted the education thing . . . And, uh, I've no idea why. I think sometimes it's either in you or it's not; she just wanted me to do it.

I really *didn't* want to do it. It was so difficult because my friends had jobs. You know, menial jobs, factory workers, apprentice this and that, but they had money. I had to scrounge a pound off my mother to go to the pub. I got three pints out of a pound, and they used to call me 'schoolboy' and everything because I was still at school. So, yeah, it was really difficult.

I could have dropped out, I suppose. I've no idea why I didn't. But I didn't know what else to do. I don't know, I just wanted to do it. I liked the subjects [history, economics and geography]. And I'd always read books. We always had books in the house, magazines, you know, *The World at War* and things like that.

And we've all done well, me and my two brothers, and we don't know why really, don't know what to say.

Gordon notes some possible reasons for sustaining his engagement with schooling but he is far more explicit about the pressures to disengage from learning: to earn some proper money and to leave the ridicule behind.

Given Gordon's story, it is perhaps surprising that *any* of the Boys remained in learning. Squeezed between institutional labelling and condemnation and more immediately attractive personal choices, disengagement was clearly the more rational response to their circumstances. Even then, though, that did not necessarily make it the sensible choice, though it made sense to many of the Boys. Tony, however, relayed his gratitude that he had gone to the Catholic school which, in his view, had provided him with an escape route to a better future. He had been brought up by a single mother and had lived in what was acknowledged locally to be the roughest part of the estate (at the heart of the 'critical patch'). Tony has since become one of the most (legitimately) successful of the Boys. Never short of a quip or two, he observed that when he went to the Catholic school, he discovered that 'not only did some kids have dads but some had dads with jobs'. His theory about the formative influences of youth is straightforward ('the school you went to and the pub you drank in'), for he is adamant that attending the Catholic school had made all the difference:

Yeah, I did have qualifications. I left with five average grade GCEs [General Certificate of Education] and a couple of CSEs. So I did have some basic qualifications. Personally I think I was exceptionally fortunate to go to the school I went to. I think it was a school that actually did have a code of discipline in place. And I totally respect that, because I remember the road I lived in . . . you know, we talk about some of the other Boys and what they've done and where they are now, and those guys were privileged compared to where I came from.

That street and the small council house in which Tony grew up could not contrast more starkly with the executive bungalow in the neat English village in which he now lives.

Tony's 'school and pub' thesis should not be dismissed lightly, for those who attended the Catholic school did, by and large, avoid the worst excesses of youthful offending, remaining more closely engaged in learning and most acquiring at least some formal qualifications. Of the three who did not, two (Marty and Mack) attached themselves to their peers from the comprehensive school at an early age and ended up in their truanting and drinking network (located around one particular pub, The Wayfarer). In contrast, Gary, the successful painter and decorator, who had attended the comprehensive school, was banned from The Wayfarer at the age of 14, and, as a result, linked up with the Catholic Boys in a different Milltown pub, The Centurion. The trajectory of his life course, and his retrospective views on learning, are much more akin to those of the Boys from the Catholic school than to those of his contemporaries from the comprehensive.

Elsewhere in the book it will be noted that the Boys – with few exceptions – now deeply regret their failure to engage with their schooling, for they have, belatedly and too late, recognized the importance that formal qualifications confer. They are keen for their children to do well in school, though they often have little idea about how to support this outcome.

The vast majority of the Boys were clearly completely alienated from schooling, resenting its authority and proclaiming its irrelevance. They saw no point in it. Coupled with the out-of-school attractions dangled before them, their disengagement is not surprising, though many have learned a harsh lesson in the longer term, as the unskilled labour market for which they were destined, and for which they prepared themselves, contracted. In its place is a crime and drugs economy, which is *always* a risky place to be. Only one of the Boys, Jamie, has made the crossover from manual labour to office-based work. Whether or not the nine CSEs up his sleeve assisted this transition at the age of 36 is hard to say, but those with nothing to show for their schooling have remained positioned much more firmly at the margins.

–5–

Teenage Dreams

Introduction

Regardless of their aspirations, the Boys' occupational options were inevitably limited by their criminal records, and their lack of educational qualifications. Those options were further constrained by the rapid restructuring of the 'youth labour market' in the late 1970s (Ashton and Maguire 1983; Ashton et al. 1990); yet the Boys had still had their dreams, despite these restrictions to their horizons.

Money, Money, Money

> I was always dreaming about money, at that time, you know, lots of money, even stealing lots of money. Yeah, basically just thinking about money – for holidays, cars, things like that.

Marty was completely obsessed with having money in his pocket, and was exceptional in that he was a lone burglar, never willing to consider collective forays or sharing his ill-gotten gains, like most of the other Boys. Of course, many of the Boys dreamt of earning 'good money' but rarely set their sights too high. As Danny observed,

> Just a good job, building site, whatever paid good. I mean, I knew I wasn't getting no qualifications, so I didn't really worry about it because I knew my [criminal] record was really bad. I knew it was gonna hold me up.

Building site work, in comparison with other prospective employment, did in fact pay 'good money', though *any job* was the humble goal of most of the Boys. Derek commented that 'in them days like, your goal was just to get out of school as soon as possible and get working, and that was it, like, you know'. Paul, rather sadly, simply dreamed of collecting his first Giro. Long before the end of compulsory schooling, he had become a regular glue-sniffer, and remained 'on the glue' until his early twenties:

> When I was in school, like, all I could think about was leaving school so I can get my dole money because that was like having your own money then. I was on the glue from

when I was 12, 13 and when I left school, I just got my dole money and I was still on the glue till I was 20, 22.

Ted learned from an early age, when his older brothers encouraged him to go shoplifting on their behalf, that there were ways of getting money without working: 'I was only a little kid and they'd give me a couple of bob and I felt rich, like; I think I learnt then that you didn't need to work to get what you wanted'.

For most of the Boys from the comprehensive school (and the two from the Catholic school who came to associate most closely with them), the acquisition of money became almost an end in itself, though it was invariably frittered away on cigarettes, alcohol and clothes. Having a constant flow of money jangling in their pockets was their abstract dream, with little sense of how it might be acquired – though some forms of criminal enterprise were already at play – or any more concrete purposes to which it might be put. Most were realistic enough to settle for the narrowly framed pathways which lay open to them.

Teenage Kicks

Most of the Boys from the Catholic school (together with Gary, who joined up with them around the age of 14) had less mercenary, and far more expressive, hedonistic dreams. Spaceman, in particular, had recently been reflecting on these matters, having been studying for his art degree with students twenty years his junior:

> And what I was thinking when I was their age was to have as much fun as I possibly could. That was it. There was no thinking about the future at all. The future didn't exist. It was live for today, without a doubt, live fast till you die. And I nearly did, but I didn't. I did die twice actually. But back then it was money, work, women, girls, clubs, clothes, music and that's all there was. Simple hedonistic pleasures of life.

Spaceman had nearly died twice and, after one fight in town, was given the last rites. Gary had had a very similar outlook on his life:

> At nineteen, I just didn't give a monkey's, really. I just really wanted to enjoy myself. It was the same with most of the Boys. I'd just pick up a bit of work here, a bit of work there – just to go drinking and having so much fun. There was no plan, nothing at all, not at that age.

Those Boys who were working got paid on Fridays and everything had gone by Sunday, for the weekends were life in the fast lane – heavy drinking, late night clubbing, and incessant fighting. It fulfilled the Boys' dreams at that moment, and few looked further ahead.

Happiness

Preparation for adult life (occupationally and socially) had simply not entered the heads of most of the Boys and, when asked to think back to whether or not they had had any dreams, many struggled for anything to say. They often resorted to an abstract dream world of personal happiness and happy families, with no concrete sense at all of how this might become a reality. Ryan said he couldn't remember ever thinking about wanting to *be* anything, except to be happy: 'so I just went from job to job, messing around, being happy; that was it basically'. Richard also said he had never had any big dreams, though,

> I just thought that when I left school I am gonna meet some beautiful woman and settle down and have a nice family and live happily ever after . . . I didn't think about how I was going to achieve it, how it was going to come about, like.

Happiness, in some abstract way, was often considered to be an important substitute if financial plenty and security did not materialize. Better to be poor and happy than rich and sad was a common mantra among the Boys, a philosophy in stark contradiction to their eternal quest for money. Even Marty, in almost the same breath as asserting that 'money is the dream for everybody', suggested that 'you know, if you're a dustman and you're happy, that's just like being a millionaire, isn't it . . .'

Que Sera, Sera

The Boys had lacked any supportive direction or guidance during their teenage years, generally living for the moment and waiting to see how things materialized. In part, this was because they felt there was no real alternative to this, and also because they perceived a risk of things backfiring if they tried to plan too far into the future. Alex had had no dreams: 'nothing at all . . . the old que sera, sera bit'. Colin simply observed, 'I had no qualifications or nothing, so it was just leave school and see what happened', while Denny elaborated on his reflections a little more:

> Well I got a job with a central heating firm and then I just thought that I'd become a heating engineer and generally have a good job and go through life and see what came really, more than dream of anything. I never had no dreams of being some millionaire or anything like that. Just to earn money, to go out and enjoy myself basically. That's all I had in mind; nothing more. I never thought too far ahead, you know, because you see you get your teeth kicked in too many times anyway, you know. Take nothing for granted. Just see what happens.

Even Tony, who is now perceived by the other Boys to have always had a burning ambition to succeed, cannot recall having any particular aspirations:

> I don't think that I had any aspirations when I was that age. It was just meandering through school. I left school with no real sense of direction, got a job as an apprentice, an alleged apprentice, and hated every moment of it. So I left that job and joined Bell & Howlett as a temporary stop gap and I have been there now for twenty-two years. So really teenage aspirations didn't exist. Nothing I can recall.

Kelvin also indicated that he had never been a big dreamer; 'it was just a case of seeing what came up', while Tommy, always matter-of-fact and to the point, captured quite clearly this absence of any defined aspiration among the Boys:

> I just wanted to get out of school. I wasn't good at anything, so I really hadn't got a clue. I wasn't going to be a footballer, or a rocket scientist or anything like that. I was just going to be an ordinary bloke. Just find a job, a decent job hopefully, and start work. That's all I wanted to do really.

Sporting Dreams

Some of the Boys indicated they had secretly harboured dreams of becoming a professional sportsman. Many, like Tommy, knew this was quite unrealistic because of a patent lack of skill, though others did perhaps possess the skills, but knew their lack of effort and commitment made these foolish hopes. One or two had, indeed, gone for preliminary trials with professional football clubs, but got no further, for even when they were asked back, they had usually not turned up.

Such dreams of stardom were not completely absurd, for the estate had produced a number of well-known singers, boxers, rugby players and footballers, some of whom were known to the Boys. Only Vic, however, took his rugby ambitions almost to the point of fruition when he signed for a northern rugby league club, but he soon came back because he was homesick and missed his mates:

> Well I suppose I always wanted to play rugby and well, as you know, I had a go at rugby league, didn't I. But I didn't have no one there to push me, to encourage me, like with my grandmother being old . . . and my mother never really had any time for me. So that went out of the window and I come back to Milltown.

Specific Labour Market Aspirations

A handful of the Boys did have specific labour market aspirations, though they accepted they would probably still just take whatever turned up. Nick, for reasons unknown to him, had embraced the traditional craftsman's ethos from an early age and wanted to be a bricklayer, although there was no member of his extended family in the building trade:

> I always wanted to be able to stand back and say 'I did that . . . that's my work'. I wanted to do something that was really appreciated . . . from that to that, it was me that done it.

For some of his working life, Nick did indeed become an exterior painter, which arguably contributed to the realization of those 'dreams'.

Mal had wanted to be a painter and decorator and did a youth training scheme to that end, but ended up working in a factory: 'other than that, I never had any big dreams, except playing for Man United, of course – that was a big dream'. Gary did become a painter and decorator, but this was something he *knew* he was going to do, following in the footsteps of his father, and had never contemplated doing anything else. Shaun had hoped to become an electrician, which he did, and still does, despite having a degree in electrical engineering.

Like Mal, a number of the Boys did youth training programmes in painting and decorating, and construction, which some considered to be 'like an apprenticeship' (see Williamson 1982), though these schemes rarely provided a route into skilled employment, and the Boys subsequently returned once more to whatever was going in the unskilled labour market.

Not all the Boys were physically able to hold their own in heavy manual labour. Tony and Eddie, in particular, were small and, although they had no idea what they wanted to do, they were clear about what they did *not* want to do, which was to avoid manual work. Tony, as noted earlier, got an 'alleged' apprenticeship as a sheet metal worker on leaving school, though he was soon searching for an office job. Eddie was so small when he left school that nobody at the careers office believed he was 16. When he was asked what he wanted to do, 'I said, well basically something clerical, that's all, and I ended up with a job in the civil service . . . So I had no high expectations or any expectations at all really, other than I fancied something clerical rather than manual or physical'.

Dreams beyond the Labour Market

Most of the Boys' dreams, where they existed at all, were integrally connected to the labour market and earning money. These, however, were rarely specific, and the realization of even spontaneous 'teenage kicks' was contingent on having the resources to indulge in some immediate hedonistic pleasure; few of the Boys had looked further afield than to the weekend spent in town.

Three of the Boys, however, dreamt of seeing more of the world, which for Tommy has remained unfulfilled, as his wife has never wanted to go abroad. In contrast, Jerry always wanted to travel and has done so in both his working and his private life. As a child, he wanted to be a lorry driver, though when he left school, he joined the army and served in Germany and Northern Ireland. He takes regular foreign holidays, saving all year to do so, and has been not only to typical package destinations such as Spain and Greece, but also to India and South Africa.

Jerry's closest childhood friend, Pete, 'came out' at the age of 16, soon afterwards moving to London to live with his brother-in-law, who was also gay, and subsequently with a partner. Pete maintains it was his homosexuality which gave him the chance to fulfil his dreams of travel, for until he was 16, he had left the city only once (apart from a short spell of incarceration in Detention Centre):

> When I was a kid, I wanted to travel. I never thought it would happen. I would sit in the woods on the mitch and dream about travelling. The 'global village' had just been coined and I wanted to be part of it. I wanted to find somebody who would take me there and show me it. I knew somebody somewhere was having it and I assumed it must be in London or New York or Amsterdam or whatever. But I didn't have the background, the contacts, the things you needed to be part of it. And then one door opened and that was enough – you only need one. My brother-in-law and, through him, my first partner Daniel. I mean, my brother-in-law was a complete and utter shit, but Daniel was my knight in shining armour. I was so very lucky. I was sixteen years old and the door to the world was opened for me.

Daniel died of a brain haemorrhage a few years later, but not before he and Pete had travelled together and embraced the vibrant gay London scene. Pete drifted for a while before meeting his second partner, Barry, and they have been together now for seventeen years. Ironically, on the first leg of a world tour they were undertaking in 1996 (Barry had sold his business to finance the trip), Barry was almost fatally injured by the nail bomb at the Atlanta Olympics, and is still undergoing physiotherapy. Despite these heartbreaks, Pete has still gone some way in realizing his dreams.

One of Pete's closest Milltown friends, Matt, became powerfully aware of his black identity when he was sent to approved school and was confronted with the prevailing Christianity promoted by the school. Resisting this, he explored Rastafarianism and before the age of 16 had 'turned Rasta': 'I had locks and got into all that cultural thing . . . I suppose I thought I was going to turn out to be a sort of preacher'. For ten years he lived in self-induced poverty, strolling round with a staff until he discovered the hypocrisy within the Rastafarian hierarchy, at which point he abandoned those dreams and 'hit the drugs big time'.

Post-16 Learning

Nathan and Tony stumbled into what they believed to be apprenticeships, while Shaun did acquire a proper apprenticeship, and some of the other Boys did youth training schemes. None of these was considered to be vocational *learning*, however; they were *jobs*, albeit with training (of some kind).

Only Spaceman and Gordon contemplated post-16 pathways that involved the continuation of academic learning. Spaceman really had dreamed of studying art and literature but, from his point of view, was 'railroaded out' of school only a few months after starting his A levels (see Chapter 4). Gordon also pursued his studies, with more success, gaining A levels and then a degree, though he made it clear that his teenage dreams were to spend more time in the pub with his mates:

> Well I *didn't* want to stay in school . . . I never did no studying. You know, homework was on the bus. For A levels that was ridiculous. Obviously I managed but the thing is, you couldn't be seen as a grafter. With all my mates going out all the time, there was unconscious pressure, I suppose. They were going out, so I wanted to go out. You know, 'cos all my mates had finished school and they were going to the pub and I wanted to go to the pub. It was 'I'm not doing my homework, bollocks to that'. What I wanted was to be with them in the pub.

So Gordon certainly did not *dream* of staying in learning, acquiring qualifications and moving into a professional career, for he wanted to stay with the Boys in the pub. His subsequent career (as something of an entrepreneur, night-club doorman and property owner) has combined the advantages of both his educational attainment and his Milltown roots, and is, of itself, quite a fascinating story.

Conclusion

The Boys had few concrete 'teenage dreams' beyond the general hope that they would get a 'good job', and thereby earn decent money and be happy. Their general position was that they would 'take life as it comes', a relaxed and casual orientation to the future which was both pragmatic and realistic (given the barriers in the way to the achievement of even modest goals), though it was also self-defeating, for there were moments of opportunity which many failed to seize.

Nathan got an apprenticeship as a tiler, but lost interest after a couple of years: 'I couldn't be bothered'. Ted had thought of becoming a physical training instructor, but two and a half years in custody between the ages of 17 and 20 'really put paid to any ideas that I had of getting on to the right side of the tracks'. Danny did a City and Guilds course in metalwork while in Borstal, but failed to complete it.

The Boys displayed an 'easy come, easy go' mentality which was rarely rocked. Only when something dramatic, and usually of a personal nature, impinged on their lives was the fatalism of their life course called into question. Gary's father died when he was 22: 'that's when it was growing up time for me. But until then it was just drinking and having a good time'. Spaceman's moment of change did not take place until his late thirties, following being told, while he was in prison, of his father's terminal illness, and medical advice that if he did not address his addictions, he would soon follow.

Such moments occurred later in their lives. When they were young, there was a well-trodden path apparently ahead of them, a future of manual labour (Willis 1978), which they did not think much beyond; nor could they, for they had few other reference points, as Shaun observed:

> I don't know whether as a teenager I actually really knew what I wanted to be. I knew what I wanted: two point four kids, four-bedroomed detached house and two cars on the drive. But as far as a job went, as a teenager, I didn't know. I knew what I was going to *do*. I knew I was going to do an apprenticeship but I didn't know whether that was what I *wanted* to be doing. Because I'd had no experience of anything. You know, I might have liked to be a social worker or a solicitor. I just didn't know. I didn't have any knowledge or experience of anything like that. You know, you come out of school, you get offered an apprenticeship and you take it, thinking that's what you want to be. If you can understand what I'm saying there.

The teenage dreams of the Milltown Boys were, inevitably, heavily circumscribed by the narrow occupational and social culture of their neighbourhood. Fathers and older brothers worked on building sites and in factories, and drank down the local pub. No wonder this was also what they expected to do. Given their limited qualifications and the added disadvantage of their juvenile criminal records (and early custodial experiences for some within the adult criminal justice system), it is not surprising the Boys' teenage dreams were largely framed by the twin philosophies of short-termism and entrenched fatalism. Live for today, they argued, for there is little personal capacity to influence the future – an approach to their lives established in their mid-teens, which became more strongly reinforced as the Boys entered early adulthood.

–6–

Employment 'Careers' – Ducking and Diving, Dodging and Weaving

Introduction

It is because they lack qualifications and skills (as conventionally defined) that the socially excluded have been marginalised, but these defects are an asset in the new capitalism, whose extremes of flexibility create spaces not just for short term jobs, but for sporadic jobs, semi-legal jobs and a variety of informal arrangements (from house cleaning and nannying to the milder forms of crime, such as selling recreational drugs or driving vanloads of beer and cigarettes across tax borders). For these sporadic and informal jobs, being 'streetwise' is all the education that is needed. At the margins of the new capitalism, knowing too much might be risky. But there is rarely a future at the margins. (Field 2000, p. 109)

The academic literature on transitions from school to work, and on job retention once in the labour market, has managed to impose an order and discipline, and produce a variety of theoretical frameworks, which simply do not stand up to the test of empirical verification if one gets close enough. From the typology of the 'careerless' and those with 'short' and 'extended' careers (Ashton and Field 1976), to the more complex view of 'trajectories', 'navigations', 'niches' and 'pathways' (Evans and Furlong 1997), there is a sense that one can somehow dissociate aspiration and experience in relation to training and work from the wider context of individual lives and then dissect this in glorious isolation. Moreover, the assessment of 'success' and 'failure' of pathways within the occupational life course has, too often, been prematurely concluded, passing judgement on young people at a point when, at most, they have reached only their early twenties.

The histories of the Milltown Boys suggest that the occupational life-course, certainly of those at the margins of the labour market, can ebb and flow dramatically in terms of its stability or volatility, even as individuals approach middle age. Working (and non-working) lives are, of course, integrally bound up with family relationships, housing circumstances – and much more; it could hardly be otherwise, for the life course is inevitably influenced by complex interrelationships between different life domains, although economy and employment is usually central. Sometimes opportunity seized in the labour market has contributed to progression and development across a wider canvas (in, for example, relationships, leisure, or housing). In contrast, however, those risks that have not been 'managed' (see Helve and Bynner 1996), and to which the Boys have succumbed, have often stalled such 'progression' and indeed sometimes put it in reverse.

Having anticipated following in the footsteps of their fathers and older brothers, the opportunities for secure and reasonably well-paid work in the local manual economy diminished rapidly towards the end of the 1970s, forcing the Boys to find alternative economic pathways. Even during their schooldays, they had blended legitimate income-generation with more dubious practices, and such combinations continued to inform their economic activities into their adult lives. Well-paid, regular, formal employment clearly reduced such a need for other activity of questionable legitimacy, but was hard to come by and many of the Boys continued to knit together, in a variety of ways, formal employment, casual work, unemployment benefit claims and criminal enterprise. This was a case of 'needs must', especially during the early 1980s when there was serious economic recession and legitimate work was at a premium. Even those proclaiming they wanted to work (and most did) found themselves experiencing extended periods of unemployment and, out of necessity (as they saw it), fiddling the dole. If they found their way back into regular work, however, they would sign off and desist from active crime. Others, though, started from the 'other side', establishing patterns of economic behaviour and a staple diet of income generation dependent on signing on, criminal activity and gambling. This was supplemented occasionally by 'fiddles' (informal work), or periods of legitimate employment. From their point of view, legal jobs paying no more than what is now the minimum wage were laughable, and they took them on temporarily only to keep the 'social' sweet, or because an offending record was becoming too 'hot' and carried the serious risk of a custodial sentence.

In contrast, a few of the Boys have almost unbroken legitimate employment histories, usually incorporating a sequence of related and unrelated jobs, and more rarely representing 'permanent' employment with just one or two companies. This has, however, been a rather different story for Tony and Colin, with Tony climbing the promotion ladder with one company to the position of regional sales manager, while Colin is still making pallets for the same company after twenty years. Beyond these questions of continuities and/or discontinuities in job histories, there has been a remarkable array in the *types* of jobs secured and sustained by the Boys. That said, only one of the Boys (Jamie) has crossed the divide between manual and office work in his adult life, though two (Tony and Eddie) entered white-collar work shortly after leaving school, and Gordon has always 'dodged' between the two.

Employment Histories – An Overview

All but two of the Boys stumbled into the labour market at the minimum school leaving age, and few had any particular intentions in mind, though there were two typical destinations: the local fruit market or a job creation scheme. Twelve of the Boys joined a scheme (for a period of up to twelve months), often ending up afterwards at the fruit market, linking up with their friends who had gone there directly from school. The fruit market was itself a stepping stone, a place for biding their time until adult employment (at age 18) became available. It was also a place for developing a repertoire of skills and scams which would often stand them in good stead in their future employment.

Tommy and Gary worked with their fathers (which they had been doing while they were still at school). Others undertook 'apprenticeships' of one sort or another, though their authenticity as proper apprenticeships was debatable. Tony and Denny rapidly gave theirs up, and Nathan dropped out after two years. Shaun duly served his four years as an electrician, as did Jamie, as a fitter machinist, only for both to be sacked at the end. Richard and Alex did some other kind of training (in bricklaying and upholstery respectively), which equipped them with skills they have continued to use throughout their occupational lives, one rather more legitimately than the other. Jerry joined the army, then became a taxi driver and now works for the Post Office.

Most of the immediate post-school occupational destinations demanded physical strength – doing building work on the job creation programme or humping crates at the fruit market. Two were not up to this, on account of their small physique. Eddie was referred to an employment rehabilitation centre, before moving on to clerical work in a Job Centre. Tony at first tried to 'hang in' with the Boys, starting at the fruit market then proceeding on to sheet metal factory work, though he was always on the look out for an office job and soon landed a temporary post with the company for which he still works.

The remainder of the Boys found unskilled labouring work or stayed embedded in criminal enterprise, though often it was a combination of the two, for the job creation programme led to unemployment more often than it did to work. Even if it led to employment, the work secured was often dirty, anti-social and poorly paid. There were strong, understandable, temptations for the Boys to remain involved in crime, even though the risks had become greater since they were no longer juveniles and a number were already or imminently on the edge of custody. Indeed, seven of the Boys had very short-lived occupational 'careers', though they did have odd jobs (ice-cream vans, supermarket cleaners, fun fairs, removals, coalman, door work and bouncing, painting and decorating), sometimes into their early twenties. The duration of this work, however, could usually be counted in months rather than years and was interspersed by periods in custody and spells of unemployment. As teenagers, they had been more 'heavy-end' offenders and steadily became more entrenched in crime as they moved into early adulthood. Most would today be described as persistent offenders and low-level 'professional' criminals, earning their living – as they themselves describe it – 'on the street'.

Four others followed such a path into their mid- to late twenties but then gradually desisted from crime. This was an outcome of getting a 'decent' job, changing personal relationships, successfully tackling drug and alcohol problems, and an emergent sense of 'maturity' and responsibility. None of the four is wholly dissociated from their past and still face temptations to return to their 'old ways', for they have worked, on a piecemeal basis, on the fiddle, in seasonal work, and in casual and temporary employment.

Eight of the Boys whose teenage offending was of a similar order to those above have moved along a very different path. They secured 'steady' work soon after leaving school and, though some have had intermittent spells of unemployment and working on the fiddle, they have generally had adult economic careers characterized by regular legitimate employment.

Only by their mid-twenties (an observation of some significance for youth research predictions) did clearer patterns emerge, as the Boys established relationships and had children. Two-thirds of the Boys were soon to reach a point where they would embark on virtually continuous employment until the age of 40, often in no more than one or two jobs.

There were, however, many surprising twists and turns in the labour market trajectories of the Boys. Housing was a key factor, with a number availing themselves of the 'right to buy' scheme. The knock-down price opened up the possibilities of owner-occupation, but also produced a new set of responsibilities, for no longer was it possible to flit between jobs, or to take time out, relying on housing benefit to pay the rent if they were on the 'social'. Though not always the case, the birth of children often produced a different sense of responsibility in attitudes towards employment. The birth of a disabled daughter transformed Jerry's outlook on both work and leisure, for he not only recognized the need for regular, stable employment in order to provide sufficiently for Rachael, but also acknowledged his own needs for space of his own if he was to maintain his commitment to her. In contrast, though, two of the Boys (Derek and Kelvin), both parents and one an owner-occupier, made completely precipitous decisions to walk out on jobs they had held down for fifteen years or so. They had simply 'had enough' and were confident something else would turn up.

Five of the Boys became self-employed. Gary runs a successful business. Alex is the sole trader in a less successful business. Richard and Kelvin do subcontracting work, wanting the flexibility to take time off when they feel like it, while Gordon is something of an entrepreneur. Having made a lot of money in the United

States, he now owns property and businesses, though he still usually does a professional job during the day.

Of the other ten, the story follows a different pattern, one heavily circumscribed by crime, alcoholism, drug addiction and physical and mental illness. Spaceman, after being 'railroaded' out of post-16 learning, joined the Merchant Navy but discharged himself after a couple of years, having served what he described as an 'apprenticeship' in heavy drinking. He embarked on a catalogue of fiddles and offending as a means of feeding his increasing alcohol (and later drug) dependency, and only towards the end of his thirties did he de-tox and resume his education. Nick experienced a short prison sentence (though he had anticipated a much longer one) before addressing his drink problem and attempting to pursue legitimate employment. Nutter, always a heavy drinker, held down a regular job at the steelworks for fifteen years until he was sacked for poor attendance, and then did not work for the next five years. Paul has never worked legitimately since the job creation programme. He admits to being a problem drinker, though he does nothing about it, and he is still in and out of prison. Nearly all the others have also experienced spells in custody, an almost inevitable consequence of trying to make a living 'on the street', though some have been more successful than others at both making a living and evading custody, with shoplifting and petty drug dealing, as well as some shifting of stolen goods and money lending, being their preferred activities.

Three of the Boys do not work for legitimate reasons. In his early twenties, Vic acknowledged he was a 'shit thief' and found work instead in seasonal industrial painting, through which he developed serious bronchial problems and is now on incapacity benefit. Marty suffers from paranoid schizophrenia, yet even before that diagnosis had never worked except in seasonal and casual jobs, while Pete has only ever worked casually in bars, warehouses and petrol stations, until he became a carer for his disabled partner, Barry.

Six of the Boys – Sample Trajectories

Shaun

Shaun, as we have seen, was the only one of the Boys from the comprehensive school to achieve any formal qualifications, his three CSEs being enough to secure him an apprenticeship as an electrician with the Docks Board, though his father working there probably helped (Lee and Wrench 1981). He 'only just' completed the apprenticeship, for in his final year he met Sue, and 'sex was much better than maths, so I spent most of my time round there when I was supposed to be in college'. His employer did not keep him on, and he struggled to find regular work. In the next twelve months, he did four short-term jobs, rewiring houses, doing electrical work for a construction firm, building motor control panels, and on the fiddle doing concreting work with his brother.

Shaun then decided to retrain in instrumentation and spent a year at a Skill Centre. After a short spell of unemployment he got a job with Allied Steel as an instrument technician where he stayed for ten years, 'and when I did leave that was more the result of the break-up of my marriage than the job itself'.

Shaun was 33 when his marriage broke up. Sue had increasingly resented missing out on her own education because of her early pregnancy and, after having three children, she returned to learning, went to university and met someone else. His dreams shattered, a devastated Shaun did not fight the divorce, and he and Sue remain on amicable terms. His immediate priority, however, became 'to find another wife'; this, coupled with uncertain circumstances at work, led to a decision to give up his job and go into higher education, where he studied for a Higher National Certificate (HNC) in electronics, then went on to do a BSc in electrical engineering. As it turned out he had no difficulty in finding another wife, for prior to starting college Shaun fell for one of his sister's friends.

On leaving university Shaun got a temporary job for twelve months, writing training and maintenance manuals for an automation company. When his contract came to an end he was out of work for a while, which he described as 'more or less a choice, there were jobs offered to me but they weren't paying enough and I thought I was worth more'. Shaun then returned to Allied Steel as an electrician, never divulging he had a degree, for he did not want to appear 'over-qualified' and had no desire to work in management. After three years, he applied successfully for another job in a paper-making factory:

I went there as a multi-skilled technician – mechanical, electrical and instrumentation. And I would have been quite happy to settle there for the rest of my life. The pay was good, the job was good, and the conditions were lovely, but unfortunately the mill shut and I was made redundant. I started in September 1997. I was there for two years and one day, just enough to get my redundancy. And then I accepted a job with a company that makes batteries for the Ministry of Defence. And I'm down there as an electrician now.

For those two years Shaun had a job that neared perfection in his eyes, and he had worked hard to achieve it. Two years later, however, he was back to being 'just' an electrician – not unhappy with the job, but not as content as he would like to be, and certainly not making full use of his manifest skills and qualifications, though this had *never* been his top priority.

Ryan

Ryan had been one of the more violent of the Boys. At 17 he owned a smart Suzuki GT250 motorbike, appeared to be indulged by his relatively well-off parents (because both were in regular employment), and was always dressed in the latest style. His preferred drink was 'snakebite' (cider and lager), which exacerbated his violent tendencies. He was courting a regular girlfriend, whom he later married (and who he is still with), and has nearly always worked, legally or otherwise. Unlike most of the Boys, Ryan does not smoke, which is significant given the job he now does.

Ryan worked at the fruit market for two years after leaving school, and then got a factory job ('where I am now, funny, isn't it') but hated it and left after a year, ending up on a couple of outdoor government training programmes, for he always preferred working outside. After being convicted on two counts of grievous bodily harm he did a spell in prison, but it was 'no big deal'. On release, he worked with a decorator for about five years, all over the country, but the business folded, and Ryan was out of work. He turned to fiddling, claiming social security and working on the side: 'I was in and out of work then, like, for the next ten years, just labouring and doing what I could'. This included working in a brewery and on building sites and then, for some years, on a motorway link road:

> I liked that, that was a good job. I was strong and fit. I suppose I was 26, 27. Yeah, that was a good job because I was out in the countryside and I was bringing home about three hundred quid [pounds] then – in 1986! – but I was working, like, five in the morning till ten in the night. That was great, but then I hurt my back. I was shifting concrete all day long, and I did my back in.

Though he was, and is, still very fit (his hobbies are walking and mountain biking), Ryan was no longer able to do very heavy manual work. He tried to find some 'lighter' fiddles but this proved difficult and, at the age of 35, he ended back in the factory where he had been at the age of 18:

> So it has sort of gone full circle. Only now I'm doing a worser job. The same place, only a worser job, because I do three shifts now and I used to do two before. It does my head in. Making seals and gaskets for cars. Mundane, non-stop production line shit.

But the money is good and that is what keeps him there, in order to indulge his granddaughter, do up the house and even consider buying it, though he really hates the job (working indoors, breathing in fumes) and is always *thinking* of moving on, but never more:

> I have thought about doing something else, retraining for something different. Since the day I started this job I have said I'll give it six months and then do something else, but it's five years coming up now. I've got used to having money now, regular money. Good money. Vicious circle, innit?

Trevor

Trevor is mixed race. He was quite deeply involved in offending as a teenager (car crime was his speciality), and on leaving school took the well-trodden path to the fruit market. For a short time, he worked abroad, but now lives within a stone's throw of where he was brought up, with his wife and three children. Having bought a former council house, he is now self-employed. He divorced his wife during the 1980s and they parted for a year, but now live together again.

Trevor recalls working on the market with affection: 'we had a good time down there, we'd get to know all the market boys and all their tricks . . . they had some good tricks, you know'. The wages were 16 pounds a week (in 1976), which was 'not bad' money for a minimum age school leaver, though it was not good either (the Youth Opportunities Programme training allowance started at £17.50 in 1979). The market, however, offered plenty of opportunity for supplementing these wages and the Boys were, at different moments, both 'wolves' and 'hawks' (Mars 1983), hunting in packs and 'working' together to liberate stock, or swooping down on items or produce left lying around. The market was the arena in which such skills were honed. Trevor worked there for two years. Offered a salesman's job with the market he refused ('just didn't interest me at the time'), though he eventually moved on when offered a job as a 'chain boy' on a building site, assisting surveyors in planning the foundations – 'the only reason I moved, more money'. As he was cleaning the surveyor's tapes one day he was offered another job by carpenters working on the site, which he took because it was, once again, more money. However, the site shut down at Christmas and, afterwards, the carpenters didn't want him back. Trevor was on the dole for a short while until, through a contact down the pub, he found work refurbishing a brewery. Workmates at the brewery then heard of lucrative building site work in Germany: 'yeah, we was offered a job in Germany and off we went to Germany', with Trevor employed as a brickie's labourer, working and drinking hard:

> And we'd go down to Hamburg in the night then, down to the Reeperbahn, the street of windows, first time we'd experienced prostitutes on a large scale. And they are asking you if you want it for thirty-five marks and you are thinking, wait a minute, that's seven pounds fifty! I'm earning three hundred pounds a week, that's not a bad price!

The heavy drinking led to some serious fighting and the Boys came home, but Trevor recalls the whole time as a great experience, for though he had spent freely, he had also accumulated quite a lot of money, and he felt *rich*. His wages had been two notes – two thousand-mark notes – and he had always sent one home by post. On returning home, he went everywhere by taxi for a few weeks, then went on holiday to Spain.

When he came home 'for good' he married Jill, whom he had met shortly before going out to Germany. By this time the money was running out and he joined a window-fitting company working on a new concert hall in the city centre. When that finished, he worked with the company around Britain, but was then laid off, and he became a Unigate milkman. After a year or so, however, he incurred a terrible injury playing football (he is convinced that had he not been 'a yard faster from working on the milk', he would never have reached the ball and not have fractured his leg) and was in plaster for ten months. During this absence, Unigate franchised the milk round and Trevor decided to take it, though he soon discovered he could no longer do the round at speed, and many customers were simply not paying their bills. With a second child on the way, he reflected on his occupational future and, after consulting Jill, decided to invest their savings of £500 in training for a Class 1 Heavy Goods Vehicle (HGV) licence. This, they agreed, would be an 'extra string to your bow that can get someone like myself a better job'.

Like Ryan, Trevor worked on the motorway link road for nearly three years, in his case from the cab of earth-moving vehicles. When the job finished, however, he was laid off and went on the fiddle, signing on and driving tippers for cash in hand. Eight months later, he set up with his brother-in-law as a subcontractor for window installation, which is what he still does, though since 1992 he has worked in partnership with another man 'who was moving in the same direction'. He has never been short of work, securing contracts through word of mouth and through the many companies with which he has been associated over the years.

Tony

Tony has done very well for himself. He lives in a detached bungalow and drives an executive Alfa Romeo company car. He married a girl from another estate (the accidental outcome of a blind date when she was 'lined up' for Gary, who didn't turn up), and they have two teenage children, both of whom are doing well at school. The other Boys believe Tony Beech was always 'destined' for this (often referring to him as 'five star Beechie') and assert he always had a driving ambition, though he himself denies it.

Growing up in a single-parent household on the roughest part of the estate and although small in physique, Tony did not shy away from the violence which, fuelled by heavy drinking, characterized the Boys' teenage lifestyles. However, he made only one appearance before the juvenile court, and got some respectable GCEs (O levels). Like many of the others, he headed off to the fruit market when he left school at the minimum age, and with two of the other Boys then worked briefly as an 'apprentice' sheet metal worker. He was, however, always on the lookout for an office job, slipping off to the Job Centre every Friday afternoon to see what was available:

And one day, down the Job Centre, there was this job with Bell & Howlett, a sort of temporary job. It was in an office environment, it was a stock control clerk. And over about seven years, from 1977 to 1984, I worked my way up from stock control clerk to a buyer and then to a buying manager.

The company was opening a new office in Southampton, and Tony was asked if he was interested in taking up a management position there. It was not too difficult a decision, for he and his girlfriend Angie had bought a small flat in Milltown and he acknowledges that he was already 'drifting away from the Boys'. Moving to Southampton as the 'admin manager, a bit like deputy manager', it was 'better money, better house, better car and all those things', and though the job did not fulfil its promise, it was a stepping stone. Two years later, Tony took a sideways step, going on the road as a salesman, and towards the end of the 1980s was offered the position of regional sales manager: 'I've had twelve years of success and I've turned the business around to the second most profitable business in the company'.

Mack

Mack, like Tony, went to the Catholic school but, unlike Tony, stopped attending well before the minimum leaving age, mitching and hanging around with the comprehensive school Boys. He was deeply involved in a range of offending as a teenager and acquired a substantial criminal record, though he was never committed to custody. He now lives with his mother, having parted from his common-law wife, though they remain on reasonably good terms and he sees his two children regularly: his son, an exceptional pool player, regularly wins national and international tournaments (at the age of 12). Mack's legitimate occupational 'career' was short-lived:

> Um . . . work wise, as soon as I left school, I worked in a big supermarket, sweeping the floors. For eleven months. Then I went to a department store, for seven months. Just doing the rubbish, picking up all the rubbish. And that's it. That's all I've ever done. I haven't worked in a proper job since.

Mack was sacked from both jobs and his career in the formal labour market ended shortly before his eighteenth birthday, though subsequently he picked up some fairly regular work on the fiddle for about six years, but 'nothing since then, nothing at all'.

Since the middle of the 1980s Mack has ticked along making a living 'on the street'. He gets a single man's social security benefit, giving this to his ex-wife 'for the kids', and is matter-of-fact about how he earns money for himself: 'just goes out shoplifting when I need to, I just make do with what I can get out of shoplifting'. Mack has a very modest lifestyle, spending most of his time in the pub or with his children. His son, Stuart, is feted by the Boys in The Fountain, who always have a whip-round to ensure he and Mack are well catered for when they have to travel away to tournaments. As Stuart's father, Mack is something of a local hero, having produced a potential star, and he never goes short of a drink, though he is usually the first to buy a round.

Work is unimportant to Mack and he gets by in other ways. He has done a couple of spells in custody, but this is an occupational hazard. Given the kinds of jobs for which he was eligible, legitimate work was never likely to appeal, for he was not going to succumb to 'slave labour', having briefly experienced it in his youth.

Ted

Ted spent most of his teenage years in care and custody. These days he does a 'bit of dealing, nothing major' and plays incessant rounds of golf, and though he lives on a poor estate away from the city his council house is well maintained and scattered with mementos of regular trips abroad. He has five children by three relationships and his eldest son is a heroin addict.

At 16, Ted had a well-paid but filthy industrial cleaning job on the fiddle, alongside other members of his large extended family, though not long afterwards he was sent to Borstal and then to prison. After this he did a couple of job creation schemes, but it was 'silly money' and he noted that 'no job has ever held enough money for me, you know, that I could live, you know, comfortably on'. For a few years he worked spasmodically on an ice-cream van but this soon became a front for some minor drug-dealing:

> Anyway, I had started to experiment with a bit of dope and I realized that I could – well, because the money from the job was so shit – so I started selling a little bit to certain people, from the van. It wasn't like people would come over saying can I have an ice-cream and a piece of dope, or anything like that. It was just a few certain people.

Ted has been doing this ever since. In Milltown, he is reputed to have hit the 'big time', and he himself claims there were some years when he was making 'fifty grand [£50,000]'. He is certainly not short of money by the standards of his neighbourhood, but nor is he a 'Mr Big' though, whether from fear or respect, he is held in some regard on his estate and gives generously to community events over the summer and at Christmas.

Ted does not trade in hard drugs, saying part of the reason is that his oldest son is a heroin addict. Through violence and intimidation he has kept heroin and crack cocaine off 'his' estate. He deals in cannabis, and cannabis alone, and is also involved in the supply of contraband cigarettes and alcohol, fake designer clothing and the distribution of tickets for major sporting events. Ted is always the man to know, describing himself as 'the nicest drug-dealer you would ever want to meet', and though there is some truth in this it is also a veneer, for he is ruthless in ensuring that nobody encroaches on his patch or threatens his reputation and source of income.

Critical Themes in Employment Pathways

Training and Qualifications

The Boys apparently placed little store by training and qualifications, which today are held to be critical. Though three of the Boys eventually acquired a university degree, not one has made any direct use of it in their employment trajectories. At lower levels of qualification, however, though the Boys generally subscribed to an 'anti-learning' culture while at school, over half have undertaken some form of vocational training since they left school (Table 6.1) – suggesting a latent recognition of its importance in securing occupational options, even if these were not always taken up. Moreover, the paucity of formal certification held by the Boys conceals a raft of less formally certificated 'skills' they now possess.

Table 6.1 'Skills' Acquired through 'Training' in Adulthood

	Type of skill	Form of training
Shaun	Instrumentation	Skill Centre
Richard	Bricklaying	Skill Centre
Trevor	HGV Class 1	Specialist course – self-financed
Tony	Sheet metal work	Apprenticeship (not completed)
	Sales/Management	Company sponsored/in-house
Mal	Supervisory	Company sponsored/in-house
Jamie	Mech. engineering	Apprenticeship ONC
Denny	Motor winding	Apprenticeship (not completed)
Nathan	Tiling	Apprenticeship (not completed)
Danny	Metalwork	While in Borstal (C&G, not completed)
Nick	Bricklaying	While in Borstal (C&G, part completed)
Pete	PSV Licence	Bus driving course
Tommy	PSV Licence	Bus driving course
Jerry	Knowledge test	Self-financed – for taxi driving
	Postal service	In-house
Gordon	Publishing	Preparatory course
	Personnel management	Institute of Personnel and Development course (not completed)
Colin	Pallet making	'Sitting by Nellie'
Alex	Upholstery	'Sitting by Nellie'
Matt	Painting and decorating	New Deal (not completed)

This short-term and on-the-job training does *not* include those (also about half) who started their working life on one of the new government training schemes designed to provide a 'bridge to work' (Manpower Services Commission 1977), for few of the Boys valued it for any training effect. All it did was provided a wage (technically an allowance), it was convenient and local, and you remained among your mates. Most were scathing about official claims that these schemes actually taught useful skills, though they might have consolidated skill and experience already acquired informally prior to leaving school in that they tended to be focused on painting and decorating and building work. Nick claimed the provision had been a 'numbers game': 'we just dossed about . . . it should have been much more structured, definitely, yeah. It was more like community service than it was like a paid job'.

Other training undertaken by the Boys rarely transmuted into commensurate or related employment, though there were some exceptions. Jamie's father got him an apprenticeship and he gained an Ordinary National Certificate (ONC) in mechanical engineering, but once he got his papers he was made redundant. With no experience ('they didn't count my apprenticeship as experience') he struggled to get a job and spent 'about four years doing nothing substantial, just a few factory jobs, some labouring and fiddling here and there'. He then got married and started work with his wife's father, who had his own building firm. For the next ten years he worked for the firm, until his father-in-law was murdered and the company collapsed. Jamie carried on in the building trade, self-employed, for three or four more years, but the work was drying up, and in 1996 he 'crossed the Rubicon' (see pp. 61) into office work.

Denny also started an apprenticeship as a motor winder, for about six weeks: 'and then I told the foreman to stick the job up his arse, because you had to stand by a bench filing these dynamos all day, it did my head in'. Nathan was an apprentice tiler but 'just lost interest in it'. He continued working with odd jobs here and there 'and then I found prison', and has lived by fiddling and crime ever since.

Both Danny and Nick tried for qualifications while they were in custody. Danny did not complete his course in metalwork, but Nick did the first part of a City and Guilds certificate in bricklaying and completed the course when he got out. Unfortunately, the issuing institution for the first part was HM Borstal Portland, stamped prominently on the front of his certificate. This, according to Nick, was good for nothing: 'I can remember getting it and I was sitting there, absolutely gutted, because I thought well I've got what I wanted, but I can't fucking use it'. Nick went on to work in window fitting, later invested in two burger vans and subsequently fiddled as an outdoor painter.

We have seen that Trevor invested in an HGV licence, which served him well, but only for a couple of years. Others made even less use of their new certification. Gordon did a preparatory course with a publishing company, but never started the job, while Tommy trained as a bus driver, but lasted in the job for little more than three months. Pete, likewise, trained for a Public Service Vehicle (PSV) licence, but had an accident soon afterwards and lost his job. Jerry's investment in the 'knowledge' test to become a taxi driver paid off for rather longer, for he drove cabs for eleven years before becoming a postman.

There appears to have been little calculation in the Boys' minds about the purpose and value of training. Usually it was approached with a crude, mercenary instrumentality, something which appeared to be a good idea at the time, theoretically offering the prospect of better, and incrementally remunerated employment. It rarely worked out that way, however, for few of the Boys continue to make use of the skills and qualifications they have acquired in the past.

There are some exceptions. Tony, in his trajectory towards a managerial position, and Mal, as he moved up into a supervisory role, have attended a raft of in-house training courses financed by their employers. Since he became a postman, Jerry has also had to undertake some in-house training. Of the others, Richard did a bricklaying course at a Skill Centre in his late teens and has worked, on and off, as a bricklayer ever since. Colin (pallet making) and Alex (upholstery) learnt their trade 'on the job' as young men and are still involved in the same activity.

The Boys generally remain deeply suspicious of the concept of 'training', tarnished as it has become through its association with government training programmes which, in their eyes, have usually been concerned simply with keeping them occupied and getting them off the dole. Only Matt, after his long period addicted to crack cocaine, has willingly contemplated participation in such a programme, briefly engaging with the New Deal, though he discovered it offered him 'nothing new', and dropped out. Danny has also grudgingly considered similar 'opportunities', but largely to get the Job Centre 'off his back'.

Such 'training' has invariably been offered to those who want it least, and those of the Boys who have had regular legitimate work for most of their adult lives possess little or no certification for the work they currently do. While they may have done bits and pieces of 'training' in the past, they argue they have acquired their skills largely through learning on the job and, as a result, they are confident they are able to 'turn their hand' at most things required in sectors of the economy in which they are likely to find work. 'Sitting by Nellie' and picking things up as they went along has served them well, they assert, and they remain sceptical about the merits of more formal training programmes in preparing them for the work available to them.

Finding Jobs

A second key theme in the Boys' employment pathways is the ways they have gone about finding jobs, though it is virtually impossible to ascertain precisely how many jobs they have had, and therefore also how they got them, for many simply cannot remember. In the early years of their working lives, in particular, they flitted in and out of what was often temporary and casual work. For this reason, though, it is reasonable to conclude that the vast majority of those early jobs were acquired through 'word of mouth', through contacts within personal and local networks. What is noteworthy, however, in these days of CVs and structured job search, is that this has *continued* to be the dominant mechanism for securing employment throughout their adult lives. Indeed, the occasions on which the Boys sought to find work through the careers service and the Job Centre, or through newpaper advertisements, are minimal. Eddie went to the Careers Office and Tony went to the Job Centre, but both needed, or wanted to find work outside the 'orbit' of the Boys' routine possibilities and beyond their personal networks. Apart from these two, Trevor tried the Job Centre and, to his surprise, became a milkman, Tommy got his first job (in a sweet factory) through the Job Centre, and Nathan used the Job Centre to find work after coming out of prison and moving to a 'strange town'. Few others recall finding work by such routes.

The early 1980s was a hard time to get 'proper' work through informal networks, for there was a severe recession which witnessed the dramatic contraction of the construction and production industries, the two main sites of employment in which the Boys tended to work. More casual fiddles, however, were still around and sometimes these had to be accepted. Derek spent three years with an opera company, building the stage set, which was 'the best job I ever had':

> I got it through a mate of mine who was working down there. It wasn't an official job, it was a fiddle. I did a few other fiddles at the same time, but I was with the opera for maybe three years. See it was hard to find work in them days, because that was when there was a lot of unemployed. You know, Margaret Thatcher was in her prime, unemployment was rife, remember. That was why I was working down there with the opera, because you couldn't get proper jobs in them days, like.

Word of mouth was critical at times when 'any job' would do, whether or not it was on the fiddle. Jerry had worked on the fruit market when he left school until his criminal record lapsed, and then joined the army as he had always planned. After leaving the army in 1981, he struggled to find work:

> Well I couldn't get a job for five years, 'cos there was a bit of a recession about the beginning of the 1980s. And I tried everything, from toilet cleaner in the post office. I couldn't even get that. No one wanted to know. And I was talking to Alex about upholstery. I went down to his place for a job as a trainee upholsterer. And the wages was £36 a week. Now I took into account that it was as a trainee. But I had just come out of the army, been on £100 a week, and I was prepared to do it, but they gave me a cock and bull story that I was too old. I was nearly 22, and they wanted someone twenty.
>
> So I mean that went straight out of the window, so basically I just got by for about five years just fiddling, signing on and fiddling. A bit of building work, but mainly on the fruit and veg on the markets, because I still had a lot of contacts there.
>
> Then when I was about 26 – you know, old enough to do it – I went on the taxis for eleven years. A friend of my father's was taxi-ing at the time and my uncle was. It was actually advertised in the paper, but they told me about it and I took the knowledge test,

passed all that and, uh, spent the next eleven years trying to get out of it! About five years ago I applied for the Post Office and I've been there ever since.

Virtually all the Boys have plugged gaps in their legitimate employment histories by working on the 'fiddle'. This kind of work can be secured *only* through word of mouth, for there needs to be a level of implicit trust between an employer who pays cash in hand, and the employee who is always anxious about being 'grassed up' to the social. Many of the Boys have had extended periods on the fiddle, some often lasting years. It is part of the culture of Milltown, a core mechanism for getting by at a level above subsistence.

Losing Jobs

The third theme concerns losing jobs, for only four of the Boys have stayed in the same work or with the same firm for most of their working lives. Colin has made pallets, temporarily moving voluntarily to a rival company but then returning voluntarily to his old place of work. Tony has remained with the same company, rising up the hierarchy. Alex voluntarily followed his supervisor to another place of work and then moved (with the machinery) to its new location and its new owner, subsequently inheriting the business, and Gary, after working for another painting and decorating firm for many years, set up his own business, with considerable success.

All the others have 'lost' jobs, often quite a number of them. Sometimes this has been an active decision, as in Shaun's case when his marriage broke up, or as Trevor did when he was simply offered better pay to work elsewhere. Both personal and occupational circumstances influenced such decisions. Richard wanted to dedicate more time to bodybuilding and so abandoned his job at the fruit market, while Derek worked in an electronics factory for twelve years, but 'in the end I just got so fed up of it, I just walked out. I suppose I must have been about 34'.

Similarly Kelvin, who had risen to the position of works manager with an engineering company by 1994, one day decided he'd 'had enough', and after living on something approaching £22,000 a year, he started work in a bakery, on a salary half that amount. Eddie, having first got a clerical job with the Department of Employment, subsequently moved to a haulage company where he rose to the position of transport manager, but struggled with the responsibility and resigned.

Many of the Boys talk about having 'had enough', being 'fed up', just 'walking away', and had few qualms about abandoning one job for a better one, if there was the prospect of a higher wage. However, as these examples illustrate, the reasons for leaving a job were often more complex and sometimes almost impossible for the Boys to pinpoint, perhaps appearing precipitous but nearly always permanent, for once the decision was made, there was rarely any chance of going back.

Some, however, were reluctant to 'walk away' even when the money was poor, for other factors 'bound' them to their employer. The classic example was Mark, who left school to work in a city centre hotel where 'I had seven great years there, best job I ever had'. The housekeeper and other staff 'mollycoddled' him and gave him confidence: 'when I first started there, I was a shy 16 year old'. As a teenager Mark was a persistent young offender, committing offences from burglary to assault. After starting work at the hotel, he was arrested for football violence, went to court, and, to his astonishment, was remanded in custody and told that he was likely to be sent to prison. His employer, however, gave him a glowing reference, which, according to the court, saved him from a custodial sentence. His job had been kept open, which engendered Mark's unswerving loyalty and a commitment to his work and to his boss. Had the pay been better, he claims, he would have stayed at the hotel for the rest of his life, though economic pressures eventually 'forced' him to move on.

These were some of the 'positive' and purposeful reasons for leaving jobs. More often the Boys lost jobs for 'negative' reasons, dismissed for thieving, fiddling, fighting, drinking, unreliability, threatening behaviour, poor attendance and so on. Nutter, always a heavy drinker and football hooligan, moved through a range of jobs at the steelworks – labouring, machine operating, furnace work, forklift truck driving – even coping with the transition to continental shift work. After fifteen years, however, he was sacked for poor time-keeping. Pete rarely 'lost' jobs because they were usually only temporary in the first place, but he often left prematurely, having been caught with his fingers in the till.

Physical and mental problems also led to the loss of jobs. A number of the Boys (Pete, Shaun, Eddie, Richard) suffered mental health problems which at times jeopardized their employment and led to dismissal or withdrawal. Richard, for example, has experienced serious bouts of depression, fuelled by heavy drinking. These have been distinct and diagnosed clinical conditions, very different from simply a failure to cope with pressure, which led to Kelvin and others giving up their jobs. Ryan and Trevor both sustained physical injuries which impaired their capacity to continue the work they were doing at the time, while Vic contracted a lung disease, which put an end to his industrial painting job, and indeed to his working life.

Drugs and alcohol have also taken their toll on some of the Boys' career trajectories. Paul continued sniffing glue into his early twenties, though he worked for a while on a government training programme, doing a bit of carpentry and painting and decorating. However, 'from then on it was like on the glue or in the local prison', and since then he has never worked, except for two days on the dustbins. He does some shoplifting but is invariably drunk, begging and scrounging the next drink from one of the Boys (who never refuse).

Denny turned to drink and gave up regular work when his second marriage broke up, instead working casually for well over a year for £25 a day, though gradually he got back on his feet and found more secure employment with a factory cleaning company. When his manager moved to another company in 1987, Denny went with him, subsequently being promoted to a supervisory position.

The most spectacular slide into alcohol and drug addiction happened to Spaceman. Unlike some of the Boys (now dead), however, he has emerged on the other side. The Merchant Navy, in his view, was a 'licence to get pissed': 'this was basically where I done my apprenticeship for boozing, just twenty-four fucking seven, you know'. He came ashore in 1979 and for four years worked as a store-keeper in a hospital, spending his leisure time drinking and fighting, resulting in having his head split open in one fight and a fractured skull in another, for which he had the last rites:

> I was in the wrong place at the wrong time but, you know, it was all drunkenness and bravado and hanging around with the Boys, all that sort of thing. We didn't run from anything. You know, just dive in and have a fight, and be a man and all that shit.

Spaceman left the hospital to work 'on the buildings' because it was better money, though he just squandered it 'on fucking clothes and music and booze and drugs'. He then met a girl and they bought a flat together, but two years later he was made redundant just as his relationship was falling apart. He vanished to Portugal, abandoning the flat, and when he returned carried on labouring on building sites, though he was more often in the pub. His wages were spoken for before they had been earned, to pay his 'slate' (drinks on credit, to be settled on pay day), and he then travelled round the country 'with a big bunch of Paddies and Cockneys who loved boozing', until he lost his job with the firm 'because I wasn't turning up for work'. There followed a string of casual jobs invariably associated with pubs (fitter, barman, painter), and he was in London just as the rave scene exploded – the 'summer of love':

> It was brilliant. Brilliant. And then I met this gang of guys, and this is where my descent, my climb into the big league of pissheads and fucking scammers and working-class yobbos *really* started. I started knocking around with them. They were fucking tough guys and I used to go out thieving with them. I lost my job, because I just couldn't be bothered working. I found that thieving with these boys was much more fucking fun. You didn't have to get up in the morning and it was more um . . . lucrative. The money was fucking great. The crime wasn't so serious: it was just shoplifting and we burgled a couple of hotels.

Spaceman's drug consumption intensified: 'ecstasy and speed [amphetamine] and fucking cocaine, acid [LSD], ganja [cannabis] – anything and everything'. The drugs gave him more courage to commit offences but eventually led to his first prosecution, though he had been arrested many times before. Previously, however, he had given a false name to the police, but this time he'd been so stoned that he signed his true name ('when you were drugged up or drunk, you lost that little bit of fucking edge') and ended up in court. He was fined £200, though this did not deter him and he continued thieving: 'I was mad on drink and drugs'. Over the next five years, Spaceman became a heroin addict and spent a lot of time in prison. His last proper job was as a barman in a holiday camp in 1992. On release from prison in 1996, he addressed his addictions and enrolled on an art course, though he is still very sick and still unemployed.

Matt has a similar history of drug dependency. On leaving approved school, he joined the youth training programme, and subsequently got a job in a plastics factory, but left after a few months 'because it was boring, you just had to stand there doing the same thing all day long and it stunk, this burning plastic smell'. Moving away from Milltown, he did legitimate building work for a while and also, for a short time, supplemented his wages as a doorman but gave this up, maintaining he was 'too spiritual to be throwing people around'. He then looked after his two young children for a couple of years after that, working next in industrial painting until he and his partner moved to London, but he couldn't settle and came home, doing a few labouring and fiddling jobs. Still only 25, this was the start of Matt's 'crack' days, and for well over a decade, he was both a dealer of crack cocaine and addicted to it, carrying out armed robberies to feed his habit and serving a number of prison sentences. Like Spaceman, however, he has now addressed his addiction and, in the last few years, has tried to return to (quasi-) legitimate employment, from toilet cleaning to door work once again. Looking back, he observed, 'I have to be honest with you, I don't even know where half my life has gone. I lost half my life in my crack days. I can't remember much about it'.

The other long-term casualty is Marty, who also started on the job creation scheme and then, for a number of years, 'just banged around building sites and then I worked in a restaurant for a couple of years'. He spent some time in prison and, apart from a brief spell working in a holiday camp, has not worked since the mid-1980s: 'yeah, after I come out of prison I came home and I've stayed here ever since. I've done the odd day on the buildings, but if I haven't been working, I've just begged and borrowed'. Marty's mental health problems probably set in about this time, though they were not clinically diagnosed until some years later. Suffering from paranoid schizophrenia, he is in receipt of incapacity benefit, most of which supports his heavy alcohol consumption, and continued use of illegal drugs.

Self-employment

The fourth theme is the extent of self-employment among the Boys, which takes both legal and illegal forms. On the wrong side of the tracks, Ted does his drug-dealing, while Danny goes shoplifting with his 'business partner' in their 'company car'. Somewhere in between, Gordon has usually held on to some 'employee' status, though often, certainly in the past, as a foundation for his more 'entrepreneurial' activities. More legitimately, Gary runs a modest but thriving business, employing core workers and casual workers he can draw on when times are busy. Trevor also has his own subcontracting business, working with a partner installing windows, while Kelvin works for himself, legitimately subcontracting building and maintenance work, as well as still occasionally working as a freelance photographer.

The Boys entered their adult lives just as Margaret Thatcher was about to secure political power, and so were the political targets for a range of government strategies of which they were sometimes the beneficiaries (such as the 'right to buy' council housing) and sometimes the 'victims' (indirectly through economic restructuring and more directly through the clampdown on 'benefit cheats' and more punitive criminal justice measures).

One of the main planks of Thatcherite public policy was the promotion of 'enterprise' and encouragement of 'self-employment', and in addition to those above, many of the Boys have, indeed, had protracted spells of self-employment. This, however, carried many different meanings and has been a mixed story.

Those of the Boys who followed the path of 'self-employment' often found themselves operating on the borders of legality, and for at least some 'owning their own business' has been something of a poisoned chalice, enabling them to maintain no more than a toe-hold in the labour market (see MacDonald and Coffield 1991). For others, self-employment has been little more than a semantic device used to justify working conditions which absolve employers of legal responsibilities, and allows them to hire and fire at will. Often this has been used as a mechanism for paying 'cash in hand', leaving the individual responsible for the payment of tax and national insurance contributions (which few ever did).

Trevor was on the sick when he took on his Unigate franchise, with circumstances propelling him into self-employment, though it is an occupational status he has sustained ever since. In different ways, Richard (in bricklaying), Alex (in upholstery) and Kelvin (in decorating and general maintenance) have followed a similar path, for they work for themselves, though their earnings are modest. They are best described as sole traders rather than entrepreneurs, for none have had the motivation or resources to invest in further business development.

In contrast, both Tommy and Nick invested heavily (in their terms) to try to get their business ideas off the ground, neither with much success. Tommy put over £5,000 into a partnership to run a delivery firm, and later committed nearly double that amount for the purchase of a new lorry, but ended up working on the fiddle to make ends meet. Nick abandoned building site work on the fiddle with a view to selling burgers to the site workers. He and a partner bought two vans, but 'the business just went downhill'.

Beyond Danny and Ted, most of the Fountain Boys described themselves as 'self-employed', and their success and failure in many respects mirrored that of their more legitimate counterparts. Many plodded along, picking up the odd day's work, and supplemented their basic social security entitlements with opportunistic petty crime, though others were more entrepreneurial in their criminal and informal economic activities, having specific customers for their illegal enterprises and more carefully thought-out strategies to 'make a raise' (earn some money).

Surviving on the Dole

There were often very blurred distinctions between being an 'entrepreneur' (legitimate or otherwise) and surviving on the dole, the fifth and final theme. A self-image of being self-employed, rather than a pariah on society, was more attractive to those who had largely eked out a living on the margins of the economy, though to depict them formally as self-employed is to stretch the bounds of credibility.

Most of the Fountain Boys said that they would prefer to work, but the jobs that were potentially open to them simply paid appalling wages. Moreover, a lawful wage would be docked to pay child support for their children, and in such circumstances they preferred to find alternative means of generating a reasonable income through benefit fraud, crime and gambling. Not that this produced a fortune. Nathan estimated he routinely made in the region of £200 pounds a week; Danny suggested £500.

There was also a lot of mutual support among these Boys. Some got lucky some weeks and were not so fortunate in others. Some had to tone down their activities because the heat was on (they were 'under pressure' in relation to the criminal justice system); others found new opportunities to exploit (during the research a housing benefit scam was in operation, though most of the Boys and their collaborators were subsequently caught). Those who were 'lucky' helped out with drinks and loans, though they would be beneficiaries at other times, for the circle invariably turned.

Most of the Boys felt little compunction about fiddling, viewing it as a necessity from time to time, though they did not always agree, like most of the Fountain Boys, that there was only a fine dividing line between making a living 'on the street', and working on the fiddle while still claiming social security. Gary, for example, thought there was a world of difference, condemning the criminals for ripping off the working man, but sympathizing with those fiddling for trying to 'make a crust' when times were hard.

Crossing the Rubicon – Jamie's Story

Eddie and Tony obtained office work early in their working lives, while Gordon combined professional and more physical work. The rest of the Boys have always been firmly entrenched in the world of manual labour, except for Jamie, who at the age of 36 gave up working on building sites and took an office job. His account of this transition is uniquely fascinating and illuminating:

The work dried up again and they said they were going to lay me off. I was thinking about packing it in anyway, with so many days off all the time. So I was out of work then for maybe six weeks, just before Christmas. And then my next door neighbour knocked the door to say there was a job going at her place: Phoenix Insurance. I asked what the money was like, as you do, and it was rubbish. But there was nothing happening in my job and so I decided to get out of the building game. Because it's working in the rain all day. I know in the summer you get a lovely tan and go to work with shorts on. People say oh look at your tan, but *you* know it's three months dry and nine months rain and drizzle. So I decided to have a complete change, although the money was rubbish. At least it would tide me over Christmas, you know, for the kids and that. I started on the eleventh of the eleventh 1996, I remember it was Remembrance Day.

I thought it'll tide me over Christmas and then I'll get a proper job. The money *was* dreadful. There was a lot more money on the buildings. I mean, if I worked overtime I used to take home two hundred plus [£200 per week]. At the insurance place, starting off, well it was monthly for a start and I had never ever got paid monthly, it was dreadful, a hundred and fifty or so. It was a bad drop.

So I started there and I was thinking so much about how it was so different. I mean, I'd never worked with women before. I just couldn't hack it first of all, although it was nicer – obviously! Mind you, you had to watch your language. And you are indoors. It would be pouring down with rain outside and I would think I would've been out in this.

Well there's just so many plusses with the job. You know, you have a shower *before* you go to work and in my other job you had a shower when you get home from work. That's so strange, it was totally different. When I tell people I used to work with, they just don't believe it. They say how's it going, and I say I'm in insurance now, and they ask me what are you doing really, honest to God, like. And now I even wear a tie and a shirt to work, how times change. I used to come home in rags, you know, and then get up in the morning and put the same rags on, because you know you will be working in tarmac and what have you, and you are going to get dirty. Yeah I have a shower before going to work, it's very strange.

Like I say, there is so many plusses working here. The work is ten times easier for a kick off. And then they made me permanent and I laughed. I kept saying, oh I'm not too bad at this then. So now I have a pension and, you know, we get luncheon vouchers and you get cheap car insurance and . . . there's loads of little perks, you know, like a free coffee machine all day, drink as much as you want. It's the conditions really, you know, and you are indoors.

I work in the post room. You are always busy but it isn't too hard. The mail comes in in the morning, of course. We have some young ones, 16 year olds, they open up the letters, we put them in separate piles and then we give them to the sections. They sort them out. And then all the mail that has got to go out, we've got to send it out, we have our own franking machine. It's just like a mini post office. But then I was also helping out in stationery and now I'm in charge of stationery as well, because the fella who did that before got the sack for fiddling the clock.

And another good part about my job I forgot to mention is the holidays. The holidays are fantastic. This year I had twenty-three days' holiday because I brought two over from last year, plus I have got thirteen days flexi-time, plus eight bank holidays, so I think its something it's something like forty-seven. Whereas before if I took a holiday, I didn't get paid. So it's a real change – and the holidays are excellent.

Jamie lucidly captures the tough occupational conditions experienced by the majority of the Boys, about which they have probably never given much thought, for they know no other working life. The Boys make great play of the freedom, autonomy and independence conferred on them by their occupational lifestyles, though this conceals the hard path that, for many, it has been. They have taken opportunities when they have arisen, occasionally creating them for themselves, but by and large they have navigated their occupational direction – with its considerable uncertainties and insecurities – in an ad-hoc fashion, according to the prevailing wind, moving sometimes into relatively stable situations, though at other times into a more precarious world of illegal and informal 'enterprise'.

Crossing the Atlantic – Gordon's Story

Gordon always stood out from the crowd, not least because he towered over most of the Boys, and because he was the one who stayed on at school. After a year out – when he too worked in a range of casual, manual jobs – he did a degree in social science, then went to the United States, which had always been his dream. He flew to Los Angeles, found cheap digs and got a job as an assistant manager in a department store. A work colleague then offered him a room, which turned out to be in a beach house: 'a-maz-ing . . . a few months ago I was in Milltown and it was pissing down with rain and now I am living on the beach in Californ-i-a'.

His girlfriend joined him a month later and they got married in Los Angeles. He forged a work permit for her and embellished his own CV. Michaela got a job in a store, while he moved on to a better retail position, and then to work for a carpentry firm – for ten dollars an hour, cash in hand. Michaela got an evening job in a live music bar that needed a doorman, and Gordon fitted the bill. More accurately, he 'manipulated the bill', charging extra for people to jump the queue, letting people in for a consideration via the fire exit and pocketing a proportion of the entrance fee. Gordon was earning more through 'scamming' than he was through legitimate earnings, but was then fired for drinking on the job: 'the reason I got fired was because of drinking on the door and partying and letting some of the locals in for free, not for taking three hundred, four hundred dollars plus a week from them'. The owner of a club down the road offered him a job as a barman:

> I became the 'Cheers' barman. Everybody knew my name. I was the Englishman at the
> bar. It was full of characters: millionaires, beach bums, the rich kids from Newport
> beach, the alco sailors who worked the boats. I could deal with them all. I used to earn
> a fortune there, because it's all about tips, isn't it.

Subsequently, he changed his day job from carpentry to cars (sales) and then
became a rep for a steel company, as he continued to be the life and soul of the
party at the club.

Michaela, however, was putting pressure on him to 'get a proper job' and make
better use of his qualifications, though he suspects she was also rather jealous of
the attention he received, and because of the time he had on his hands between
jobs, for Gordon would 'lounge around, watching all the girls on the beach'.

They had made so much money they decided to stop work and travel the world
for a couple of years, though this was put on hold when Gordon had a serious car
crash. During a period of recuperation, however, he took over the management of
a club, receiving a percentage of the profits in lieu of wages, so he quickly clamped
down on the fiddles and scams, and as a result the profits shot up!

Michaela's mother died and she caught the next plane home, and when she tried
to return, inconsistencies were discovered in her immigration papers and she was
given thirty days to leave the United States. She and Gordon had a brief holiday in
Hawaii, then came back to Milltown. They had saved a considerable amount of
money in a Channel Islands bank account, which they subsequently invested in
property and business.

Gordon quickly got bored, for though he worked as a residential social worker
and as a night-club doorman ('just something to do') he still had itchy feet and
wanted to go back to the United States. Michaela, however, wanted to settle down
and their relationship became strained, though Gordon was determined to set off
once more, and with a couple of the Boys went off round the world. He and
Michaela got back together when he returned, but parted again, and Gordon left
for the United States, rubbing shoulders with the very rich and being offered a
lucrative job with a major international company.

In 1994, however, Michaela joined him for a backpacking trip through Central
America, after which, it seems, his wanderlust was over, for they returned to
Milltown and bought more property. Gordon worked once more as a social worker
with disadvantaged young people, then studied for a certificate with the Institute of
Personnel and Development before a friend in human resource management wrote
him a fictitious reference and he became a manager with a manufacturing company.

Gordon is fundamentally bored, for he is very wealthy and does not need to
work. However, he now has two young children who tie him (willingly) to his
locale, and he lives in a rambling Victorian house less than half a mile from
Milltown. He works and studies now almost for the fun of it, for he has been

extraordinarily successful, working very hard to achieve what he has, yet he talks more or less in riddles when reflecting on his 'career', almost denying his quite evident success:

> Yeah I suppose I have worked hard, even if I give the veneer of being a lazy bastard. But I was a lazy bastard. I was intelligent enough to scrape through on everything I did. I wanted to do all the lazy things that everybody else did, so I did as much as I could to do that. I did the both, so I could get away with the one and with the other. And you talk with any of the Boys and they will always say that I'm a lazy bastard . . . 'this manufacturing thing is the first proper job he's ever had but somehow he's always had money falling through his hands, he's always had things come to him easy . . .'. And, yes, that's the perception they have of me and in some ways it's stuck. But I think you make your own luck.

Gordon has 'worked' *both* his formal credentials *and* his legacies of Milltown to his full advantage, and has charm and charisma, like many of the Boys. More importantly, he also has the intellect to make it pay!

Conclusion

In their occupational 'careers' the Boys had one thing in their favour and many things against them. In their favour was the fact that they knew how to 'twist and turn', but against them was the rapidly transforming labour market and a prospectively increasingly marginal position within it. They had not expected to have to twist and turn, though many have proved remarkably resilient in doing so. They have survived, some succeeding against all expectations, maintaining regular and reasonably remunerated positions in the legitimate labour market. Some of course have not, succumbing to adverse occupational circumstances for a variety of reasons, getting by through 'ducking and diving' on the margins.

Why some have succeeded and some have succumbed is hard to discern, for the only observation to be made with any confidence is the striking diversity of occupational career pathways taken by a small group of individuals from essentially comparable backgrounds. As teenagers, most had some general idea of where they would be going; as adults, following the collapse of their anticipated occupational destinations, few have had any idea about what lay in store for them, and have had to 'dodge and weave' in relation to the opportunities which became available. Some did so more successfully than others, though more stayed on than strayed from the unmarked occupational road-map on which they were travelling. Given the historical moment of their journey, this is something of a testimony to their resilience and versatility, and Gary conveys, in a strikingly concise analysis, the uncertainty of the labour market pathways the Boys have sough to navigate during their lives:

At the age of 13 I knew I was going to be a painter and decorator because I was going to work for my father. I think if that had been different, and it is a lot different today, then you've got to try that little bit harder. Like if I'd never had a job when I left school, in those days, there was still a lot of possibilities. I mean, if your dad worked in the paper mill or steelworks or whatever, *you* would go straight into the steelworks, you would go straight into the paper mill. It was mapped out for you, basically. But now all those father and son jobs are gone. You know, the docks, it's all changed, the paper mill has shut down, the brewery has shut down. It's more difficult. You speak to guys like Ryan's father, he's had two jobs in his life – two jobs. My wife's father had two jobs, British Dredging and then he finished his time with Blue Circle Cement. For those guys, if you had a job, it was forever. But nothing is forever today. And I've always tried to explain that to the Boys. Things can always go pear shaped. You've got to be ready for something new. I realize that and I'm ready for it as well, I think. You know, nothing is forever. And if things did go pear shaped for me, you know, if the business folded, I know I would get on. I would find something. I would work for somebody else. I know I can make a living and get on and do something else. And most of the Boys usually find a way to get by, one way or another.

–7–

Criminal Careers
– More Monty Python than Al Capone?

Introduction

Three of the Boys, perhaps surprisingly, had done jury service. Like so much else in their adult lives, their reactions and perspectives on this experience could not be more diverse. Pete actually did his service just a few weeks before being convicted of 'cottaging' (committing an indecent act in a public place) and had taken the role very seriously, wanting to ensure that there was a proper discussion of the case:

> I mean, I've been brought up on welfare all my life and I'm living on welfare again. We owe a debt to society. It's easy to keep saying let someone else do it, but somewhere down the line you've got to say, right, this is my share.

Pete endeavoured to strike some balance between the responsibility of being a juror and his direct experience as an offender. Denny and Jamie drew more exclusively on their own experiences of the criminal justice system. Denny was convinced that if people had got as far as a court appearance, then they were 'probably' guilty (as he always had been), while Jamie was equally adamant the accused were innocent, victims of being 'stitched up' by the police (as he had nearly been on one occasion).

Elsewhere during his interview, however, Jamie expressed indignation about offenders often 'getting off' on a technicality, making a telling observation in the process:

> I know a lot of the Boys have got off like that and I suppose if it happened to me I'd be perfectly happy, but it's still wrong. The system is wrong: it's about time they filled these loopholes in.

This captures well the Boys' position on concepts of crime, courts and custody, which is one of complete self-interested hypocrisy, for essentially they all want a firmer line and a stronger hand, so long as it is not applied to them!

The common defining characteristic of the Boys is that all had been 'juvenile delinquents' in their youth, to a greater or lesser extent. As teenagers, they themselves had always played down their offending behaviour, regardless of where it lay on a continuum of 'seriousness', routinely invoking 'techniques of neutralization' (Sykes and Matza 1957), arguing their offending had been petty, they had never been caught (and therefore never been to court), they had never been convicted, they had never hurt anyone, or they had only ever fought among themselves. Moreover, some had 'taken the rap' for offences they did not commit (Williamson 1980), sometimes voluntarily (to protect a mate from a more severe sentence) and sometimes after being 'stitched up' by the police.

However, their actions had *not* been 'more Monty Python than Al Capone', as Tony had somewhat flippantly alleged, though none had been of the order of 'Al Capone'. Though the Boys' offending had rarely been *very* severe, neither had it been transitory or insignificant, for most were persistent young offenders. Their offending behaviour was diverse and they themselves made the distinction between 'instrumental' and 'expressive' crime (Williamson 1978), for though much of their teenage offending had been to make money through theft, burglary and shoplifting, it had also been undertaken for the kicks or for a dare. Both types of offences were sometimes calculated, sometimes spontaneous and opportunistic. These are not, however, crisp distinctions, for the two blur into one another in both parallel and linear ways. Cars used for joy-riding, whether planned or spontaneous, could also be stripped of saleable parts. Shoplifting, which often started as a 'bit of a laugh' for the challenge and excitement, could evolve into a way of making money, and ended, for some of the Boys, as a way of life. Moreover, the Boys both went on purposeful forays into town (for example, to steal glue, before it was banned from the shelves) and at other times simply seized the moment.

There is considerable current interest in 'pathways' into and out of crime. For many of the Boys their involvement in crime ended, for a variety of reasons, in their late teens and early twenties, thus fulfilling the promise of delinquency theorists that most young people 'grow out of it'. For some of the Boys, however, offending behaviour persisted and has continued, though the nature of that offending has taken different courses.

The Boys have rarely had a distinctive modus operandi, and most have combined a range of offending patterns, crossing the instrumental/expressive and calculated/spontaneous divide. However, these have been adjusted over time as a result of personal calculations of risk, changes in policing and surveillance practices, and their own endeavours to desist.

A number of the Boys were removed from home as teenagers on account of their offending behaviour and their (often related) non-school attendance. Three (Ted, Danny and Matt) were taken into care and sent to residential establishments. Others were removed for shorter periods of assessment. Five of the Boys (Marty, Pete, Nick, Vic and Paul) were sentenced to the 'short, sharp shock' of three months in Detention Centre. Four (Ted, Danny, Nick and Vic) were committed to 'Borstal training', an indeterminate sentence of between six months and two years. The short, sharp shock of DC had little effect on offending behaviour – all were subsequently reconvicted, though in Pete's case not for some years. Of the four who went to Borstal, three (Ted, Danny and Nick) subsequently did time in prison, as did Marty and Paul, who had been to DC. Indeed, ten of the Boys have spent some part of their adult lives in custody as convicted prisoners, while Mark spent time on remand in custody, though when convicted he received a non-custodial sentence. Most of them have sustained criminal lifestyles throughout their adulthood.

In contrast, fourteen of the Boys have had little or no contact with the criminal justice system as adults. Six have hovered on the edge, not actively engaged in offending, but neither clearly distanced from it. Of course, as we have seen, many of the Boys have been involved at some time or another in working 'on the fiddle', though none has ever considered this to be a dimension of *crime*, as fraudulent abuse of the social security system is something else.

Defining 'crime' is contentious not just for criminologists but for the Boys themselves. Gordon, for example, who had a couple of minor convictions as a teenager, but then went on to make a lot of money through what was in effect theft from his employers, observed: 'so of course there was nothing else I ever done because if you never get caught it's never a crime, is it?'

Experiences of Offending: Four Illustrative Case Studies

Paul

After steadily 'disengaging' from school and immersing himself in the 'wicked buzz' of glue-sniffing, Paul admits to going 'downhill'. He started shoplifting and 'screwing' houses, occasionally being caught and cautioned, and was also regularly involved in fights in town, invariably ending up assaulting the police, with the result that he was in prison on remand for his eighteenth birthday. Warned that any further offending would lead to Borstal or DC, he was fined, but within two months 'I had a mad head on me again' and was sent to Detention Centre: 'I thought never again. It was a quick sharp shock, you know, but as soon as I comes out, it all started again'.

Paul did not want to go to prison for fighting and 'stupid things like that' but continued stealing, serving three months for the attempted burglary of a warehouse and then eleven months for the burglary of a shop ('the longest sentence I've ever had'). He was then 21, and commented wryly that 'during those seven years, from 18 to 25, I did five birthdays inside'. Constantly in prison for three or four month stretches, he eventually decided to change his approach and started stealing from cars, 'smashing the window and taking out whatever was in there'. For one such offence, he got nine months in prison.

When he was interviewed, Paul proudly told me he had not been in prison for twelve years (since 1988), when he, Mack and Danny – as a shoplifting team – had been remanded in custody for conspiracy to steal, though they all subsequently received a community sentence.

Paul estimates that, since 1988, he has done about a dozen community sentences for offences largely related to shoplifting – though he has also been convicted of threatening behaviour towards the mother of his 5-year-old daughter. Indeed, since the break-up of both of his parallel relationships, he has been drinking even more heavily and committed further assaults on the police. Paul reflected on his offending 'career':

> Like in my teenage years I was getting into trouble with fighting, but that's what all young men do. And then I stopped all that. And I mean, like a lot of the Boys, we all done burglaries, whatever, to get money. But when you gets to a certain age it's time to stop, but then you're just not earning no money. So you turns to shoplifting, just to get your beer money, because I thought it's not that bad an offence. But when you end up getting caught a few times, it mounts up, and then the court looks at it more seriously and you're looking at committals [to the Crown Court]. So I tried to give up shoplifting, but then you get desperate, so you start again. And with all these problems with my daughter, and because of my drinking, everything I'm getting done for now is for violence.

Denny

Denny enjoyed riding in stolen cars when he was a teenager, and was not averse to benefiting from stolen property, though he was never involved in burglary. He would maintain that he 'was never much of a crook', despite his penchant for stolen cars almost leading to a custodial sentence when he was 19, though he escaped with a heavy fine. In his adult life, when he was unemployed, he worked on the fiddle, never resorting to theft, and indeed he has largely had a 'respectable' adulthood, his criminality restricted to a five-year period in his late teens:

> Yeah, mainly petty things, mostly between when I was 16 and 20. The odd fight, and stolen cars. I never actually pinched a car but I used to go in them. But since then, just a few little fiddles. I haven't stood up in a court for many years. I've been pretty good. I'm an upstanding, honest, working-class bloke. I can hold my hand up to that.

Like so many of the Boys, Denny played down the seriousness of his particular line of offending. Joy-riding had been just 'a bit of fun', no more, no less, for which he received a number of heavy fines, paying them off conscientiously at £10 a week. He prided himself on always having worked (albeit sometimes on the fiddle), and deplored the culture of thieving and burglary which prevailed among some of the Boys:

It's their way of getting money, thieving and breaking into houses. But that's the wrong way to me. Breaking into somebody else's house is the lowest of the low as far as I'm concerned. If I was really desperate I might go and break into a warehouse, but not somebody's house. I mean, I've bought some dodgy gear in my time, but if I had an inkling it's been nicked from somebody's house I wouldn't touch it. Because I know how hard people work to get this stuff. And then some sod who's never worked in his life pinches it and tries to sell it for a couple of bob, for half of what it's worth or less, so they can have a bit more for fags and beer. I hate that.

Denny clearly saw a 'moral' distinction between stealing from institutions and stealing from individuals, condemning the *behaviour* of those Boys who failed see that difference, though he did not condemn *them*: 'I'll have a drink with them, I grew up with them, but from my point of view they've gone the wrong way'.

Denny continues to live in the middle of a culture of active and passive criminality, but now has a strong sense of right and wrong, attributing his teenage offending to an episode during his late adolescence, not as some apprenticeship for a life of crime. Relatively secure in employment throughout his adult life, he is convinced he was never *really* a crook. Moreover, he knows that his third wife Annie would 'go poppies' if he ever got into any more trouble: 'she'd kill me'.

Nick

Nick has also benefited from the influence of his wife Karen, though it took some time and trauma for this to take effect. Unlike Paul, he eventually decided to do something about the drink (and drugs) problems which appeared to lie behind his violent tendencies and criminal activity.

Nick went 'off the rails' at an early age and his committal to Detention Centre at the age of 15 put paid to any possibility of educational achievement. Yet he is certainly one of the more articulate of the Boys, and it is quite conceivable he could have done well at school and perhaps established a very different pathway in his adult life:

We was always out robbing and thieving. I was coming up to the last year at school and I couldn't be bothered with it, although I had it all according to the teachers. I could have gone on to do O level, even A level if necessary. But I got sent to DC, and after DC it was totally different. I was totally different.

Prior to being sent to DC, Nick had acquired a string of convictions for theft, so he was not surprised to be 'sent down' ('the judge [magistrate] had to do his job, I suppose'), though it was still a shock: 'as far as I was concerned I was going to court and I would get another fine, or extended probation, or something'. The Boys *always* expected one 'last chance' and, like Marty, Pete, Paul and Vic who also went to DC, Nick testified to the loneliness and isolation he experienced during his first days (and nights) in custody:

> God, the effect was immense for the first few days. It was terrible. It frightened the shit out of me. It was like a nightmare at first. I thought it was a dream. I remember waking up the first morning and seeing this food tray slid underneath my door. And I tried opening the window and it only went so far and then made a clanging noise against the cage. And it was then that I thought, oh shit, it's real.

It may have been a shock at first but, like all the Boys sentenced to custody, Nick soon learned to cope. Any potential deterrent effect those first few days in DC might have had soon wore off, for Nick came out of DC and went straight back to his thieving ways. At the age of 18 he was sent to Borstal, convicted of 'another accumulation . . . theft, loads and loads of theft'. Though no longer proud of his juvenile offending record, he is proud of the fact he was only ever a thief, never a burglar, and like Denny, deplores those who burgled private dwellings:

> I've never screwed a house in my life. I just went robbing and raiding and stealing. Even though I say live and let live, crime is going to go on regardless of what we do about it, but screwing somebody's house is still a no, no . . . definitely.

Nick served fifteen months in Borstal, which had no more effect than DC: 'as soon as I come out, I was back on the criminal scene'. However, he then dropped out of it, because 'I met Karen', and got a legitimate job with some of the other Boys, installing windows. Earning about £180 per week at the time, he saw no reason to steal, but he was made redundant after three years, and admits he 'nearly got tempted back into crime', because he had become accustomed to good money. However, he resisted going back to stealing 'to prove to Karen that I could stay out of trouble'.

Although his marriage to Karen put limits on Nick's offending, he was still a heavy drinker and a substantial drug-user. On occasions, when finances were low, he did go on a few raids with Matt, robbing warehouses for significant sums of money, which he always considered to be crime with a purpose: 'I didn't see the point of having a big wad of money and not doing anything with it, but when I needed money for something, I'd go with Matt on his commercial burglaries'.

Most of the time, however, Nick tried to work legitimately, even trying to set up a business with one static and one mobile burger bar, serving building sites during the day and clubs and pubs in the evening. Karen had encouraged him to stay on the right side of the law, yet, paradoxically, she inadvertently fuelled Nick's final and most serious brush with the criminal justice system. A detailed and convoluted story, in essence it involves Greg, a former boxer and one of Karen's in-laws, who falsely accused Nick of a crime that he himself had perpetrated. Nick and Karen were both arrested, though they had a reasonably solid alibi. Subsequently the charges were dropped, but Nick still threatened revenge – 'every dog has his day and mark my words, one day I will break every fucking bone in your body', biding his time, despite constant taunts from Greg that he had got away with the offence by setting Nick up. Four years later, fuelled by drink, Nick exploded, and now accepts the injuries he inflicted on Greg would not have been so great had he been sober: 'yeah, the truth of the matter is that if I had been sober, then I would have thought about things a lot better'.

Stewing over the events of the previous four years, Nick decided he'd had 'a fucking gut's full of the bastard', and in his drunken state, went to Greg's flat and kicked the door down. Greg had smashed Nick over the head with an ashtray ('a big fucking jelly mould thing') and then, as Nick recalls, 'something really clicked'. Seizing a T-shaped piece of window frame from a skip in the street, Nick remembered his promise to 'break every fucking bone in his body' – and kept it.

When Nick, who was initially charged with attempted murder, saw the photographs of his victim, he could hardly believe what he had done: 'I shit myself . . . I thought this is the fucking big one now'. However, for various reasons, the charge was ultimately reduced to one of Grievous Bodily Harm (GBH) and Nick was sentenced to twelve months' imprisonment, eight of these to be suspended:

> And so I done four months, which was probably the worst sentence of my life. One, because it was so short and every day seemed like a week; and second, I was with Karen and I had somebody to miss for the first time, apart from my mother.

Nick remembers feeling that he could have 'kissed the judge' for the leniency of his sentence, for he had been told to expect seven years. He had inflicted horrendous injuries on Greg, almost to his surprise, for he really thinks he did not fully realize what he was doing. Nevertheless, he still has no remorse about his actions, claiming 'the sad thing about it is that I enjoyed it, not the physical part of battering him, but it made me feel good that I had kept my promise'.

The prison sentence caused Nick to reflect deeply on his propensity to violence after having too much to drink, and, somewhat ironically, he was introduced to Alcoholics Anonymous (AA) by a drug-dealer he met in prison. He read the AA book while he was inside ('it was me to a fucking tee off') and determined to do something about his drinking. Furthermore, he had missed Karen terribly ('like she could come to see me, but it was never enough'). With Karen's support and through his own willpower, Nick eventually stopped drinking when he was 30, and has not touched a drop of alcohol for ten years, nor has he committed any further offences:

> Yeah, that was the last time. It's something I'm immensely proud of. I'm proud of a lot of things I've achieved, but stopping drinking and staying out of trouble comes out somewhere near the top.

Nick's prospective seven-year sentence for GBH (which at the time meant serving *at least* four years) constituted a form of 'wake-up time' where he re-evaluated the course of his life and decided to try to change.

Gary

Gary also experienced this kind of 'wake-up time', although in very different circumstances. Initially very much a core member of the group of Boys from the comprehensive school who were heavily involved in instrumental crime (burglary, theft, shoplifting), Gary linked up with the Catholic Boys almost by chance. The Catholic Boys, in contrast, were much more involved in expressive offending (fighting, criminal damage), as a result of constant drunkenness and 'going over the top', and while the Boys from both groups often overlapped in terms of social activities, few crossed over in relation to their offending behaviour. Only two of the nine Catholic Boys (Marty and Mack) became heavily involved in instrumental offending (though Spaceman also started to steal for a living after he moved away).

As a young teenager Gary earned some money putting the skittles back up and collecting glasses in The Wayfarer. For a laugh, however, he put up flagons (beer bottles) instead of the pins and was banned. As as result, around the age of 16, when he started drinking as an 'adult', he decided to go to The Centurion, the pub in Milltown favoured by the Catholic Boys. Up to that point, he hung around with the comprehensive Boys and committed his share of burglaries and theft. After that, he was much more involved in fighting (earning his money through casual work with his father), until a Crown Court appearance for affray (with Jamie and Kelvin; all three were acquitted) caused a reappraisal of his wild drinking and clubbing forays into town:

> Oh yeah, I screwed houses and went shoplifting like most of the Boys. But I hardly ever went to court. We did the football club, you remember, me and Trevor and some of the others. And then I was with the Centurion Boys, going to town on the weekends. We were always in fights . . .
>
> The last time I offended? That would have been 1980, for the affray. That was a big one. We were looking at prison. And that was waking-up time for me. You know, being in court for two weeks. It was an experience you don't want to experience again. In the end the three of us got acquitted, but it was a bit of a lesson. We were, at that time, on the borderline. Everybody was going out drinking and fighting and doing a lot of violence. We were having a good laugh and enjoying it. But then Spaceman got glassed and then he got a chair smashed over his head. And the fun started going out of it then, as far as I was concerned. You realized that somebody was going to get badly injured. That brought it all home to me.
>
> We were on that scene for a long time. For about five years, from a Wednesday to a Sunday basically. On the piss, getting into rucks. In town, doing the clubbing scene. Drinking, drinking, drinking and it was all good fun. I loved it. But the time came when

I had to stop. I know some of the Boys carried on. Some of them are still doing it. But for me, after that court case, I knew it was time to stop. That was enough for me.

Gary had come to the end of his offending career, deterred by a possible prison sentence staring him in the face and by the endemic violence of his social life getting out of hand. He immersed himself in his work and has never been in any trouble since.

These cameo accounts of just four of the Boys illuminate the diversity of the offending careers they followed and (sometimes) curtailed. Paul and Nick were quite clearly 'heavy-end' juvenile offenders, experiencing custody at a relatively early age, engaged in systematic instrumental offending and offences against the person as a result of seriously dependent drinking. In Nick's case, this was recognized and addressed, with the critical support of his wife Karen, but only after a traumatic experience of imprisonment produced his particular personal 'wake-up time'.

Paul recognizes his drink problem, but accepts custody as an occupational hazard and, since both of his (parallel) relationships collapsed, feels he has no motivation to change, and cannot do so.

Denny and Gary reached what they felt was the brink of custody, then, for them, 'enough was enough', and they both settled into work and family life. Denny maintains he was never really a 'crook', despite his love of riding in stolen vehicles. Gary concedes he was 'lucky' to become associated with the Catholic Boys, which helped him to establish some distance from the culture and behaviour of his more 'natural' associates with whom he had gone to school, though he also had the self-discipline to refrain from offending before things went 'too far'.

Gary and Denny curtailed their offending in their early twenties; Nick managed to do so only a decade later, while Paul continues to offend, for his thoughts are less about desistance and more about adapting the nature of his offending behaviour to minimize his chances of going to prison. Even in this, however, he has proved unsuccessful, for neither personal relationships nor employment opportunities (which in different ways have supported Denny, Nick and Gary in staying out of trouble, and what Trevor calls the two Ws of women and work) have exerted any external influence on Paul. Moreover, he does not possess the personal resilience or motivation to face up to his offending behaviour alone, explaining away his inability to do so on the grounds of a weak personality and dependency on drink, and in this this respect he is certainly not alone among the Boys.

Critical Themes in Criminal Careers

Types of Offending

Danny, the 'greatest' recidivist of all the Boys, came out of approved school skilled in the theft of motor vehicles, and most of his early convictions were for stealing cars and motorcycles, and driving without insurance. It was only later that he turned to committing burglaries, for the cars and bikes had been fun, but now he wanted money. Later on, in his early adulthood, he gave up domestic burglaries and turned to commercial break-ins and robbery, before taking up shoplifting and money-lending as a way of life.

Nathan, who started as a burglar, then moved on to shoplifting, specializing (like many of the 'criminal' Boys) in toiletries from high street chemists. Currently he does some low-level drug-dealing: 'bits and pieces now and again, ganja and speed; people phones me up and I just drops it off – makes a tenner, fifteen, twenty or whatever, here and there'.

This is a humble version of Ted's more entrepreneurial drug-dealing activities, though as a teenager Ted was more inclined towards burglary and the robbery of petrol stations. Matt was equally entrepreneurial as a drug-dealer after he was released from his first prison sentence (which he felt had been unjustly given). Unlike Ted, however, Matt became drug-dependent, and for over a decade was addicted to crack cocaine. As he described his first successful week in 1989 dealing in crack – when he made over £1,000 – he noted poignantly: 'I never thought I was going to be skint again, to tell you the truth, but then again I never thought I was going to be a crackhead'.

Matt then moved on to armed robbery, involving 'Danny and a few of the Boys', and describing those days as 'good times . . . or they would have been if, in my case, it hadn't all just been wasted on crack'. The raids were, he said, well organized though little was planned:

> As soon as the money was going down, we was starting up for the next raid. We just went out. We would steal a car, put £20 of petrol in, have no cash left and so we've got to make cash to get back home. It wasn't planned. It was only planned on the basis that, well, you couldn't come back on nothing. That was the only plan.

Matt was caught only once for 'raiding' and escaped with what he pointedly described as being a 'slap on the wrists', though he was sentenced to four years' imprisonment for dealing crack cocaine. He was at the sharp end of some serious offending, not only committing robbery, but also using firearms, after concluding that baseball bats and martial arts were powerless in the face of guns.

Matt's offending behaviour was very much at the extreme end of the Boys' criminality. Much more commonplace were crimes of burglary and theft, offences concerning motor vehicles, and shoplifting. Though domestic burglaries were committed regularly when the Boys were young, they yielded relatively little return (mainly the money from gas meters), and diminished in frequency as they got older.

Many of the Boys desisted from all but 'incidental' or 'accidental' offending once they had reached adulthood, though some were drawn back, usually temporarily, into instrumental offending for expedient reasons. Those who persisted in crime tended to have a limited repertoire of offending preferences, by far the most common being shoplifting, some of which was carefully planned and some of which remained essentially opportunistic. The drugs culture did provide new opportunities for income generation, though it also sucked some of the Boys into offending in order to finance their dependency. Furthermore, alcohol-related offences (mainly to do with violence and damage) continued to be committed by some of the Boys well into their adult lives (see Table 7.1). The types of offence committed throughout their lives include:

- domestic burglary and theft
- motor vehicle offences (take and drive away; 'ringing' cars)
- robbery
- shoplifting
- violence – assault, GBH, affray
- criminal damage
- drug-related (selling and supporting habit)
- fraud.

More 'sophisticated' criminality such as fraud and deception was rare, for the Boys were not connected to the right networks for such 'enterprise', though Trevor, at a time when he was out of work in young adulthood, engaged briefly in some credit card fraud, in response to an offer which, at the time, he felt he could not refuse. As a teenager, he was involved in burglary and theft, taking motor vehicles, and violence, but in his adult life, apart from this brief spell of fraudulent credit card use, he has desisted from offending.

Quite a few of the Boys were ardent followers of the local professional football team, and were involved in (and sometimes convicted for) offences associated with football hooliganism, such as assault, the possession of offensive weapons, criminal damage and resisting arrest.

What is of particular note, however, is how patterns of offending changed not only *among* the Boys as a whole, but on the part of individuals over time. It is difficult to sustain a picture of the Boys having any specific modus operandi, though some were reputed to have a particular speciality. Marty, for example, had always been a burglar and had never engaged in car crime, while Denny was the opposite.

Table 7.1 Offending Trajectories into Adulthood

Active involvement		Incidental/accidental		None
Ted		**Richard**		Gary
Danny		Mark		Denny
Spaceman		*Derek*		*Tony*
Marty		Colin		Alex
Matt		Tommy		Jerry
Paul		Mal		Shaun
	Ryan		*Jamie*	
Mack		Pete		*Eddie*
Nathan		**Vic**		*Kelvin*
	Gordon			
	Nick			
		Trevor		
		Nutter		

Black or mixed race: **bold**

Catholic school Boys: *italic*

Notes: some of the Boys did not *sustain* their criminality beyond early adulthood. Gordon did his 'fiddles' in the United States. Nick was a regular offender until his late twenties but has desisted since then. Ryan did a prison sentence but then 'settled down'. Vic has always hovered on the edge of the criminal fraternity. Trevor had a brief foray into illegal enterprise but otherwise has remained law-abiding. Nutter has largely been done for alcohol and football-related offences. Jamie has been convicted as an adult for assault, but otherwise is one of the more 'respectable' of the Boys.

Active involvement generally means continuing to live life 'on the street'.

Incidental/accidental refers to unexpected brushes with the law or 'passive' engagement through, for example, the receipt of stolen goods.

None refers to those Boys who have significantly stayed *completely out of trouble* during their adult lives.

Some of the Boys were clearly more dynamic and proactive in their criminal enterprise, while others tagged along with the crowd, and as a result taking some share of any financial pickings, or getting embroiled in fights. For most of the Boys, however, their offending behaviour as teenagers ranged across both instrumental and expressive territory. As they got older, they either 'left the circle' (as Shaun put it), or became more focused on one type of offending pathway or another.

Pathways into Crime

It would be surprising if the Boys had *not* generally become involved in offending when they were young. Deviance of one form or another was all around them, though this was certainly not always active criminality, and some parents went to considerable lengths to delineate boundaries between 'right' and 'wrong'. Such boundaries were, however, often very permeable, for even the more law-abiding of the Boys' parents rarely adhered completely to the preachings and warnings they issued to their children. Indeed, they may have been condemnatory of active offending, but were sometimes willing to benefit from its consequences. The receipt of stolen goods, for example, was rarely considered to be an issue, with no questions asked. Moreover, there was a culture of avoidance of official regulation: cars were driven without road tax, television licences were rarely purchased.

The culture of the neighbourhood was therefore firmly oiled both by an unwillingness to meet official obligations (taxes, rent, rates, fines, debts and so on) and a willingness to engage with the informal and illegal economy, if only from the margins. Working on the fiddle was routine, and 'borrowing' from the gas meter towards the end of the week was one strategy to make ends meet if times got hard. Shopkeepers split packets of biscuits in half for trusted customers, simultaneously providing a service and increasing their profits, and they were willing to sell individual cigarettes, or 'separates' as they were called.

The Boys were therefore surrounded by a culture of petty deviance, and would have also been aware of, if not directly connected to, more serious offending. Some parents and neighbours served prison sentences, many more appeared in court on charges of theft and shoplifting. The offer of 'cheap' (i.e. stolen) goods came round recurrently.

Closely linked to such deviant activities was a culture of opportunism and 'enterprise', and before they moved to secondary school many of the Boys had collected firewood then sold it door to door, retrieved and returned pop bottles which, at the time, had a small monetary value if returned, and washed cars. Socially, they hung around in the woods, lit fires and messed around with the stolen cars already abandoned there. Meanwhile, fighting was already endemic, to 'resolve' even the smallest problem.

The Boys therefore served an 'apprenticeship' in a neighbourhood which prepared them well for their subsequent offending behaviour. As Matt recalled, 'we all had an apprenticeship in making money – without working', learning how to steal and to fight, how to break into and drive motor vehicles, and how to open gas meters. Used to freedom and 'having fun', on their own terms, these activities became more pronounced as they moved through their teenage years and started smoking, drinking and sniffing glue. In turn, this generated greater need for financial resources, and these were secured through casual jobs and more frequent instrumental offending. Having fun and wanting money were therefore key factors in their largely unobstructed pathways into crime and delinquency, and it was, initially, a relatively risk-free activity, for the chances of being caught were slim, and the chances of being taken to court and convicted even slimmer. Even if that happened, then most of the dispositions of the juvenile court hardly impinged on their lives in any significant way (Williamson 1978).

Expressive and financial imperatives were differently balanced by the Boys, in relation to each other and in relation to other priorities and pressures in their lives, the latter becoming more relevant to the equation as the Boys got older, as the negative impact of the criminal justice process started to cause at least some of them to reflect on their behaviour. For a while, however, offending was an integral part of the Boys' everyday life, and was in no significant way disconnected from other aspects of their daily round. Doing burglaries was discussed in the same matter of fact way as playing football; going to court was almost a social event akin to going to a match, for defendants were often accompanied by a crowd of their mates. In keeping with the 'que sera, sera' and 'devil may care' attitude which prevailed, most simply joined in whatever was going on, and took the local and the formal consequences in their stride. Only much later in their lives did any of the Boys really reflect on what they had done, for at the time, money and excitement were the driving forces of their everyday existence.

Ted is cautious about attributing his involvement in crime to some kind of peer pressure (which should not be surprising, as he was often the instigator), though he clearly attaches some importance to the influence, first, of his extended family, and second, to the culture of the neighbourhood. Indeed, it was this latter influence that caused him to move away at a relatively early age, as he made a rather half-hearted attempt to stay out of trouble (he has been 'in trouble' all his life):

> I just started doing what all the Boys were doing. It was like you almost had to do it. Well that is what I had in my head at the time and I thought, well if I can escape from Milltown then that, maybe, is half the battle. So I did. I got married in 1981 and started living in other places.
>
> But when I think about it, I was surrounded by crime. All my older brothers were into it. And they got me to do things because if I got caught, at the time it was likely to be just a slap on the wrists.
>
> I think if I had stayed there I would have ended up doing five, seven, maybe a ten year stretch for something really serious. People got to expect me to be involved in the heavy things 'cos of what I'd already done and 'cos of who I was, you know, like the family I came from.

Ted was 'sent away' to a community home when he was 12, the same age that Danny was sent to approved school, where he learned a broad repertoire of offending skills:

> I learned to operate a car, so I knew how to rattle [break into, hotwire and steal] cars. I got to know how to open gas meters and electric meters. There's two hundred boys in a place like that – you can learn a lot!

The third of the most heavy end young offenders was Vic, who, alongside Ted and Danny, got involved in a range of serious offences, including burglary and theft, motor vehicle offences and violence. Vic was sent to an attendance centre and subsequently to Detention Centre, and later was committed to Borstal. He describes not a 'drift' into offending (see Matza 1964) but an incremental slide, starting with petty shoplifting, but rapidly developing into more serious crime:

> It started off with the shoplifting when I was still at school. It was more of a laugh than anything else. Just fun. I never got anything out of thieving, not until I got a bit older and needed money. Yeah, so it was shoplifting first and then the cars, with you know who [Danny]. And then when I was a bit older I was doing some serious robbing and making money. You had to, the dole in them days was forty odd quid a fortnight.

Vic makes light of his progression into crime, though one of his first convictions had been for 'slitting a kid's wrists', and he was sent to Borstal for burglary and car theft. He is, however, quite clear as to why he 'got into' crime: first for the fun and not long afterwards for the money.

Ryan, in contrast, was not really sure why he started getting into trouble. He came from a comfortable background (by Milltown standards) and took a relatively well-paid factory job on leaving school. He describes himself as 'not that criminally minded really', though he had done 'little things . . . nothing much', which included stealing lead from houses (with Danny) and a few 'little burglaries, just for the money to stay out, basically'. Apart from one prosecution for theft, when the police found 'watches and stuff' in his house, Ryan evaded conviction until his early twenties, when he was sent to prison for 'affray, two counts of actual bodily harm, and something else, I can't remember'. Since then he has largely stayed out of trouble, apart from occasionally liberating wood that is 'lying around' to save paying for his do-it-yourself activities. His closest friend, Trevor, was also actively involved in offending as a teenager and is very clear as to why he got involved: 'you know, you are like little sheep then, just doing what everybody else is doing'.

The Boys from the Catholic school, though often from very similar home backgrounds to the rest of the Boys, had different explanations for the (different) kinds of offending with which they became associated. Tony, for example, now a successful businessman, attributed it to little more than the 'high spirits' of youth:

> We all just liked to have a drink or two, or twenty! And inevitably when everybody got pissed up, there'd be a bit of trouble. Yeah, there was a lot of fighting when we went to town, but it was just the way things were. It wasn't so serious really, despite what happened to Spaceman. And it was the same at the football. We'd have a few beers before the game and the fighting there was, I think, a fashion – you know, 'football violence'. I think we used to follow the fashion rather than set it.

Kelvin, likewise, felt that he had been led along by the crowd. He was prosecuted for painting on the school walls and for attempting to steal a car, 'but it was silly things like that, really, we were little buggers but we were never crooks'.

Explanations and Attitudes

Ted was always completely amoral about his offending, taking what he could get wherever and whenever he could get it. As a young man he had been seriously immersed in criminal behaviour across a spectrum of offending and fully expected that one day he would end up in jail:

> I think I always knew when I was younger that I was heading that way. I knew I was going to spend some time in prison. Given what I was doing it was bound to happen sooner or later, wasn't it?

Legitimate employment never paid enough, and instead Ted has made a good living dealing 'soft' drugs around his local community, where he is very much the linchpin of the neighbourhood. Danny also views crime as integrally bound up with trying to earn a living, for he felt he was never likely to get a job which would pay what he considers to be a 'sufficient' wage. Even working on the fiddle is unattractive to him, in that it would probably pay no more than £150 a week, £200 at the most. As a result, he has to find alternative means of making money, his current preferred activity is shoplifting, and he does not believe he will ever work legitimately, though he knows the price to be paid for his criminality is occasional spells in prison:

> I'm at that stage now when I know I'll never work. I'll go shopping [shoplifting], I'll get caught, I'll do my bit of jail ... But I'm earning enough. If I get eight weeks over the wall [in prison], I'm covered.

Danny still maintains he would stop offending if a suitable (and suitably rewarded) job became available, for he is aware that his criminal involvement produces constant uncertainty and insecurity: 'every day you go out and you don't know if you'll be sleeping in your own bed that night'. Of course Danny could stop offending, but he could not possibly support his lifestyle on social security or in a job paying the minimum wage, for he always likes to be able to afford 'the best'. His offending finances a comfortable though certainly not extravagant living, enough to have a well-furnished house, run a couple of cars, buy a few drinks and pay for the keep and care of his daughter's horse. To Danny, offending is not a matter of choice but a necessity.

Instrumental crime was committed wherever and whenever opportunities arose, the sole considerations being the money to be made, and the convenience of the 'enterprise'. In their younger days the Boys had burgled local domestic premises, mainly to steal from gas and electricity meters; the theft of money or jewellery was regarded as something of a windfall. Later in their lives, the commonplace activity was shoplifting in the city centre, until slowly but surely their faces became known. Nathan is banned from many of the chemists in town, where he had specialized in the shoplifting of toiletries and razor blades:

> Yeah it's sad really, some shops I can't go into any more. It was good money. We used to sell all the stuff to the boys on the markets. It was something they could always sell.

As the Boys became increasingly 'known' in the city centre, they changed track or roamed further afield. Nathan gave up shoplifting, electing instead to supply soft drugs, while Danny and others became more 'professional', organizing forays to other towns and cities where they were unlikely to be identified.

Trevor defended his temporary venture into credit card fraud on the basis of the need to 'look after my family', when he was on the sick for almost a year, after incurring his serious ankle injury playing football. The opportunity to make money in that way arose by chance, and Trevor seized it, though it was never planned or intended:

> A couple of my mates showed me what to do and said did I fancy going out 'shopping' with it. I said, yeah, go on then, I'll have a little go. And I found it was so easy, it was unbelievable. So I done a bit of shopping. I used to go out and get some clothes, only clothes, for the kids. The wife used to go potty and to keep her happy I'd get a couple of dresses . . .
>
> I only did it for about three months but it was good at the time because I needed the money.

Matt came out of approved school with every intention of trying to 'go straight', for he had embraced Rastafarianism, and got a labouring job paying over £200 a week ('that was a decent wage in 1989'). Unfortunately he then got involved in a serious fight for which he was sent to prison, generating within him a profound sense of injustice and a determination never to pay a penny in tax ever again. Since then, he has never worked legitimately, maintaining that his 'unjust' imprisonment propelled him back into crime:

> There would have been some purpose to keep me outside, have me paying a fine, than putting me away for four and a half fucking months. I was the only one they put away and it just seemed like I was the one who should have stayed out, because I had a better job than them. That turned me negative, that did. Because I'd been legal, right and when you're legal you try to forget about that other side of your life, like the things you've done in the past, like as if you've always been a legal person. So I never talked about drugs or crime with my friends at work. I was talking about normal things that workers

talk about. And it was like that part of my life when I was a young kid was disappearing. But going to prison put me right back in the lion's den, where there is no chance of it disappearing. You can't make it disappear because it is all around you – just crime, more crime and more crime.

Matt said that, given his wayward youth, he got no credit for having tried to work legitimately, and then being unexpectedly propelled into custody was, to him, like getting 'a funny handshake'. He would never again pay 'a third fucking taxes', and instead ended up in heavy-end drug-use and persistent serious criminality.

Expressive crime had very different antecedents, as Kelvin testified: 'to us, it was just having a laugh, it wasn't the money, it was the laugh'. Spaceman, one of the few Catholic Boys who persisted in criminal activity into his adult life (to feed his drug and alcohol addictions), continued to 'celebrate' the expressive dimensions of his offending, even when it was committed for essentially instrumental reasons, though he detected the point when the 'fun' started going out of his offending, and it became more planned and purposeful:

> Yeah, it did get more serious but for a long time it had been just petty crime. I really enjoyed that life. I loved walking out of places with stuff that didn't belong to me. I must admit that. After a couple of beers I'd always go and fucking steal something.
>
> I wasn't really a compulsive thief. It was just such a good buzz. But it got to the stage where I had to become more organized. We knew people who'd buy everything off us for a third or maybe a half. If we had a grand's worth they'd buy it off us for three and a half hundred, four hundred maybe. Which ain't bad for a day out! And the rest of the time I'd be on the piss. Go on the piss, get into town, do about an hour's work and then you are fucking made for a couple of days. It was a good way of earning money but it was also a good way of spending money, because I needed drugs and drink.

Eddie, another of the Catholic Boys, speculated on the possible reasons why the Catholic Boys had been more inclined towards 'expressive' delinquency and less prone to committing more 'instrumental' offences, attributing this neither to parental upbringing nor to differential access to legitimate resources, but to the different disciplines of schooling:

> I do think that at the time [the Catholic school] was a more disciplined school, and I think that rubbed off on a lot of us. I think that it did set boundaries, whereas I can remember the Boys from [the comprehensive school] saying, when we were 11 or 12, oh we can get away with this and that, we can get away with anything. You couldn't in our school. I'm not saying that everyone in my school was this and everyone from up there was that, but I think there was a significance. Definitely. I mean, most of the Boys from my school were never robbers or burglars. What they got done for was more opportune, like. They were more fighters and drinkers. I don't think most of them ever meant to get involved in crime.

Pathways out of Crime

Gary was one of the Boys who experienced a critical moment (wake-up time) in their deviant 'careers' which made them decide to stop completely, though this was a relatively rare occurrence. There were, instead, various shifts or changes in offending behaviour towards more legitimate lifestyles, influenced by a range of factors.

Some of the Boys, like Danny, have continued to be deeply embedded in criminality, but the frequency or severity of their offences has diminished, while others have sought to desist from active offending but are still involved more 'passively' (for example, in showing no qualms about receiving stolen goods). Many of the more law-abiding Boys have, through necessity or preference, carried on fraudulently exploiting the social security system by working on the fiddle, and the vast majority of the Boys see absolutely nothing wrong with this. Only a few of the Boys, therefore, have completely severed their links with illegal activity, purportedly for ever, though substantially more proclaim they have stayed 'out of trouble' since their teens.

The *deterrent* effects of custody (or the prospect of custody), or a greater likelihood of *detection* appear to have had relatively limited impact. Mark's unexpected experience of being remanded in custody certainly caused *him* to be more determined to stay out of trouble in the future. Nick's last custodial sentence, at the age of 30, made him reflect deeply *and act* on his drink dependency, which had precipitated so much of his offending behaviour. The same applied to Spaceman when he was in prison at the age of 36, though the catalyst for change was also to do with his failing health and the sight of his dying father. Vic concluded in his early twenties that, having been caught and convicted so many times, he was a 'shit thief', and decided to find more legitimate ways of earning a living.

More typically, however, those of the Boys at the sharper end of offending adjusted their patterns of crime according to the perceived presenting risk. Danny, for example, abandoned commercial burglary when the police started using helicopters. Knowledge of alternative 'escape routes' became redundant, 'because when they get the helicopter out, it'll fly over the top of you and pick you out, so you can't sneak away no more; it's going to follow you and they'll catch you'.

Danny turned to shoplifting instead. He had already served many years (about twelve in total) in prison and his only child was born while he was inside. He could no longer bear the thought of another protracted spell in custody: 'I can miss my daughter for a couple of weeks, maybe even a couple of months, but I couldn't miss her for a couple of years, it would do my head in'. Shoplifting was a safer bet, carrying less of a risk of a lengthy custodial sentence.

Some of the Boys simply lost their 'bottle', no longer possessing the 'courage' or bravado to continue in their old ways. Nathan became 'scared' of going into shops, aware that his face was probably known and believing that he was always being watched (and therefore likely to be caught), and turned to minor drug-dealing instead. Colin had never really had the stomach for active offending: 'I know what a lot of the Boys do, but I wouldn't do it . . . yeah, I'll buy the gear off them, if it's something I want, but I wouldn't do it myself. I haven't got the bottle to do it myself, it's not in me'.

Court appearances, in and of themselves, rarely served as a deterrent (the Boys had become only too familiar with them), though they sometimes provided the catalyst for change if they coincided with 'wake-up time' brought about by other circumstances. Even 'last chances' were usually treated complacently, for the Boys doubted their sincerity and were often genuinely surprised if, on their next appearance, they were committed to custody. One exception here was Tommy, for whom the threat of a 'final chance' was taken very seriously:

> I haven't done crime since I was 15. That was the last time, for breaking and entering. And the judge [magistrate] said next time I see you, you are going away. And I haven't done anything since. I will always remember his words and I've never . . . well, I'm not saying I've never done anything criminal since, but I've never done anything like that since. I don't know why it affected me like that. Most of the other Boys didn't seem to care. But I didn't want to go to prison. If they put me in prison I'd kill myself. I couldn't handle that. I like to go out. If they stuck me in a cell for twenty-three hours a day, I'd hang myself or something. I just couldn't handle it.

Many of the Boys, like Tommy, did endeavour to curtail their offending behaviour as they moved into young adulthood, but less as a result of the threats and risks of the criminal justice process, and more as a result of wider personal circumstances. Trevor is convinced it was his family responsibilities that propelled him out of trouble: 'You get older, don't you . . . I said to myself I've got a family now, I've got to lead by example. How can I moralize to my kids if I'm taking drugs or boozed up every night or robbing and stealing everywhere? I suppose you just get older and wiser'. Kelvin, one of the Catholic Boys who felt that their offending was more 'comic strip' than calculated, was of the same opinion, and dropped out because he felt the Boys' violent behaviour was escalating and getting out of control. Moreover, he got married:

> When I got married I decided that my commitment was to my wife, not to my mates. I thought that if I still hung around with the Boys we would end up in bloody prison. And I thought, well, as a married man, I can't afford to be in prison. Don't get me wrong, we'd had a great time. But I felt that things were starting to get out of hand.

Alongside Gary and Jamie, Kelvin had been charged with affray, which he described as 'one of the big frighteners of my life'. All three were found not guilty, but two weeks later the Boys had another 'ruck' in a hotel, and even on Kelvin's stag night the Boys caused £10,000 worth of damage – 'Nutter started that, it was his fault . . . Things were going crazy, like' – and Kelvin felt it was time to get out.

It was not just children and partners who influenced the Boys' decisions to change their ways. The most striking example of 'wake-up time' related to Spaceman, although rather belatedly at the age of 36. He was serving yet another prison sentence when he was informed his father was dying of cancer, and he secured a sympathy visit to the hospital, though his paramount reason was in fact to get hold of more drugs:

> I didn't even recognize him. His fucking weight was down to nothing, his hair had fallen out. But the thing is that I'd arranged to meet someone at the hospital who was going to bring me some drugs. I'd arranged to meet him in the toilet. And I did, but I told him to fuck off. So I didn't bring nothing back. I was very confused about doing that because I wanted the drugs as well. But my old man dying was a turning point.

Spaceman came out of prison, acquired a sketchpad from a toy store to see if he could draw again, then enrolled on an art course for young offenders, and went on to do an art degree. He still smokes ganja, but that is all.

Matt told a similar story. After more than a decade of crack cocaine addiction and robbery to support his habit, he opened his door one day to find his father standing there with two suitcases in hand, explaining that he was homeless because his house had been repossessed. Matt had been oblivious to his father's inability to pay the mortgage and reflected that, had he been more aware, he could have easily paid off the arrears, but instead:

> All I was thinking about all the time, all I ever wanted to do was go and get my smoke for the day. But when my old man knocked on the door that day, carrying his suitcases, I think that was the start of me coming off crack.

Decisions to desist from offending have rarely been so spectacular. Jerry had had to wait for his juvenile convictions to become 'spent' before he could join the army, but now spoke at length about his inherent honesty, describing how he had recently returned an expensive watch he had found in the street, 'whereas I suppose twenty years ago I would have been wearing it'. The birth of his first daughter and the onset of her disabilities had contributed to an early sense of responsibility and, in his judgement, the need to forge a legitimate pathway in life. His job with the Post Office had cemented this: 'I mean, I had responsibilities and now, with the Post Office, everything is centred on honesty'. Jerry considers his juvenile delinquency as something of an errant episode in his life: 'I mean, I was brought up to be honest. I just ignored it for a few years! I just think that you tend to set your own standards as time goes by'.

In this respect, Jerry (like Trevor) supports the conventional wisdom about young people 'growing out of crime'. With the onset of family responsibilities and occupational trajectories, both developed different moral and expedient perspectives on the offending behaviour with which they had once been firmly associated.

Many more of the Boys maintained that there was no need for 'desistance', on the grounds that their offending had hardly been 'crime' in the first place. Tony asserted it had mainly been 'pathetic stuff', while Eddie and Alex said that, sure, they had hung around with the Boys but had never really got involved in any serious offences. Shaun was adamant that his offending had only ever been 'trivial' and a very temporary episode in his life. Mal had been convicted on two occasions (for burglary and for possession of an offensive weapon), but had stayed out of trouble as an adult apart from two moments of aberration (one for assault, the other for being drunk and disorderly). Derek, likewise, had not been in trouble as an adult apart from (unknowingly) purchasing a stolen motorbike for his stepson.

By their early twenties most of the Boys had taken one of two paths. The majority had, for the most part, dissociated themselves from the routine offending that characterized their teenage years, largely through the dual influences of 'women and work' (relationships, families and employment). A significant minority, however, pursued, deepened and diversified their offending behaviour, which inevitably led to experience of custody.

Inside – Experiences and Perspectives on Imprisonment

Twelve of the Boys have, at some point in their lives, received custodial sentences. One other, Mark, was briefly in prison on remand. Ten of the Boys have been sentenced to prison custody as adults. Four of these had *not* experienced custody or removal from home (to community homes or approved school) as juveniles, and two who had been incarcerated as teenagers were never locked up again (see Table 7.2).

Danny has been in prison more frequently, and for longer, than any other of the Boys. It is an occupational hazard he treats with fatalism and humour, taking things as they come, handling unexpectedly severe treatment with stoicism, and unexpectedly lenient treatment with satisfaction. A charismatic figure, he is always ready with a sharp (and conveniently embellished) anecdote and unfailing in his capacity to see the 'bright side' of life, in spite of a history mapped by experiences of custody, which, indeed, is what he talked about in response to a question about *employment*. Work has far less meaning in his life than crime and imprisonment, and 'work', since his early twenties, has consisted solely of criminal activity, which he has adjusted according to changing policing practices, calculations of the risks involved, and the needs of himself and his family.

Table 7.2 Experiences of Custody as Teenagers and Adults

Only as teenagers	Both as teenagers and adults	Only as adults		Never
Pete	Ted	*Spaceman*	Gary	Colin
Vic	Danny	Ryan	**Richard**	*Jamie*
	Marty	*Mack*	Denny	*Gordon*
	Matt	**Nathan**	*Tony*	*Eddie*
	Paul	[Mark*]	Alex	*Kelvin*
	Nick		Jerry	**Trevor**
			Shaun	Tommy
			Derek	Mal
				Nutter

Black or mixed race: **bold**

Catholic school Boys: *italics*

* Mark was remanded in custody but received a community sentence.

After going to approved school at the age of 12, he was later sentenced to Detention Centre and then to Borstal. His first prison sentence was for six months at the age of 20, and subsequently he had further sentences of eighteen months, two years, fifteen months, and then another two years. During his last seven-month sentence (in 1991) his daughter was born.

Danny has served further time in prison on remand (awaiting trial) and for non-payment of fines, and admits to being a pathological thief, unable to go into a shop without stealing a Mars Bar. His offences have shifted across the years from house burglary, taking motor vehicles, robbery of commercial premises, to shoplifting – which is well planned and done to order.

The custodial records of the other Boys are neither so profound nor so sustained. Paul has done a series of prison sentences, but most have been for less than a year. Matt did a four-year sentence for drug-dealing after a four-month sentence for violence, though those are the only times he has been inside. Ryan also did a six-month spell for violence, while Nick (after Detention Centre and Borstal as a teenager) received a twelve-month sentence (eight suspended) for Grievous Bodily Harm, and Mack has served short sentences for shoplifting. Spaceman has also served a number of custodial sentences for shoplifting, culminating in a fifteen-month sentence in his mid-thirties. Since going to Detention Centre at the age of 14 for burglary, Marty has served adult prison sentences for similar offences. After leaving the community home at the age of 16, Ted then spent fifteen months in Borstal and twenty-one months in prison for burglary, and since then has done short sentences for intent to supply illegal drugs.

Only Nathan matches the longevity of Danny's custodial experience; he was sent to a maximum-security prison for assaulting a police officer: 'Yeah it was a bit of shock. Twenty-seven months in Dartmoor for fighting with the police. I was only 21'. Like Paul's and Nick's, Nathan's offending profile was heavily drink induced. When he recounted his other spells of imprisonment, both on conviction and on remand, he noted that 'they were all around drink'. He served five months on remand for robbery with a firearm but was then acquitted, then was sentenced to seven months for drink driving and assault, which became twenty-seven months following prison riots during which he 'turned a fire hose on a screw [prison officer]'. Towards the end of the 1980s he had a couple of 'little ones' for 'drink driving, criminal damage, assaulting police and things like that'. In the 1990s, he has been in prison twice, both for drink and drug-related offences: 'it's just drink it is – stupid. I drink and then I get into these predicaments. I try to get my act together, but it hasn't really made no difference'.

No one wants to be locked up and deprived of their liberty. The Boys were no exception, and though they may have appeared blasé in anticipation of a possible custodial sentence, privately most were terrified at the prospect of imprisonment, always hoping the courts might give them one 'final' chance if they adopted the right stance and argument.

Mack knew that, sooner or later, he would end up in custody, having been a persistent juvenile offender, but 'I always dodged it when I was a kid'. Eventually sentenced to custody at the age of 30, he was 'shocked' – though imprisonment did not serve as a deterrent, because by then offending (shoplifting) was his way of life and as soon as he was released 'I was back to normal, like'. Fatalistic about occasionally having to do time inside, Mack reflected: 'you've got to get caught now and again, haven't you, when you do what I do'.

Danny had already been in an approved school (for the 'deprived and depraved'), but when faced with the prospect of a more punitive custodial regime:

> I screamed for my chance . . . I tried to pull the wool over their eyes. I swore I'd never commit no more offences, please give me community service or a fine. I'll get a job, I'll try my best . . . anything, don't send me to jail.

So even though the Boys faced the possibility of going inside with fortitude and fatalism, they always hoped that somehow they would find a way of avoiding going to prison. The more persistent offenders accepted the inevitability of custody, and given their social and cultural background, usually had some prior, if partial, knowledge of what lay in store for them. As Danny put it, 'you know a lot before you've even got there, you know, with the stories'.

Ryan observed that when he was sent down for six months and committed to the *local* prison:

> I didn't care. I knew what it was going to be like and I knew everybody. No big deal. One of the Boys was a red band and he sorted me out. All of them was helping me.

Home from home really. All you miss is the beer. It wasn't no fucking big shock like it should have been.

Unfortunately, the prior knowledge imparted to the Boys *were* just 'stories' – incomplete, distorted and invariably romanticized, certainly providing some clue as to what life would be like inside, but rarely preparing them completely for the impact of imprisonment, especially when – *unlike* Ryan, who found himself immediately in the company of people he knew – the Boys were sent to institutions far from home.

Danny's first night in Detention Centre was characterized by complete disorientation:

First night was fucking hell. People had told me you've got to have the bed made in the morning before the doors open. That was one of the things I knew, from the stories. So anyway I got into bed and I'm falling asleep and I hear 'ding, ding, ding' and I thought it was morning. I thought, the night's gone quick. So I jumps up, makes my bed, gets dressed – now what do I do? Then this screw slid the bolts on the door and I am just standing there. And the screw screams at me to get out of the cell. So I poked my head around the door and they are all in the centre with fucking fire blankets on them. It's a quarter to one in the morning and it's a fire drill. I thought it was time to get up! Anyway, I had a few slaps for that, for not moving fast enough. It wouldn't happen now; they'd be out of a job.

Early days in custody were often disorienting, with the Boys experiencing an overwhelming loneliness, anxiousness and helplessness. This initial powerlessness was exploited ruthlessly by prison staff – before the new prisoners were acclimatized and absorbed into the main prisoner population, and greater 'safety in numbers' was secured – and the Boys were subjected not only to physical violence, but also to more subtle humiliations, such as shapeless haircuts. However, they quickly learned appropriate strategies of avoidance, resistance and survival, as we shall see.

Marty captured these initial feelings, conceding that he had 'cried like a baby' when first sent to Detention Centre, and, moreover, suggesting his subsequent spells in prison had not been markedly different:

The first week inside it's fucking murder . . . scrubbing floors, all the banging and all sorts of things. Unfamiliar surroundings, you don't know anybody. But you get used to it. You have to.

Not only do prison officers and prison routine seek to subordinate and control new prisoners, but also the internal hierarchy of the prisoners themselves is set up to evaluate the vulnerability (or strength) of a new prisoner, just as the new prisoner, in turn, seeks to evaluate it. New prisoners have to learn fast – how to simultaneously present a sense of humility to the prison staff and an aura of toughness to the prisoner community if they are to avoid the degrading and often violent rituals of humiliation. On his first day inside Matt found himself in a cell with someone with whom he had a few scores to settle. He decided to 'take him on' and, in doing so, incurred some cracked ribs in the process. Once they'd thrashed things out in this way, however, 'we were together after that', and Matt had converted a potential enemy into a loyal ally.

The Boys soon became acclimatized to their new surroundings, for, as Danny said, not only do you get to know other prisoners, but also you 'know which screws to avoid if you can, and the ones you can get on with, get some favours out of, like'. To survive (emotionally and sometimes physically) in custody, all prisoners need to construct a framework for action, incorporating alertness to institutional power, the meeting of personal needs and attention to the culture of one's peers. This is a see-saw exercise, where too much attention to one at the expense of another is likely to produce significant difficulties in 'getting by'.

Danny can tell a catalogue of tales about different approaches to getting by. Never averse to being deferential to the prison staff, though this was sometimes for motives beyond simple compliance with the rules, he was always able to exploit weaknesses in the system that would confer on him additional privileges or opportunities. Moreover, he did not run shy of engaging in maverick pranks, which, though they sometimes cost him privileges and occasionally lost him time when some of his remission was revoked, earned him kudos among his fellow inmates. Based on Danny's extensive experience and corroborated by the other Boys who have been inside, one can usefully distinguish between 'playing the game', 'playing the system' and 'playing up' as a tripartite strategy for making the best of prison life.

Playing the Game

Playing the game was essentially about behaving according to the prison rules and the demands of the prison staff – 'yes, sir, no, sir, three bags full, sir' – and it guaranteed a quiet life from prison officialdom. If used as an exclusive strategy, however, it invited ridicule and possibly victimization from the other prisoners.

Playing the System

Playing the system was about pushing the boundaries of the prison rules to greater personal advantage, or the advantage of other inmates. Danny recalled joining a voluntary service working party as part of a pre-release scheme. Each day he ventured outside the prison in two sets of overalls, selling one set to local workmen for a packet of cigarettes. The Boys also 'cultivated' friendly prison officers, partly as protection against the more vindictive ones and partly to secure additional favours. Matt held 'parties' in his cell, where contraband tobacco and alcohol were available; al though the prison officers routinely searched the cell, so long as the contraband was kept to a modest level it was rarely confiscated, for they were keen to maintain harmony on the landing. Matt, as he said, learned 'not to push things too far' where these parties were concerned.

Playing Up

Playing up was a more risky strategy but commanded respect among the other prisoners. The secret, according to Danny, was timing. You did not mess around without weighing up the likely outcomes, for it was important to sense the lie of the land and to get the measure of both the staff and other inmates. The skill of playing up lay in winning status with the other prisoners, while not eliciting too draconian a response from the prison authorities. The important thing was to 'have a laugh', and if you could get the screws laughing too, despite the transgression or flouting of regulations, this was an added bonus. Some such humour, however, was threaded with the pathos of being locked up:

> I mean, no one wants to go to jail but once you're there why be worried? You've got to do the time, you've got to have a laugh. Everyone who's never done it before says they couldn't do it. I say to them, what will you do then – commit suicide? I say, well carry on, I want to get up the next day. There was one like that with me in the cell one time; he did my fucking head in. So I went and got him a bowl of water and he put his head in it. So I rang the bell. And the screw come and I said look he's trying to commit suicide 'cos he don't want to be here. And the screw looked at him and kicked him right up the arse – get your fucking head out of that water. We *all* had a good laugh about that.

In playing up, Matt engaged in wars of attrition with prison staff in the sewing room, sometimes refusing to work, sometimes working on to finish a job when he had been told to stop. Often hauled in front of the governor for 'loads of charges, mutiny charges and all that', on many occasions he would enlist the support of a prison visitor and argue a rational case for his behaviour: 'I got off with so many charges that way, it was stupid'. He also opted for a vegetarian diet because he didn't want to eat pork, but one day decided – contrary to the rules if you were down as vegetarian – to eat chicken. The head chef (whose food Matt had always insulted) immediately scratched his name from the vegetarian list:

> But I already had it sussed out. They were giving me fish, which is white meat, and chicken is too. And I got the prison visitor to put this down in writing and when I went to see the governor he said he could see my point and told me to tell the chef to put my name back on the vegetarian list. But the chef wouldn't do it. Dinner time came and the governor himself came down and put my name back on. The chef glared at me. We hated each other. But, you know, so many times I got off with them kind of things.

Matt was a polished performer in first playing up but then finding ways to *downplay* his behaviour, thus avoiding more serious penalties for breaching prison rules, and usually striking exactly the right line between rebellion and reason. To his fellow prisoners, he was a self-declared rebel always trying to get his own back for what he considered as unfair (and perhaps racially discriminatory) treatment by the prison staff, while to the prison authorities, he was clearly an awkward case, though one who was generally able to advance a reasoned and reasonable argument.

Prison is always a tough place, though the Boys found ways of making it tolerable. Their public recollections of being inside *always* gloss over the more private pain they often felt about their lack of control, and the separation from their loved ones. (Danny's marriage collapsed when he was inside; Ted, Danny and Nathan became fathers while they were in custody.) Nevertheless, they had to display rectitude when they were banged up, and sustain the stories afterwards. It was the only way, it was all they could do, for, as Danny noted poignantly, 'it was all about having a laugh. That's what stopped me from going under, messing about'.

The Boys don't often look back – it can be painful. Those who did made some additional, instructive observations about their experience of custody. Nathan and Vic recalled it was the first time they had thought about their cultural and ethnic identity. Both are mixed race: Nathan of Arab and Irish parentage (though born and raised in Wales), Vic, African Caribbean and Welsh. Nathan did not find his ethnic background problematic, and attached himself 'naturally' to the *Welsh* boys in prison ('the Welsh boys would all look out for each other'), whereas Vic, in contrast, was rapidly alerted to his *black* identity:

> I mean, you've come from an area where there is black and white everywhere and then you go to a place where everybody is separated. You know, my idea of getting on was the black and the white all together, but when I went inside it was either I was with the blacks or the whites. If I wasn't with the blacks or the whites I had to be on my own, so that's the thing I didn't like. Because the whites didn't want me. So it made me feel more black. I *had* to be more black. It had never bothered me before. I'd never thought about it until I went to those places. I'd never been called names before, you know, like nigger. There it was in your face.

Vic, along with Marty, made some telling suggestions about improving the impact of custody, arguing forcefully for much more robust through-care support:

> When I come out of DC I was straight back on the street again. I done my six weeks of marching up and down. But there wasn't someone meeting you outside and saying well OK, you've done your sentence, you've had the discipline, you know what it's like to get up early in the morning, you might have learned something a little bit useful in

there. Now here you are, there's another place to go, this is what you should do next. They put kids in there and then dump them on the street. They should try to keep their education going. Because everything you learn in places like that is no good to you. A lot of kids go in there, they are blind. And they come out of there, they know how to steal, how to open doors, and everything – terrible.

Marty advocated a version of the 'short, sharp shock', though considerably shorter (and therefore, in his view, sharper) than three months in a Detention Centre. Like the other Boys who had experienced custody, he noted he had adapted quickly to the circumstances, though this was *not* immediate:

Well you just get acclimatized, don't you. You get used to it because you can't avoid the situation. You have got to learn to live with it. I've often thought about it. You know, if they'd let me out one week after going through what I went through, after the first week, half of these Boys wouldn't go back in there. But they just get so used to it in there, do you know what I mean?

Moral Boundaries and Philosophies of Crime

The more instrumental offenders among the Boys generally had little compunction from whom they stole, though some (like Denny and Nick) condemned unequivocally those who burgled private dwellings. The Boys who had been engaged in more expressive delinquency were far more forthright about the distinction between an almost 'accidental' criminality and more calculated offending. Tony maintained he was 'never a thief', though he admitted to sometimes 'keeping watch' and to some petty shoplifting, while Kelvin argued that 'yeah, we got into a lot of trouble and there was a lot of violence, but we wasn't violent people'. His view was that when fourteen or more of the Boys were walking around together 'you just draw attention, you attract trouble'. None of them was really 'that bad', he maintained, emphasizing where his 'crowd' drew the moral line by reiterating that 'we didn't go breaking into people's houses and stuff like that. I mean, I know some of the Boys did but that was because they got in with a different crowd'.

Derek, another of the Catholic Boys who had been convicted for fighting and criminal damage to motor vehicles ('playing rugby with a brick', as he put it), asserted he 'had never been a criminal . . . I mean, I've got into scrapes like drunk and disorderly but I've never been a burglar or a thief. I wouldn't do it. More high spirits, really, alcohol induced'.

Gordon had been convicted in his schooldays for stealing a car, receiving stolen goods and shoplifting. In his adult life he has executed a range of illegal strategies which have made him a fortune, but has never been caught, and has an essentially pragmatic view of offending:

And of course there is nothing else I ever done because if you never get caught it's never a crime, is it? Anyway, everything I've ever done has been trivial, just trivial. You know, I've never hurt anybody on purpose. But if somebody came in here now and had a mountain bike and said give me £40 for it, I'd give it. I suppose it's a Milltown thing. I think it's how you're brought up, you know.

Richard has always been more closely associated with the more criminal of the Boys, but was keen to distance himself from them, aligning himself more with the perspectives of the Catholic Boys, though he remained more sympathetic to the position of the 'criminals':

> Oh I'll buy knocked off [stolen] stuff. I wouldn't bat an eyelid to that. But it depends where it comes from. If it's from burglaries and I know it is, I won't entertain it, honestly. I don't like anyone who is into burglary. I don't associate with any burglars, not any more. I wouldn't give them the time of day. But as far as shoplifting is concerned, I don't see anything wrong with that, because the Boys who do that are not working. They have got to find money from somewhere, so they take stuff from shops. I don't see that as a big problem.

Matt also defended the offending trajectory which had led to the commercial robberies he'd committed to feed his crack cocaine addiction: 'I was never a person who would kick in people's doors . . . I used to do warehouses, but I would never rob a house'.

Even within the sphere of violent crime the Boys made distinctions between what was and what was not acceptable. Vic was one of the more violent of the Boys, along with Danny and Ted. Indeed, the three of them had worked as nightclub bouncers long before they were technically old enough to drink. Yet Vic maintains they had their boundaries and their 'standards'. In the following observation, he refers to an incident in Milltown in the mid-1990s when a man walking home from the pub reprimanded four youths for vandalizing a traffic bollard, and they kicked him to death:

> Yeah I was heavily into fighting when I was 16, 17. And I'm not saying that it was really any different then, but it does seem worse now. Like the Lenny Ross thing . . . There was none of that with us. Like we wasn't going home kicking people in when we was that age, me, Danny and Ted. It was harmless fun, stealing somebody's car, things like that. And if we had a fight, we had a fight, but we wasn't going around beating up old men. We was fighting with guys of our age and maybe a bit older. But no picking on some pissed-up man on his own. And *we were the vicious ones*, us three. Like there wasn't many in Milltown who could come and deal with us. Everybody knew that we could look after ourselves.

Vic's depiction of his and others' offending as being 'harmless fun' does not really stand scrutiny, but this was his way of defending and justifying it. Nutter, whose speciality was football violence and who has always been a heavy drinker, was at pains to emphasize his 'clean' record. Never having been in prison and only ever fined, he had once been convicted of an offence other than drunkenness or violence, a burglary which he claims was not a 'real' burglary for it was the theft of copper from houses being renovated. Nutter asserted that being 'disorderly and stuff' was 'not real trouble', and anyway he viewed his fines as a *de facto* tax that was almost his licence to offend (though he has rarely paid more than the first instalment or two).

The Boys constantly and invariably invoked 'techniques of neutralization' (Sykes and Matza 1957) in defence of their particular brands of criminality or to explain away its seriousness. Those who have, by and large, desisted from crime in the adult lives, use a range of 'vocabularies of motive', which serve in a variety of ways to justify or excuse their teenage delinquency; they were young and wayward, they wanted money and craved excitement. Sometimes, they admitted, things got out of hand, though they insisted they had never been vicious, malicious or wantonly destructive. Trevor encapsulates some of these perspectives:

> I mean, I done a couple of bad things as a youngster. But I was only a kid in school then. I mean, we were teenagers, we just liked messing about. And like down the market, well that's not crime, is it? It was just taking a little opportunity here and there.
>
> Yeah, we stole cars but we never wrecked them. I know that doesn't make it right, but we never wrecked them. We just used them. We didn't even take the radios out of them.

Even at the furthest end of the offending spectrum, Matt found grounds to justify his behaviour, defending it *in relation to* the 'normal' activities of those in similar circumstances:

> I had to feed my habit, you know. That was it; that was what I had to do. And I could afford it, that was the worst thing. I wasn't like a crackhead on the street, who have to go and nick a chain and got to go and break into someone's house and take their television and video. I didn't have to do all that. I would go and make a good raid and I could afford it.

Few of the Boys look back on their offending careers with any sense of shame, self-reproach or regret. It has happened. It is what they have done. Some now identify particular forms of offending about which they feel bad, especially the burglary of private houses, for they recognize now that they were stealing from 'their own'. Not surprisingly, those of the Boys who did reflect more deeply on their offending behaviour, whether or not they feel any shame today, embedded their remarks within a context of cultural determinism. They had simply behaved, to a greater or lesser extent, like those around them, particularly those in similar circumstances.

Theories of criminality and delinquency are legion, yet it is difficult to locate the Boys' offending behaviour confidently within any specific theoretical framework. The Boys did much more than 'drift' into crime and out of it again, though there was also little evidence of 'status frustration' or 'subterranean values' at work here. The Boys wanted, like anyone else of their age, to have fun and to have money in their pockets, and they found mechanisms to achieve this, which does correspond with theories of delinquent subcultures arising from 'blocked opportunities' (Cloward and Ohlin 1961). The moral boundaries which may constrain criminality to achieve these ends were arguably more permeable in Milltown, for many of the Boys' parents were hardly in a position to condemn their behaviour; and much of it, anyway, was out of sight and therefore conveniently out of mind.

The concepts of 'differential association' (Sutherland and Cressey 1966) and 'differential identification' (Glaser 1956) may continue to be useful: all the Boys were attached in some way to a repertoire of offending behaviour when they were young, but the attachment of some was relatively marginal, and though they hung around with the Boys, they were reluctant offenders. Others engaged in the normative delinquency of the time, but were hardly embedded in the kind of criminal subculture which, for those like Ted, Danny, Matt and Vic, informed much of their everyday behaviour, and was reinforced during their spells away from home in care or custodial institutions.

Wherever the Boys were along the spectrum of delinquency, however, they invariably developed their own moral justification and defence for it, and positioned themselves *against* those who were further down the track.

A long-held prevailing wisdom is that young offenders 'grow out' of crime, which has certainly been the case with the majority of the Boys, though some have remained partially attached to offending networks, while others have had occasional 'accidental' brushes with the law. For around one-third of the Boys, however, the offending lifestyles they established when they were young have persisted into adulthood, though the nature of their offending behaviour may have altered. This, they would argue, has been as much a product of necessity as of 'choice' (though some of the other Boys would disagree). Crime is, for these Boys, an integral component of their efforts to produce what they consider to be an acceptable income, even though, at times, it has also been a consequence of heavy alcohol and drug consumption. It is a necessary, though not always desired, component of living 'on the street', and those of the Boys who pursue this way of life have learned to reap the benefits as well as take the consequences.

Housing Careers – Space Oddities?

Introduction

Like other 'trajectories' and 'navigations' in their lives (work, crime, relationships, drug-use, and so on), the Boys' housing careers became similarly polarized. Colin, for example, *never* moved from dependent to independent living, continuing to live with his mother, though now in a house across the road from where he grew up. In stark contrast, Gordon and Tony now both live beyond the estate in expensive owner-occupied accommodation. Within such extremes lie a mix of stories, though housing has been one of the more successful dimensions of many of the Boys' lives. At the time they were interviewed, no fewer than twelve lived in owner-occupied housing (though Nathan just happened to be living with a woman who owned her own house). Two of the Boys (Nick and Nutter) lived in private rented accommodation, while half were still living in social housing, including two (Mack and Eddie) who, though they have lived independently, were once more living in their parents' home.

Table 8.1 Housing Status and Location at Time of Interview (2000)

	Social housing	Private rented	Owner-occupied	Total
Top of the estate	9	1	4(1)*	15
Elsewhere on the estate	1	1	2	4
Very close to the estate	2	—	2	4
Elsewhere in the city	3	—	1	4
Beyond the city	1	—	2	3
Total	16	2	11(1)*	30

* Nathan in parentheses is an owner-occupier by proxy

Two-thirds (nineteen) of the Boys still live in Milltown and four others very near to the estate, though this snapshot conceals a complex set of pathways in the housing careers of the Boys, for many have moved away from the estate but then returned. Twelve of these Boys live in social housing, two in private rented accommodation, while nine live in privately owned houses. Margaret Thatcher's 'right to buy' scheme in the mid-1980s, which permitted tenants of social housing to buy their property at a concessionary rate, provided the springboard for some of the Boys to consider the idea of owner-occupation. The scheme gave them a foothold in the private housing market from which some progressed to housing destinations ('never council', they always pointed out), through a combination of good fortune and calculation, guided by personal belief and financial circumstances. Others, however, became owner-occupiers but later abandoned or forfeited their property, and are now living once again in social housing, the victims of the extortionate interest rates that prevailed towards the end of the 1980s. None of the Boys as children would even have dreamt of owner-occupation, for *all* had grown up in social housing, and their housing aspirations in young adulthood rarely extended beyond this. Indeed, most started out on their path to independent living in tried and tested ways consistent with the traditions of the neighbourhood.

A Typical Pathway to Independent Living

Housing and mobility, predictably, has been closely linked to the formation and subsequent breakdown of personal relationships. Typically the Boys did not move away from home until they met a 'serious' girl; typically the young woman was also from Milltown, or close by. The relationship would reach a point when *he* moved into the house of his girlfriend's parents (it was rarely the other way around), or they would both move in with one of her older (married or co-habiting) sisters. Then, whether or not this actually strained household relationships, as a result of overcrowding and/or personality clashes, the time came when the young couple were 'evicted' – sometimes on spurious grounds, sometimes for genuine reasons – and were therefore, as far as officialdom was concerned, 'unintentionally homeless'. This made them eligible for council accommodation, more so if the girlfriend was pregnant, though there often ensued a period of waiting during which time the young woman on her own, and sometimes the couple, were housed in temporary hostel accommodation. Eventually, however, they were allocated social housing often, though not always, in Milltown, and where accommodation was taken up away from the estate, it was often possible to 'exchange' houses, flats or maisonettes, and return to Milltown, as Ryan's experience illustrates:

> It was the usual thing. We were 'kicked out'. She was having a baby. When I come out of jail, I was living at home, she was living at home but I was really living down hers. And she was having a baby so we made out we were kicked out. We was put in a hostel then, the usual thing, for four or five months. Both of us. And then they gave us a house down [another area of the city]. I said I don't care where it is, that'll do. We were down there for a year and I was talking to this fella in a pub and he was living in Milltown and he fucking hated it. So we put it down that we wanted to swap, swapped six weeks later and I've been here ever since. Eighteen years.

Ryan now lives just around the corner from where he grew up, though his story does not reveal that, like some of the other Boys, for many years he maintained a separate flat elsewhere in the city as part of a 'scam' for fiddling the social security. Indeed, for over a decade, he was officially separated from his wife, though in fact they have *always* lived together.

Trevor, who now owns his own house at the top of the estate (where all the Boys grew up) went through a similar process, initially living with his wife Jill at her sister's house, before moving to bed and breakfast and then hostel accommodation, after being 'kicked out':

> I mean we weren't really kicked out. That was just the way the system worked. See, you've got to make yourself homeless. Jill was pregnant at the time. And then they gave us that house, that one right across the road. That's the first house we ever had.

Trevor subsequently exchanged that house for the one in which he now lives, which he bought through the 'right to buy' scheme some years ago.

Mark and Veronica were also 'kicked out' of her mother's house but, because they were not married, Veronica and their baby daughter were placed in a hostel, while Mark moved back, temporarily, to his parents:

> The only way to get a council house was to pretend she was kicked out. So she went down to the housing place with all her bags and they put her in a hostel. I used to go down there and see them. But she was only there about six weeks and then they put her in a hostel up here and after that she got a house in Jameson Road. I moved in with her. We were there for ten years and then we come here about six years ago.

Veronica was technically a 'lone tenant', while Mark officially remained at home (thus maximizing *her* state benefits), sustaining the charade for the best part of those ten years. It was only when they moved to their current house, a stone's throw from Mark's mother, who still lives in the same house where he grew up, that they went 'legit', for Mark had had enough of playing cat and mouse with the social security (a story he recounts later).

Tommy married Suzanne at the age of 20 when she became pregnant with their first child, and for eighteen months they lived with her sister, until they had 'a bit of bust up'. They were allocated a maisonette on the south side of the estate, and when the maisonettes were sold by the council to a private developer, Tommy and his family were rehoused in a nearby council house, where they have lived since 1983.

Shaun found himself adopting similar tactics when he was in his early thirties, after separating from his first wife Sue and moving back to his mother's. He and Sue had bought a house in Milltown, which yielded only a small profit after they split up, for Sue was unable to keep up the mortgage repayments after Shaun left, and most of the profit went to the building society. Soon after meeting his future second wife Gaynor, Shaun moved with her into her father's house. Her father's decision to sell the house was the catalyst and pretext for Shaun and Gaynor to become 'homeless':

> We put our name on the council list and got a house within about three months. We did this by putting ourselves in a bed and breakfast for a while. It was about three months before Eve [their daughter] was born. The point is that we made ourselves homeless and that made us eligible quicker for a council place.

Pregnancy or parenthood certainly accelerated the process, and Nick deeply resents the fact he and his wife Karen were 'less eligible' for council housing because they are unable to have children. They first lived with Karen's sister and then moved, according to form, into bed and breakfast accommodation on the grounds that her sister's place was overcrowded:

> Basically we wanted to get a council place. It was a bit of a scam, obviously. But we just met with a brick wall because . . . well we were told to our faces: want a council place, have a kid. And this was when we discovered she couldn't have kids.

Refused council housing, Nick and Karen moved initially into private rented accommodation, though eventually they were allocated a council maisonette in another part of the city and later, through an exchange, moved to a council house back in Milltown. This did not turn out to be what they had hoped for, and they gave up the house in favour of another private rented flat on the south side of the estate.

In their early adulthood, the acquisition of a 'council place' was considered by the Boys to be the best they could achieve, for the quality of such housing stock was generally good (though there were exceptions), and rents were relatively low. Private sector accommodation was quite the opposite, being usually poorly maintained with extortionate rents, and, not surprisingly, few of the Boys ever contemplated renting privately. Pregnant girlfriends or wives conferred advantage in the queue for council housing; otherwise they remained at home. The course of housing transitions in their young adulthood was not quite predetermined, but it was a well-known and well-trodden path usually requiring little active decision-making, though at times it demanded some careful management to achieve the desired outcome.

Kelvin and Julie were set on getting a council house, though after getting married in 1983 they moved into a private flat in another part of the city where they lived for seven years, before getting a housing association flat where they lived for a further two years. The flat was 'absolutely fantastic' compared to the first one (half the rent and much better maintained), but they still wanted a council house in Milltown, telling the council they were still living with Julie's parents and were under pressure to leave because of overcrowding. As a result, they were allocated a council house ('we were lucky, we've always been lucky with housing'), later taking advantage of the 'right to buy' and moving steadily up the housing ladder, and they now live in a well-presented private house on a small private development on the edge of Milltown.

The Boys have different perspectives on what constitutes 'success' in the housing market. Many of those who have secured social housing in Milltown, in a location of their choice, are quite satisfied, like Tommy, who 'got' a house he was happy with in his early twenties and has remained there ever since. Others, like Tony or Shaun, have been faced with different possibilities and opportunities at different points in their lives, as a result of their changing occupational and personal circumstances. Such crossroads in the housing market have produced not only success but also loss and failure, for it has certainly *not* been an incremental and unproblematic journey of the kind routinely associated with climbing the housing 'ladder'; many 'snakes' have been experienced too.

Domestic Factors: Moving Away from Milltown – and Moving Back

Girlfriends generally, and pregnant girlfriends in particular, provided the Boys with a spur towards independent living. Most of the Boys' relationships *and* their housing aspirations remained firmly focused on Milltown, though relationships formed with individuals from beyond the estate presented the strongest rationale for moving away. Few, however, did so permanently, for the Boys retained a deep loyalty and attachment to the estate, to which even relationships were sometimes subordinated, and when relationships further afield crumbled, those involved invariably returned to Milltown (see Table 8.2).

This was not, however, always the case. Ted met a young woman from a town some twelve miles from Milltown, where they married and moved into a flat close to her parents, and though the marriage did not last, Ted elected to stay in the area, meeting his next partner soon afterwards. It was perhaps significant he did not have a 'home' in Milltown, for both his parents were dead, though his sister and some of his brothers still lived there, and he has never returned.

Nor has Tony who, after forming a relationship with a young woman from another estate, bought a flat in Milltown but moved, soon afterwards, for occupational reasons, to Southampton; and Alex, who, after living with his wife in Milltown, moved away to another part of the city.

Shaun's second wife came from a neighbouring town and he moved there, before buying a house in the city, while both of Vic's partners came from other towns and he lived elsewhere until he returned with his second partner to live in social housing in Milltown. Nathan also went to live in another city with a young

Table 8.2 Those who Moved Away 'for good' and Those who Moved Away but then 'came home'

Reason	Moved away 'for good'		Moved away but 'came home'	
			With a partner	Alone
Personal	Ted		Nathan	Matt
relationships	Tony		Vic	
	Alex		Kelvin	
	Shaun			
			Mal	
			Gordon	
	Pete	Jamie		Marty
Other	Derek			Nutter
	Spaceman			

Notes: Gordon and Jamie do not live in Milltown but some five minutes' drive from the estate; Kelvin and Mal live on a private housing development adjacent to the estate which they insist is still Milltown.

woman who had been visiting him while he was in Dartmoor, though later they came back to Milltown until the relationship ended and she returned home:

> So when I come out I just went straight to hers. I didn't come back home. I thought I'd try it and I did try my best. But I wanted to come home, so she moved back to Milltown with me. She sold her property up there to come back here. But it didn't work out and she went back to where she came from, although we are still friends to this day.

Matt came back to Milltown alone, following the breakdown of a relationship he formed with a young woman from London while working in a nearby town, where they had lived together for a while. She had then decided to return to London and Matt went with her, but hated it: 'so I told my missus I was coming back home for a weekend, and six months after that she brought all my clothes back down because I wasn't going back to London'.

Some of the Boys decided to leave Milltown for other personal reasons, though subsequent relationships often strengthened their resolve to stay away. Like Matt, Pete also went to London, in order to live with his gay brother-in-law. Having declared his homosexuality when he was 17, he was convinced he could no longer live in Milltown. Shortly after arriving in London, he set up home with an older man who died a few years later, and then, after a sequence of brief liaisons in different parts of the country, formed a long-term relationship with Barry, with whom he now lives in the east of England.

Derek left Milltown in his late teens to live with his mother on the other side of the city (he had been brought up by his grandmother), until he bought a house with his girlfriend at the time. When that relationship ended he met another young woman on a visit to a nearby town and moved there for a year and a half, though he could not settle and they came back to the estate where his mother lives.

Both Jamie and Gordon now live in owner-occupied property just outside Milltown. Technically they have left the estate, though they are not far away. When Jamie married Pat she had already bought her own house, and he moved in with her, while Gordon left Milltown to go to university, subsequently seeking his fortune in the United States, accompanied for much of the time by his girlfriend Michaela, before buying a house nearby.

Kelvin and Mal both profess to live in Milltown, though they live on a private housing development adjacent to the council estate, and both want to stay in Milltown, even though their respective partners, Julie and Jane, detest the place. Mal left briefly in his teens for family reasons and then spent two years living with Jane's parents on a neighbouring estate, while Kelvin and his wife Julie lived away from the estate for approaching a decade, though Kelvin had always wanted to 'come home'. Julie eventually agreed to do so for an 'experimental' three years, which will soon be up, but Kelvin does not want to leave and hopes he will persuade her to stay. Mal stubbornly refuses to move from Milltown, but observed that Jane would leave tomorrow: 'she's never settled here, this house has never been her home . . . she'd go to Australia or wherever, no problem. Anywhere but here'.

A few of the Boys left Milltown briefly for a range of different personal reasons. Nutter followed his landlord to a new address, but then returned to lodgings on the estate, while Marty went to see Pete for a couple of weeks and ended up staying for nine months, before coming back to Milltown. Spaceman, on the other hand, has stayed away, having drifted from place to place for many years, before finally 'settling' in a small flat on the other side of the city.

The Boys have generally, however, been determined to stay local, for their identity is bound up with Milltown, both psychologically and physically. The vast majority have established relationships with local girls, who themselves have wanted to remain close to 'home', and as a result, the *location* of their housing decisions has rarely been an issue. Some, however, have been 'pulled away' by their personal relationships (and occasionally 'private troubles'), though they have also often been 'pulled back', not only on account of their loyalty to Milltown, but also their dislike of other locales, and the collapse of the personal ties which took them further afield in the first place. Of those who initially moved away but have since returned, some persuaded partners to come 'home' with them, while others have returned alone.

Employment and Imprisonment – Leaving Milltown for a Time

Just under half of the Boys would claim they have never lived anywhere but Milltown, though many of them have actually spent sometimes significant periods away from the estate, following in the traditions of both working away and being 'put away'. Jerry served in the army, and Spaceman in the Merchant Navy, while Trevor, Nick and Richard worked on building sites in Germany. Vic and Spaceman travelled round Britain, doing industrial painting and labouring, and Gary still works all over the country, though he lives in the house where he was born. Vic spent a short time in digs while playing professional rugby in the north of England. Gordon went to university in Birmingham, and then to the United States. Marty and Spaceman worked at Butlins. Ted, Danny, Nathan and Paul, among others, have had recurrent spells in prison. The Boys' self-perception that they have 'lived' in Milltown all their lives therefore conceals these extended periods of both voluntary and enforced absence from the place they would firmly assert has always been their home.

Living 'Alone'

Eight of the Boys live 'on their own', though three live at home with their mothers. Colin has never left, while Mack returned to his mother's house some years ago when his marriage broke up; he is close to his kids and close to the pub, and that is good enough for him. Eddie went back to his mother's after yet another mental breakdown, for he needs her nurture and support, though he once bought a flat on the estate, but hardly ever lived there because he was anxious about being alone.

The other five currently live alone, though in very different housing conditions and with very different housing histories, often contingent on the ebb and flow of their personal relationships (or the lack of them). Spaceman had a brief relationship in his mid-twenties and he and his girlfriend invested in their own flat, but the relationship ended and he 'walked away', subsequently spiralling downwards into criminality and substance misuse and usually living in temporary accommodation or with relatives and friends who were willing to put up with him. He also spent time in rehabilitation and in prison until, in 1996, on release from prison, the probation service found him a small council flat on the other side of the city, where he is surrounded by the brilliant art he now produces and dirty washing soaking in the bath. Though 'desperately lonely', he knows his self-isolation is necessary if he is not to be sucked back into drug and alcohol abuse.

For the past few months, Paul has also been very lonely, living on his own for the first time in his life in a sparsely furnished maisonette close to the estate. For many years he shared his time between the two women in his life until both rejected him, and now most of his time is spent in the pub. Richard lives in an identical maisonette across the road from Paul. He lived at home until he married, and through the 'usual' mechanisms was allocated a council house in Milltown, where his wife still lives. When his marriage ended he worked for a while in Germany, returning home to live with his parents, where he still spends a lot of time despite having had the maisonette for the past few years, for – like Paul – he gets very lonely and his mental health is fragile.

Marty also suffers from mental health problems. Diagnosed with paranoid schizophrenia, his domestic situation is bleak in his one-bedroomed flat in the heart of the estate. His windows are regularly broken by children going to school (they are aiming for the empty flat above where all the windows are either broken or boarded up), and he is surrounded by empty beer cans and dog food tins. The dog is his sole companion ('I don't really see nobody else'). Most of his disability living allowance is spent on alcohol, drugs and the dog, for his grandmother provides his meals, and his auntie cleans the flat once a week.

Nutter lives in a house nearby, illegally subletting a room from the tenant, who receives full housing benefit to cover the rent charged by a private landlord. He lived at home until his late twenties, when his parents 'got fed up of my drinking' and he moved out, taking on a mortgage, though he paid just one instalment and was eventually evicted (after three years), since when he has lived in a series of rented flats and lodgings. Like Colin and Eddie, Nutter has never been involved in a personal relationship. They, and others, live on their own, in different levels of contentedness.

Dual Abodes – Autonomy, Income, Escape

Paul had acquired his council maisonette some time before his relationships with his two women were conclusively over, for he anticipated the 'writing was on the wall' and knew he might need an 'escape route', even though it was hardly his desired option. For the Boys to have their own 'independent' accommodation while concurrently living with a woman was not common but nor was it unusual, though there were different rationales for such practices. Matt had always retained either a private rented flat or a council flat (over the years, he has had three in all, in different parts of the city), despite having lived with Camilla in her council house for over a decade. As he was officially in receipt of income support the flat rental cost him nothing (it was paid through housing benefit), and it served as a retreat when his relationship was strained, and a place where he could freely and more privately indulge his drugs habit.

The illusion of living separately from Camilla also produced an economic benefit for Matt, though this was not his primary reason for maintaining the 'scam'. First, his dole was paid as a single man's benefit; Camilla worked and disclosure that he was her live-in partner would have significantly reduced their official income. Second, since he did not use the flat regularly, he let it out for a small rent and within this rather expedient and calculating scam lay a kernel of altruism, perhaps deriving from the days when Matt had wanted to become a Rastafarian preacher-man:

> Sometimes I feel annoyed that I can't say to one of them [homeless] people on the street, go and live in my place. But of course I can't because they're on the dole and the social wouldn't pay me! But yeah I rents it out. Only for £25 pounds a week. Just to have someone there, because otherwise it's just a fucking waste. It's a nice flat, you know, properly kitted out.
>
> You know, I am glad I can give this guy a place to live, because he is a foreigner, see. I like to help folk and he needs a place to stay. He's a waiter but he only works two nights a week and he only gets £70. At first I wanted forty [pounds a week] off him, but he only gets seventy and I thought I can't fucking leave him with just thirty quid, so I said give me twenty-five.
>
> And the joke is that the landlord gets fucking £75 a week for that flat off the council. And he does fuck all for anybody.

Ryan was even more explicit about the economic benefits of appearing to live 'independently'. He has been married to his childhood sweetheart Laura for over twenty years but shortly after they married, when Ryan started working on the fiddle, they decided on a 'phantom separation':

> We was always together but we made out that we weren't. That we'd split up. Because then we can both claim off the social. I had my own dole then, my own pocket money. And then whenever I worked, that went to her and the house and I just had my dole money. And some of the rent money. Remember Bardsey? I had a place in his house. Marty was there as well for a bit. A few of us, yeah. We used to rent rooms off him. Well the social paid the rent. He'd have some of the rent and I'd get some. It was like that for years and years. Until about five years ago, I suppose.

These arrangements worked in different ways for the Boys, to the advantage of all parties concerned. When Denny's second marriage ended he lived with one of his brothers and then, for a short time, sublet a council flat:

> I had it off this guy who was living with his bird [girlfriend] but he still wanted to keep the flat on, so I was paying him rent . . . the wobbly [social security] was paying his rent, so it was a fiddle for him.

Clearly there were powerful financial reasons for exploiting the housing context in this way, though of greater importance to some of the Boys was the fact such 'second homes' provided havens and boltholes for themselves (and their mates). They were a place for 'escape', both from officialdom (having different addresses was always useful) and from fractious relationships, and also offered a personal space for greater autonomy, which was at times put to use for the Boys' unofficial and often criminal enterprise.

Exchanges and Transfers

The social housing system in the 1980s and 1990s permitted individuals to exchange by mutual consent. Exchanges, 'swapping' and transfers thread through many of the Boys' housing careers. Sometimes they were cleverly planned and sometimes they were just seized opportunistically. Often they were 'sensible' internal swaps within Milltown. The Boys, with their growing families, exchanged smaller accommodation for larger houses, with people they knew whose families had grown up. The most important transfers, however, as far as the Boys were concerned, were those which provided the opportunity to return to Milltown.

Ryan, as we have seen, quickly secured an exchange back to Milltown through a chance encounter in the pub. Nick's route back was more protracted, for he and Karen – after their problems getting any council housing because they were unable to have children – had eventually been allocated a maisonette on a neighbouring estate (where Paul and Richard now live):

> And from there we exchanged. Karen's sister met this guy and they got married. He had a council house in Milltown and of course he was going to move in with her sister, so he was going to give his place up. So I said exchange with us. We exchanged our flat with him and then he immediately gave our old flat back to the council.

Kelvin's move back to Milltown was even more fortuitous. He and Julie were living in their 'lovely' housing association flat, but it was on the top floor, and after their son Damien was born it 'was a bit awkward'. Julie played bingo in Milltown every Wednesday with her mother and one evening another older couple who also played 'jokingly' suggested an exchange, for their children were grown up and they were looking for a smaller place. Kelvin went to look at their house, which was just down the road from Julie's mother's, and the exchange was agreed:

> It was ideal for them because they was older people and ours was a one-bedroomed flat, it was lovely and warm and everything. So we just exchanged, so we were, you know, now in a council house.

This was Kelvin's first fortuitous step towards owner-occupation, whereas Trevor, once he became aware of the 'right to buy', had always aspired to owner-occupation, but it had to be the 'right' house. The council house he had been allocated at the top of the estate was *not* one he wished to buy, so Trevor sought to engineer an exchange to one he considered to be more desirable – the house across the road!

We had two children and the one we had was the wrong shape house. I couldn't do anything with it. As cheap as I could have got it [through the 'right to buy'], it would have cost me more money to build an extension on the side, with all that rising and, you know, the foundation work. It was the house across the road I wanted. And I persuaded him to exchange with me. The houses are just the same; it's just that this one has more space round the outside and the land is flatter. So we moved here and I bought this one. We've been here thirteen years now.

Owner-occupation

One-third (eleven) of the Boys, like Trevor, have become owner-occupiers, many benefiting from the 'right to buy' scheme during the 1980s, and some more by chance than judgement. Some have taken further incremental steps in the property market, while others have regressed and returned to council housing or the private rented sector.

Tony was without doubt the greatest beneficiary of the vagaries of the housing market and, since leaving home, has never lived in a council house, for he and Angie put down a deposit on a small flat with the windfall they accrued from the cancellation of a foreign holiday. His first steps towards owner-occupation were, therefore, hardly planned but ultimately paid enormous dividends:

I would have been about 24 when we bought the flat. We were both working and we were going to go on holiday with my brother-in-law and his wife, and my sister. None of us had been abroad before and we started saving some money. And then it all fell through. So we had this small amount of money. I was perfectly happy at home with my mum but I said to Angie we've got this little bit of money, let's go and get a mortgage. And so we bought the flat.

When Tony's work took him to Southampton, they sold the flat and took out a huge mortgage on a house. Tony observed that 'with hindsight it was probably the best thing we could have done', but, at the time, interest rates rocketed, 'and, boy, when that happened we didn't live, we survived'. House prices also ballooned, however, and the house they had bought in 1984 for £24,000 was sold four years later for £75,000 when they moved north. They bought another house for £83,000 and sold it ten years later for £103,000, enabling them to purchase their current house for £92,000, 'but then we spent about £50,000 on it . . . I suppose it's worth nearly two hundred grand now'.

Kelvin and Julie also gained dramatically from the housing boom of the late 1980s. Two days after exchanging their flat for a council house in Milltown, Kelvin rang the council to see how long he had to wait before he could consider buying it. It turned out that the two years they had spent in their housing association flat counted, and so they could *immediately* get one- third off the price. They bought it for £13,000 and sold it two years later in 1987 for £40,000, when they moved else-where into a large Victorian terrace house, which cost them £39,000 and required considerable renovation and maintenance. When they returned to Milltown in 1997 (though Julie had never wanted to do so), they purchased a relatively modern house for about the same price as they had sold the old one:

> We wanted a newer house. Julie didn't want to go back to an ex-council house and I wanted something a bit more modern that was not going to be hard work. I mean, I do fabulous jobs in other people's houses but when it comes to my own.

Kelvin lives close to Mal, on the very edge of Milltown in housing which has always been private – it was once compared to Mayfair in the Boys' localized version of Monopoly – though both Kelvin and Mal assert forcefully that they still live in Milltown. They are, however, economically and socially, if not geographi-cally and psychologically, a long way from their roots, and Mal readily acknowl-edges this. Having been thrown out of home at the age of 16 after a fight with his father, he rented a room elsewhere in the city, before meeting Jane and living with her parents for two years, both prior to and after they were married (in 1984). Jane's parents lived on a neighbouring estate, but Mal wanted to get back to Milltown: 'so we bought a house in Grant Road, down the bottom. I had a regular job so I got a mortgage. Thirteen and a half thousand I paid for it. And we lived there '85 to '96'. Grant Road deteriorated dramatically during those eleven years. Mal said that when they first moved there it had been a 'lovely street', but by the time they left it was 'like fucking Beirut', and he did not want his daughters growing up there any more: 'I wanted to give them better than what I had'. Mal had mixed fortunes in the subsequent move, for he made a limited profit from the sale of the house in Grant Road (valued at £34,000, it sold for just £24,000 because 'it had got that bad down the street'), but got a concessionary price on their next house, since they bought it from Jane's uncle, who would accept no more than £57,000 (the price he was paying for his bungalow), though it was valued at nearer £70,000. As a result, Mal and Jane came out 'evens', theoretically losing £10,000 on the sale of his first house, but 'saving' a similar amount on the next.

Jerry's move into owner-occupation arose from his desire to build up some col-lateral for his profoundly disabled daughter, should anything happen to him. After he married Sam in 1983 they lived with her sister for six months and then, for a further six months, with her mother. They were then allocated a two-bedroomed council house where they stayed for eighteen months before exchanging with Jerry's brother-in-law's mother for a three-bedroomed house with a 'massive' back garden, which enabled them to extend and modify the house to meet their daughter Rachael's needs. Under the 'right to buy' scheme, they purchased the house in 1992, later selling it in 1999 for a 'good profit' and moving into a modern house in a secluded private housing development high on the hill in the far southern corner of the estate:

> This place cost £65,000, which I can't really afford. We couldn't afford it if Sam wasn't working. It stretches us, makes things pretty tight. Some of the Boys think I've become a snob because I've moved over here, but it's for Rachael really. It's like an investment for her.

Once Trevor had exchanged his council house for the one with greater potential 'across the road', he immediately arranged to buy it, for he was determined not to 'hang around'. His parents had bought their house through 'right to buy', but only towards the end of their working lives, and Trevor 'didn't want to end up doing it like them'. He took out his mortgage at the age of 27, planning to have it paid off by the time he is 50, and has negotiated with his building society to pay substantial 'lumps' (as he calls them) whenever he can:

> This is just between you and me. I don't tell the Boys, but I paid off £7,000 last year. I want this out of the way as soon as possible. I'll have another lump to pay off now at the end of the year.

Recognizing self-employment can be fickle, Trevor pays off 'lumps' whenever he has completed a successful contract.

Gary has not had to face this issue, for although he is also self-employed, with a successful painting and decorating business, he inherited his house from his parents who had taken advantage of the 'right to buy' when he was a young man. His father died when Gary was in his early twenties and his mother then moved into smaller accommodation, leaving him the house in which he had been born and grown up. At the time he was interviewed he was contemplating moving to a bigger house 'not far, just down the road', though he was adamant he would never sell the house: 'I'll rent this house. I'll never sell it. I love it. This is where I grew up'.

Some of the Boys became owner-occupiers by proxy, through the partners to whom they became attached. For Jamie, this has proved to be a permanent situation, whereas for Nathan, it was a relatively brief episode early in his adult life, though recently he has once again moved in with a woman who has 'her own place'. Jamie married his childhood sweetheart who had already bought a house through support from her father: 'Yeah, she had her own house, very nice! And then about 1990 we came here. We made a killing on the other house. She bought it for seventeen [£17,000] and sold it for forty [£40,000], it was in the middle of the boom'. Jamie and Pat live five minutes' drive from Milltown.

Nathan has spent most of his life in precarious economic circumstances, making his living 'on the street', though immediately after his first prison sentence, he went to live with a woman who was an owner-occupier and they subsequently returned to Milltown to live in a private house *she* bought. After that relationship failed, he lived with his wife in her council house until the marriage collapsed, moving then into private rented accommodation. At the time he was interviewed, however, he had just moved in with a woman in Milltown who owned her house – 'so now I'm helping to pay the mortgage. 'Cos we've bought this house . . . well she bought it, but she's my partner, so it affects me as well, doesn't it'.

At the other end of the spectrum, Gordon completed his university degree and went to the United States, before returning to Milltown laden with both legitimately earned cash and ill-gotten gains, which he invested it in property. He and his wife Michaela bought one house for themselves and another to rent, and they also invested in a hairdressing salon. Though Gordon went off to the United States again, he returned to settle down with Michaela in a large Victorian house overlooking a park a few minutes away from Milltown, and they have since invested in more property:

> And then me and Michaela got back together and we bought this house. And we bought the building the salon is in, and the shop next door, and then we bought her mother's house, then we bought another house to rent out and a coach house . . . oh, and then we opened up another salon up the top of Milltown.

On a much more modest scale, Denny also ventured into owner-occupation later in his life, having had a roller-coaster housing career, first living with the parents of his first wife, then in a council house in Milltown, followed by an exchange to a more desirable house on the other side of the estate. When his marriage collapsed he spent some time in bed-sits, before meeting his second wife and moving into a privately rented flat above some shops on the edge of Milltown, where they experienced harassment and ended up living rent-free for nearly a year before being moved into temporary accommodation, and then briefly to another council house on an estate on the other side of the city. Another exchange brought them back to Milltown, where they had a council house until they split up, and Denny then lived with different brothers and sublet a flat from a 'mate' before getting a housing association flat on a neighbouring estate, where he met his third wife Annie, who moved in with him and they decided to buy an ex-council house in the centre of Milltown:

> I was fed up with chopping and changing, moving from one place to another, so we came over here and bought this place. Yeah, it's not rented, we're buying this. I mean, my mortgage isn't much more than the rent I was paying.

The Boys therefore moved into owner-occupation in a myriad of ways. Some almost 'stumbled' into it, their circumstances and resources suggesting it was the right decision at the time, while others worked towards it, taking advantage of opportunities which presented themselves. Some had a clear idea of the kind of place (and location) they wanted, whereas others did not. Some stretched their resources to the limit, whereas others purchased more modest property well within their means. Some profited enormously from the vagaries of the housing market; others suffered and struggled, but at least managed to hold on to their owner-occupier status. A few of the Boys were not so fortunate. They had once been in owner-occupation but had returned to renting privately or to social housing (see Table 8.3).

Table 8.3 Owner-occupation: Past, Present and Future – At Time of Interview

Current owner-occupiers		Past owner-occupiers			Future?
'Never council'	Ex-council	Repossessed	Sold up	Walked away	
Jamie*	Nathan*	Vic	Derek	Spaceman	Ted
Jerry	Denny	Nutter	Eddie		Danny
Mal	Trevor				Ryan
Tony	Gary				
Shaun					
Kelvin					
Gordon					
Pete*					

* Owner-occupation 'by proxy'.

Like Mal and Trevor, Derek had always contemplated buying his own house and in 1985, together with his girlfriend at the time, he did so ('I couldn't live with my mum forever, could I?'). When he split with his girlfriend, he took over sole ownership and lived there until 1990, but 'the government kept hiking up interest rates all the time and eventually the mortgage repayments was more than I was earning'. Derek couldn't keep up the repayments and so decided to sell the property: 'It wasn't repossessed. I sold up fair and square, but by the time I'd paid the building society what I owed them I didn't come away with much at all'. Later he met his future wife Danielle and, after living with her in another town for eighteen months, they were allocated a council house a few streets away from his mother.

Eddie bought a flat in Milltown in the early 1980s and owned it for ten years but, on account of his fragile mental health, made little use of it (though both his sister and his brother did, from time to time), spending most of this time at his mother's. For very different reasons, then, Derek and Eddie sold up, while others just 'walked away' or had their properties repossessed. Spaceman earned very good wages in his mid-twenties, though he 'blew' most of it on 'clothes and fucking music and booze and drugs', but in 1983, he decided to buy a flat with his girlfriend. Less than two years later he lost his job and the relationship fell apart:

I moved back home with my mother. I signed the flat over to her, everything, because I wanted a clean break. I just wanted out of all this fucking mortgage business and responsibilities.

She did all right out of the flat. We bought it for twenty-two [£22,000] and about two years after I signed it over, she sold it for thirty-eight [£38,000]. Me? I went on a self-destruct trip after that.

Two of the Boys had their houses repossessed. Nutter eventually left home and decided to buy a house because, so he maintained, a mortgage was cheaper than paying rent, which in his case was certainly so, because he only ever paid one instalment – the first, though it was three years before he was 'kicked out'. Throughout that time he was living 'mortgage free, everything free', and since then he has lived in a succession of flats and lodgings.

Vic was brought up by his grandmother until, in order to try his luck at professional rugby, he went to the north of England, where he lived in digs but was homesick and came home. He met a young woman from a nearby town, living with her for a couple of years at her mother's house, then after their child was born in a council house in the city where 'she ended up with some fella, I ended up on my own'. He met another girl from another town and moved in with her, for she had inherited her house from her parents and they lived there until 1990 before selling up and buying a house 'up the top' in Milltown. They were unable, however, to keep up the mortgage repayments, 'so it was repossessed . . . I was gutted. We ended up in emergency accommodation. Then we rented a place off some guy and then we got this place off the council in 1997'.

Those who have ventured unsuccessfully into the private housing market have generally not tried a second time; for both psychological and economic reasons, they have been unwilling to take the risk, or unable to do so. The sole exception is Shaun, who stayed in Milltown until 1990 and took full advantage of the 'right to buy' scheme but this backfired on him when his marriage split up:

> Well first of all, me and Sue lived in shared rooms in somebody else's house and then we got a council house ourselves. And then we decided to buy a house 'cos this was the time when Margaret Thatcher was in power and everything was being done to assist people in council houses to buy their own homes. So we bought a house and it was probably seven or eight thousand pounds cheaper than the market value. We were up there for about five years until the marriage broke up.
>
> And then I went back to my mum's because I had nowhere else to go. I didn't hand over ownership of the house to Sue, but I packed in work so I could no longer meet the demands of the mortgage. But that meant that Sue was able to turn to the social security and they paid the interest on the mortgage for her. Within eighteen months she was about six and a half thousand pounds in arrears. We sold the house before it went any further and I came out with £250. That was devastating. I'd invested over ten years of my life and I come out with that. That was a bitter pill to swallow.

Shaun later met his second wife Gaynor, living in her father's house until they became 'homeless' in order to accelerate their eligibility for council accommodation. They lived briefly in a bed and breakfast and then moved into a council maisonette where they stayed while Shaun studied for a degree. Six months after getting a permanent job, at the end of 1995, he put down a deposit on a three-bedroomed house in a new housing development in the city, some four miles away from Milltown.

Pete has never directly 'owned' a house, which is hardly surprising given his errant employment history and personal life, and he admits 'I've never had a place of my own', confessing he has always had to rely on somebody else – from his mother to his current partner Barry. He proclaims he grew up in a 'happy hovel' before coming out as gay and going to live with his brother-in-law in London, where he met Daniel, who owned his own flat, and lived with him until Daniel died. Pete subsequently moved around many different places until, in the mid-1980s, he met Barry, and they have shared many different housing contexts since – hotels, houses and flats. They have also run a pub together, and since Barry's dreadful injury in 1996 they have lived in a council flat which they recently decided to buy. Like Shaun, therefore, though more frequently and in very different circumstances, Pete has moved in and out of contexts of owner-occupation but this has been a consequence of his personal relationships rather than any active decision-making on his part.

Routes *out* of owner-occupation have taken various forms, ranging from voluntary decisions (such as Spaceman's), through constrained 'choice' (in the case of Derek and Eddie), to having little choice as a result of changed circumstances (as with Vic and Shaun). Only Nutter displayed gross irresponsibility in his approach to owner-occupation. Those who moved out of owner-occupation were, in many respects, the 'victims' of wider circumstances, while those who remained owner-occupiers were, ironically, the beneficiaries of often very similar circumstances. The housing context of the 1980s (high interest rates but also rapidly increasing house prices) produced a combination of risk, to which some of the Boys succumbed, and opportunity, which many of the Boys seized to their advantage. Of those who succumbed, only Shaun has started again on the private housing ladder.

Three of the Boys who have never been owner-occupiers are still toying with the idea. Two of them (Ted and Danny) are modest criminal entrepreneurs, who would find it difficult 'justifying' their capacity to buy, though they have never ruled it out. Ted has had his tenancy for seventeen years and estimates he could therefore buy the house for around £15,000, but does not want to buy that particular property, though he does not want to move far from the estate where he now lives. Danny moved out of home into a housing association flat when he got married in 1983, but he and his wife separated after just six months and divorced while he was serving his next prison sentence. He spent much of the 1980s in prison, then met his current girlfriend in the early 1990s, and after living with her on and off for some years, moved with her into a council house in Milltown in 1998, from which he has no intention of moving:

> No I'll stay here now. It's well kitted out and we're happy here. I'll probably end up buying it. I mean, I'll get it cheap enough. The longer I'm a tenant, the cheaper it'll be. I don't want no mortgage, I want to buy it outright. I'll find a way to do it.

Ryan and Laura are also happy to remain in their council house, despite its position in the most notorious core of the estate:

> Unless we were really rich I wouldn't move from here. We've thought about buying the house. But, you know, next door but one, they just can't sell it. They've been trying to sell it for thirteen years and they've only ever had three people come to see it. So it makes you think. They want £35,000. But if we can get this one a lot cheaper then we would think about buying it. It'd be nice to have your own place.

All three of these Boys are attracted by the idea of owner-occupation. Ted and Danny need to do something with the proceeds of their crime, and investing in property seems to be a sensible idea, if they can think of a suitable cover. Danny has already conjured up the illusion of an inheritance from a long-lost aunt! Property investment where Ryan lives is certainly not a sensible idea, in economic terms, but he does not intend to move and 'home ownership' has more of a psychological appeal, providing the price is right.

There are not pipe dreams, for Ted and Danny have significant sums of cash stashed away, while Ryan has had a regular job for the past five years, and all are therefore in a realistic position to buy their homes. Many of the Boys are not, and have never been, in this position, so any claims they make about not being interested in owner-occupation are certainly in part a rationalization by those unlikely to achieve it.

There is, nonetheless, some basis for their arguing against owner-occupation, for the taking on of mortgage commitments did have a knock-on effect in constraining occupational flexibility and freedom. When a place was rented, housing benefit covered the cost if one became genuinely unemployed or was working on the 'fiddle', whereas with a mortgage occupational uncertainty also jeopardized their housing position, as some of the Boys found to their cost. Owner-occupation therefore bound the Boys to the labour market in potentially undesirable ways, for they were less able to 'get up and go' or 'take a break', as at least some were accustomed to doing.

Some of the Boys without a mortgage recognized this, asserting they did not want such a 'millstone round my neck', yet both Tommy and Alex indicated they would have liked to convert to home ownership, but acknowledged their wider circumstances precluded them from doing so. Tommy conceded that when he was in a 'permanent' job he 'never got round to doing anything about it', admitting he had been a bit wary of the responsibility, and the opportunity had therefore passed him by. Alex divulged he had a number of old County Court Judgments against his name, which had presented some difficulty in obtaining a mortgage. Moreover, being self-employed, he admitted to being economical with the truth when declaring his true earnings to the taxman (not that they were anything extraordinary, but they did enable him to live above subsistence level and follow Arsenal). Even after he married Honora in the mid-1980s, he had lived at home until 1994, when they moved to a rented council house nearer to his place of work in an area of the city some miles from Milltown:

> Yeah, the house is rented. Couldn't afford to buy one. Well I probably could. I probably earn enough to buy the house. But now I'm in a Catch-22 situation. If I declare that I earn so much that I can get a mortgage, then you've got to pay mega-tax, haven't you. So I'm a bit stuck. I just have to live with it.

Other Housing Problems

In their housing trajectories, just as in other aspects of their lives, the Boys generally proved themselves to be creditably resourceful and expedient, usually having somewhere to go if things got tough – if only back to their mother's. Few experienced real housing crises, and only two of the Boys found themselves in situations they found intolerable. Between his first and second marriages Denny lived an itinerant life between a number of bed-sits and flats. He started life with his second wife in a private flat above some shops, which turned out to be an illegal let by the tenant shopkeeper and, as a result, Denny was subjected to intimidation and threats by the owner. In an atypical move for any of the Boys, he called the police and the 'heavies' backed off, and though the owner then took him to court, the 'judge' ruled in Denny's favour, saying he should remain in the flat – rent-free – until he could find alternative accommodation with the council:

> And that's what happened. I was there for another six months, rent free, everything. I never paid for no gas, no electric, it was all in with the shop downstairs. And he [the owner] hated me for it. His cronies used to drive past now and again and park outside. The owner was worth a fortune but he was worried about renting this one shop because nobody would take the shop on, because if you had a shop there you would want to live upstairs, and I was living there.

Nick also found himself compromised in the housing market, for the exchange he eventually secured to get back to Milltown turned out, in his view, to be a house unfit for habitation – 'a fucking house of death', with massive subsidence, damp and woodworm. So, having at last got the council house they wanted in Milltown, he and Karen had to give it up, and as far as Nick knows it is still empty. They moved back into private rented accommodation, first away from the estate, then back once more in Milltown.

Loyalty to Milltown

Two-thirds (twenty-three) of the Boys currently live in or relatively close to Milltown. Some, like Gary, Mack and Colin, have never left, while in contrast, only three of the Boys (Ted, Tony and Pete) left when they were young and never returned, though Pete has recently considered coming 'home', now he realizes his sexual orientation is tolerated and for the most part accepted by the Boys. Even those who are glad to have 'escaped' from the estate through choice (like Shaun) or circumstance (like Spaceman) feel some pull from their 'roots', and others, such as Kelvin and Mal, have moved back to Milltown, but not to Milltown per se, electing to live in what was once considered by them and is still considered by many of the Boys, to be the 'snobby' edge of the estate. Here they have the best of both worlds: the maintenance of their Milltown identities but far less of the crime, violence and anti-social behaviour which is endemic at the heart of the estate. Ten of the Boys, however, still live in this 'heart', at the top of the estate, five less than five minutes away, and nine more within a fifteen-minute walk of it. For both economic and relationship reasons, or a combination of the two, some would always have struggled to leave, even had they wanted to, but others who could have 'escaped' have chosen to stay at that very heart. Trevor has even bought a house there and Ryan is still thinking of doing so, while Gary was also still living there at the time of his interview, though was seriously considering moving 'down the road'. He feels bound to the area even though he could easily have afforded to leave long ago, and deplores what he feels is the undue and unjustified negative labelling of the area by officialdom and the media, despite some truths in their accounts, though he interprets these rather differently:

> We're happy here and we've never had a problem. Never had a break-in, never had my vehicles touched. Even if we do move I'm still Milltown. I love this place and I just find some people so narrow-minded when they speak about Milltown – you know, in the papers and on the telly – and I just want them to wake up. They haven't got a clue. Milltown gets such a bad press but it's the same in a lot of other places too. Yeah, we had the 'riots' but of course the papers made a much bigger thing of it than what it was. The press gets hold of things because it's Milltown and they just write crap, don't they, just for a story.

Gary may well have underplayed the severity of the 'riots' which took place in Milltown and other parts of Britain in the early 1990s (see Campbell 1993), but this is undoubtedly how he sees it, drawing deeply on his own personal experience. This is, inevitably, the basis on which the Boys evaluate the 'quality of life', for they know Milltown is an area where a disproportionate number of burglaries, thefts, damage and motor vehicle offences take place, and accept some parts are like 'mini-Beirut', but so long as they personally are not affected, they remain deeply attached to the estate. Trevor is adamant that he will never move away:

> Personally no. I'm Milltown born and bred. I love the place. I've never had any trouble. No one has ever attempted to break into my car. No trouble whatsoever. I think it's because I know most of the rogues and, well, they do tend to have a bit of respect, don't they, for people they know.

Only Kelvin, of all the Boys who have 'come home', thinks he may well move away again, for despite his love of Milltown he concedes there is 'a bit of gypsy in me' and knows his wife does not wish to stay. As a result, he does not rule out moving on once more, perhaps to Ireland, where he and Julie have spent a number of holidays. She would certainly like to live there and is determined they will *not* remain in Milltown for the rest of their lives.

Conclusion

Like all the other 'transitions' experienced by the Boys, housing careers have been far from linear and incremental. Some typical patterns have prevailed at different ages and stages, notably when first moving from the parental home and when there has been a possibility of the 'right to buy'. Personal relationships have had the most significant effect on both the Boys' geographical mobility and their decisions in the housing market, though many of the Boys exerted considerable pressure on their partners to remain in, or return to Milltown. Rarely did this, in and of itself, cause the breakdown of personal relationships, but where relationships broke down, in Milltown or elsewhere, the Boys invariably returned home and 'started again'.

Housing careers were something of a cyclical process often culminating, where relationships were stable, in securing council housing in Milltown, which at an earlier point in their lives would have been the pinnacle of the Boys' housing aspirations. However, the wider policy and economic context of the 1980s assisted many of the Boys in continuing further in the cycle – towards owner-occupation. The 'right to buy' scheme was accessible and often desirable, even for those on modest incomes, and as a result a significant minority of the Boys became owner-occupiers, though modest incomes sometimes could not cope with the rising interest rates at the end of the 1980s, and some of the Boys had to sell their properties for minimal profit, or had them repossessed. With one exception, they never again ventured into the private housing market, often having to 'start again' in emergency accommodation while they waited for the allocation of a council property. For those who were able to manage the challenge of ever-increasing mortgage repayments, the 'prize' was property which itself conferred the opportunity for further progression in the housing market – to houses which were always proudly depicted as 'never council'.

Many of the Boys used the provision of the exchange and transfer system to move back to Milltown, sometimes seizing an unexpected opportunity, sometimes using a more calculated strategy, and in this way, even those who had been compelled to move away came 'home'. Milltown was where the Boys literally felt at home, where they were safe and secure, where they knew everybody and knew 'the score'. All but one of those who have returned or, indeed, have never left, say they would never leave.

Of the twelve Boys who lived in owner-occupied housing at the time of the research, seven live in Milltown and two others live very close by. Admittedly, some like Jerry, Mal and Kelvin live on the periphery of the estate, but others, like Trevor and Gary, still live at its heart. Only Mal – himself fanatically loyal to the area – conceded some of the more brutalizing aspects of life on the estate, giving this as the reason for moving from 'mini-Beirut' to the quieter edge, whereas the others erred towards an almost romantic celebration of the qualities of Milltown. There *are*, however, good reasons for living there, for there is comfort in familiarity and there is a real sense of solidarity and comradeship, and those of the Boys who value these things most have endeavoured to stay firmly connected to it. Their housing careers are clear testimony to this.

–9–

Domestic Lives and Personal Relationships

Introduction

Over one generation the domestic lives of the Milltown Boys have transformed dramatically. Virtually all of them grew up with both of their natural parents and with a number of brothers and sisters, though there were, of course, some exceptions such as Jerry, who had just one sister, and Danny and Vic, who spent much of their childhood with their grandparents. Marty also lived with his grandmother for much of the time, because his mother was struggling to bring up her five children on her own. Only Pete, Tony and Spaceman were brought up by single mothers, their fathers having left when they were very young. Ted's parents died when he was 12, and he lived with an older sister for a short while, before being taken into public care.

The Boys' own relationship and family formation has been much more varied, though thirteen have had one long-lasting stable relationship, for fifteen years or more, despite, in two of these cases, the relationship being interrupted by at least one temporary period of separation. Indeed, Trevor actually divorced his wife but, after a year, they got back together, though they have never remarried. Ten of the Boys have had more than one 'serious' relationship, of which some were relatively short, particularly when they were quite young, though they often produced children. Four of the Boys (Ted, Denny, Matt and Nathan) have had three serious relationships, whereas, in contrast, four others (Marty, Colin, Eddie and Nutter) have never had an adult relationship, and another (Spaceman) had only a relatively brief relationship in his mid-twenties.

These relationships have produced sixty children (and one more died at birth), though two of these children are not in fact their own, but they were very young when the Boys met their mothers and were 'taken on' as their own (see Table 9.1). On average, then, the Boys have had two children each – a far cry from the families in which they themselves grew up, which typically comprised five or six siblings or more.

Seven of the Boys, however, have no children. Nick and Karen are unable to have children, though they would desperately like to have done so. Pete has only ever had gay relationships, while Marty is schizophrenic and has had no steady relationships since a long-term teenage love affair. Spaceman has spent most of his

Table 9.1 Relationships and Children

	Relationships and children			Total no. children
	1st	2nd	3rd	
Ted	1	2	(1)1	5
Danny	0	1	—	1
Spaceman	0	—	—	0
Marty	—	—	—	—
Gary	2	—	—	2
Matt	2	2	0	4
Paul	3	1	—	4
Richard	2	—	—	2
Denny	1	(1) 2	0	4
Ryan	2	—	—	2
Tony	2	—	—	2
Alex	2	—	—	2
Mack	2	—	—	2
Mark	2	—	—	2
Jerry	2	—	—	2
Nathan	0	2	0	2
Shaun	3	1	—	4
Derek	0	1	—	1
Colin	—	—	—	—
Jamie	2	—	—	2
Gordon	2	—	—	2
Eddie	—	—	—	—
Nick	0*	—	—	0*
Kelvin	3	—	—	3
Trevor	3	—	—	3
Tommy	3	—	—	3
Mal	2	—	—	2
Pete	0**	0**	—	0
Vic	1	3	—	4
Nutter	—	—	—	—
				60

( ) Not 'natural' children

* Unable to have children

** Gay relationships

adult life in a daze of drug and alcohol dependency, while Eddie would have liked a relationship and children, but his life has been plagued by recurrent episodes of mental illness and the 'right woman' never came along. Neither Colin nor Nutter appear ever to have shown much interest in the opposite sex.

Three of the Boys are already grandparents. Ted's first son, from a teenage relationship, has three children by two different women, and though Ted saw him briefly as a baby when Ted came out of prison in his late teens, they did not meet again until he was 16, and he has little contact with his grandchildren. Shaun's eldest son also has three children by two different women, and Shaun has no contact with his first grandchild, though he does see the other two (a third child from that relationship is on the way). Ryan and Laura regularly see their baby granddaughter, who was born to their younger daughter just over a year ago.

In the space of two generations, one can detect both continuities and change, for despite evidence of family stability akin to that experienced by the Boys during their own childhood, there is also evidence of family fragmentation and loss of contact with children, which was rare in the previous generation. There is significant polarization going on here, with those who have maintained long-term stable relationships prospectively raising children with greater opportunities than they have had, but those with a history of more unstable relationships producing children who are arguably more vulnerable and prone to risk than even they ever were. Paul has a son who has already served time in prison, while Ted's eldest son is a heroin addict. The Boys with the most chaotic relationships tended to have children earlier, and of the twenty children already over the age of 16, only one (the eldest daughter of Mal and Jane, who have been together for twenty years) is in post-16 academic learning, while two other children (also daughters) are in post-16 vocational learning. This picture is, however, likely to look less bleak as the younger and generally more successful children of more stable relationships grow up.

Table 9.1 provides an overview of each of the Boys 'serious' relationships and the number of children produced within them, though it does not reveal, of course, the complexities and dynamics attached to the formation and breakdown of those relationships. The Boys' contact and relationships with their children are discussed in Chapter 10; here the focus is on how they established, sustained and sometimes failed in the many partnerships formed throughout their lives.

Relationship Formation

Nine of the Boys ended up in serious adult relationships with their teenage girl-friends though some, like Danny's, did not last, whereas, in contrast, Tommy proudly proclaimed he and Suzanne had been together for twenty-six years, having started going out together when he was 14. (He was interviewed the day before his twentieth wedding anniversary.) Ryan and Laura have also been married for twenty years, though official records would not tell this story, as we shall see. Indeed, no fewer than thirteen of the Boys were still with the women they had met in their late teens or early twenties, though for some it has been more of a rocky road than for others. Their partners were mainly Milltown 'Girls', or young woman from nearby areas, and a further eight of the Boys also had relationships with local girls, which later broke down.

The formation of such relationships followed very different patterns. After the failure (after just six months) of Danny's marriage to a young woman he had 'courted' throughout his teenage years, he started seeing Naomi 'on and off' who then, to his surprise (for he had come to believe he could not father children) became pregnant, and they have lived together ever since. Mack and Andrea's relationship followed a similar pattern, though they had known each other for years before they 'fell into' a casual liaison which led to her becoming pregnant, and they then lived together for many years and had a second child.

Casual encounters such as these, which produced children and led to more serious relationships (at least for a while), were flanked on either side by calculated intent and cunning, or by partial or complete 'luck'. Nick had 'set his sights' on Karen the first time he saw her, though he was 'knocking off' another girl at the time: 'I went out with Marie to get through to Karen. It was a nasty ploy, I admit, but from a man's point of view, it's what you do. It worked – took longer than expected, though!' Nick married Karen in 1984 and they are still together. At the other end of the spectrum were complete chance encounters, as in the case of Angie, Tony's wife, who turned up for a blind date with Gary, but Gary did not show up, and Tony spotted his opportunity and chatted up Angie to long-lasting effect.

In between these two positions were instances of both chance and seizing the moment. Mark had known Veronica since she was at school (he had worked with her brothers), and he had always fancied her: 'she was very pretty, she still is, but she was *very pretty* when she was younger'. Mark describes their getting together as 'actually a mistake', for he was going to a party with another girl:

> Now I was on to a sure-fire shag, if I can put it like that. And Veronica's brother said 'do me a favour, let me go with your girl and you go with my sister Veronica'. He suggested we swap. At first I said 'piss off, I'm on to a good thing'. But we swapped. And so I ended up going with Veronica. He had the shag, I never!

Mark and Veronica started 'courting', later having two children, and they are still together. Shaun married his childhood sweetheart Sue as soon as she was 16, for she became pregnant at 15, but the marriage ended a decade later when she met someone else. Shaun, who was in his early thirties at the time, decided to give up his job and go to university – a good place, in his view, 'to find another wife'! Before he did so, however, he met his future second wife, Gaynor, the 21-year-old friend of his sister's, 'across the ironing board' at his mother's house, where he was living after his marriage ended:

Gaynor used to come back in the evenings and have a bit of tea before they used to go clubbing. That's how I got to know her. They used to get me to do the ironing for them before they went out. And one night she asked me out for a drink. And then a few months later she asked me to stay over. I stayed and I never went back.

Most of the other Boys met their partners in tried and tested, conventional ways. Gary spent his early twenties on the clubbing scene ('always with women, good fun but nothing ever, ever serious') until the day he met Amelia, whom he subsequently married. Derek met his second, current, partner Danielle at a christening 'and I asked her out . . . that's how it started'. More typically, though, the Boys' future partners were often already relatively 'close' to their own networks or connected to their frenetic round of social activities. Kelvin had taken out one of Julie's friends, and he and Julie were introduced; before Julie, he observed, 'the longest relationship I'd had was about two months'. Trevor had known Jill for some time before they went out together and subsequently got married, Jerry met Sam at the local social club, and Denny met his third wife Annie in the same way. Alex and Mack also established long-term relationships with girls from Milltown – local girls 'on the scene' – though Mack's relationship with Anthea later collapsed as the two of them 'grew apart'. Danny's first marriage was to Nutter's sister, while Jamie had gone to the same school as Pat: 'we started courting when we were 16 and then we might have broke up for a bit, but not much, and we got married in 1985'.

Some relationship formation was, however, more unusual. Once Pete had declared his homosexuality he moved to London and met Daniel in a gay club, then when Daniel died, floated around for a few years until he met Barry in a gay bar in 1983, and they have been together ever since.

Nathan met his first partner through a friendship forged with another inmate in Dartmoor, who asked if Nathan 'fancied' writing to a (female) friend of his:

> You know, we were 21 at the time and he said, do you want to write to this bird, so I wrote to this girl and she came to visit me. So when I come out, I went straight to live with her.

Phantom Separations and Living Apart

Trevor and Jill actually got divorced but later moved back together, though there was a moment when their relationship had clearly broken down. In contrast, temporary or more prolonged 'phantom' separations, to be carefully distinguished from real ones, were one of the expedient tactics exercised by the Boys when times were hard and income needed to be maximized. Living apart generated extra resources from the social security, especially when children were involved. Ryan married Laura in 1980, but an early 'separation' was necessary when he was sent to prison and lost his job, after which he resorted to fiddling, and for the next ten years he was theoretically living elsewhere:

> We got married in 1980. She was pregnant. But, you know, after I come out of prison it was the usual front. We pretended we wasn't married no more. You have to pull these little scams to get by, live on your wits, isn't it. But we are back together now, proper, legitimate. We was always together but we made out that we weren't, because we could both claim then.

Unlike Ryan, whose 'scam' was never detected, Mark's attempt at a similar ploy was discovered, and he subsequently engaged in a prolonged game of 'call my bluff' with social security officials, in order to ensure his spurious circumstances were established as authentic. They lived together in Veronica's council house but, for almost a decade, Mark was theoretically living at his mother's. Throughout this time, he was working legitimately (though on a very low wage) and Veronica was in receipt of benefit, for her and their two children. Mark concocted a range of stories about Veronica's 'wickedness' in preventing him from seeing his children, and the threats he received from her brothers, simultaneously portraying himself as a responsible father, doing his best in difficult circumstances – making some financial contribution towards his children, though he was being denied access to them. All this was completely untrue, but it elicited the sympathy of the 'social': 'I got them on my side'. Things came to a head, however, when, towards the end of the 1980s, the Child Support Agency sought both to formalize and increase his contribution towards the upkeep of his children. Until that point he had been paying 'voluntarily' some £20 a week, which was deducted from Veronica's social security entitlement but still left them considerably better off than if they admitted to living together. Mark was taken to court, with a demand to start paying £60 pounds a week, and felt compelled to invent yet more 'stories':

> I said look, she don't let me see my kids, but I buys them everything. I've bought the washing machine, the cooker ... I started to lose my rag. I said, you're running after me for my money but you're not willing to help me see my children. And then they said I would have to start paying sixty pound a week. I was dumbstruck. I started ranting and raving. I'm a compulsive gambler, I said, I've got blokes after me that you think only exist on the telly. I said they're going to kneecap me if I don't pay my debts. They said they were sorry to hear this but that I would have to increase my payments from twenty-odd to sixty pound a week. So I just said I can't afford that. No way. I'll jack my job in, simple as that, and then you can keep the lot of us.

Mark offered to pay £30 a week, which was accepted, and eventually this was deducted directly from his wages, but only when his wages were above £140 a week. To avoid reaching this threshold, Mark simply stopped doing overtime, though he came to realize the long-term scam was hardly financially worthwhile any more. He also became increasingly paranoid about getting discovered, for the social security were constantly checking up on him, 'so I said to Veronica we should go down to the social, go straight, tell them that we'd started living together':

> So I went down the social and said to the woman, look we're going to give it a go. Now she'd dealt with me through all those years, so she shook my hand and said, 'I hope you make it.' Because she really wasn't so bad. I mean, I'd told her some wicked things about Veronica, and when Veronica used to have to go down there, she'd look at her and think she was a horrible cow because of the things I used to say about her. But it was all part of the game to me. You've got to try to be as clever as them if you're going to beat the system. You've got to be up to their level and call their bluff, type of thing. After that, for a bit, we just about survived and then, when the kids were old enough, Veronica got herself a job and since then we've had a bit more to spend on ourselves.

The social consequence of 'giving it a go' was to be freed of the anxiety of detection, but the economic consequence was that Veronica and the children were no longer entitled to many of their benefits, though Mark could now earn more, through overtime, without fear of deductions.

Things may have been 'tight' for Mark and Veronica, but Mark, like many of the Boys, had always ensured he had money 'for a pint'. The Boys had very clear ideas about having money 'for themselves', and phantom separations facilitated this 'understanding'. Social security benefits for their partner and their children were the basic income for the household (for rent, food and other 'everyday' needs), while their own income (from the social, through crime and fiddles, from gambling, from subletting their 'independent' flats, and from earnings) was for themselves, and for 'extras' for the family. This was the way in which real, as well as 'phantom', separations were managed, though the dividing lines were not always so clear-cut and often blurred. Mack, for example, still gives all his social security money to his ex-partner, to support their children, and makes his own money 'on the street', while Matt also gives his 'social' money to Camilla, with whom he has lived for ten years, though theoretically he lives in a flat elsewhere – earning a living through subletting that flat and 'on the street'.

There was not, therefore, always a huge chasm between real and phantom separations, and some of the Boys had regular spells of real separation from their partners before they returned, for it was part and parcel of their unpredictable and sometimes volatile relationships. As Derek observed, he had only been 'kicked out' three times, but he and Danielle were still together. This was, indeed, another 'justification' for having separate income streams, for, when such episodes occurred, if the man had been earning legitimately or claiming benefit on behalf of the family, it would then be necessary, on each occasion, for the mother to make a fresh claim for social security. It was much better, some of the Boys argued, not to be there are all, and their partners often agreed, colluding willingly in the 'scam'. As a result, the women secured a relatively stable source of income for themselves and the children, topped up quite regularly by their menfolk. Such arrangements were self-evidently desirable – for both parties – especially when the Boys themselves were unemployed, working on the fiddle or, like Mark, in low-paid legitimate employment.

Rarely were phantom separations as carefully planned as Ryan's, but any such 'scams' demanded some level of strategic thinking if they were not going to be detected. Social security investigators once discovered Mark's clothes on Veronica's bed, and it took some vocal assertiveness on Veronica's part to persuade them he was not living there. Ryan and Laura were always meticulous in covering their tracks, and none of Ryan's clothes were ever left at the house. On one occasion, however, they nearly slipped up, for, when the investigators knocked, there was a pair of men's wellington boots in the hallway. Laura was terrified they had been caught out, but 'fronted it out' effectively through telling the investigators her daughters' father was a vicious, violent man, but he still had a right to see his kids from time to time. He had come round the other day to take the children over the woods, and obviously must have forgotten to take his wellingtons home with him. This explanation had worked, for investigators did not pursue their suspicions, and though they had returned now and again there was never any further evidence Ryan was living there.

As Mark testifies, however, such scams required a high level of watchfulness and generated considerable paranoia about who might be watching them. The Boys were, as a result, not over-enthusiastic about living their everyday lives in such an atmosphere, though some grew more accustomed to it than others, and if their resource base improved, for whatever reason (such as securing more regular or better-paid employment, or children leaving home), they were inclined to abandon such arrangements.

Relationship Breakdown

One-third (eleven) of the Boys have experienced the breakdown of what they would view as a 'serious' relationship, four of whom have suffered the ending of two serious relationships. Inevitably there were many reasons why relationships came to an end, though in some cases (Ted, Matt, Paul) they were temporarily retrieved, in others (Denny, Nathan, Paul) reconciliation was desired and sometimes attempted, and in three cases (Ted, Gordon and Trevor) they were re-established.

Despite getting on so badly with his first wife (and second partner) Amy, and splitting up (their daughter Natasha was conceived almost immediately Ted and Amy got together, and was born after he had left), Ted briefly got back together with her. By that time he was seeing Lucy (with whom he still lives), but after living with her for a couple of years, their relationship hit a rocky patch, and they separated. He went back to Amy, and though he was with her for only a matter of weeks she became pregnant, though just as before, Ted had left (and gone back, once more, to Lucy) before Jenna was born.

Gordon also temporarily parted from his wife Michaela, though they had married in California after living together during his final year at university. They returned together to Milltown but Gordon then went on a tour round the world, and when he came back, Michaela had left him. He stayed around for a while and briefly they got back together again, but then split up once more and he went back to the United States. Michaela then joined him for a backpacking holiday in Mexico and Nicaragua where they had 'great fun' together. She wanted him back, and he wanted to come back, so they came 'home' together, bought a house and started a family; they now live near Milltown with their two young children.

After having three children together, Trevor and Jill were divorced in 1993. In the early 1990s their relationship had been characterized by 'non-stop bickering', which Trevor attributed to hormonal change in Jill following her hysterectomy. Jill had asked him to leave but he refused, so she left instead, taking the children with her and instigating divorce proceedings, which Trevor did not contest. He continued to see the children most days and now maintains 'we never really fell out and then we sort of reconciled and we decided to go on holiday together'. They went to Tenerife for a week, 'sorted things out in the sun and come back and then she moved back in' – and they have remained together since. Trevor still insists their divorce was significantly 'to do with that operation . . . well I don't think she has ever been the same since'.

Both Denny and Nathan separated from their wives but retained, at least for a while, some possibility of returning. Denny parted from his second wife when he discovered she was seeing another man, yet despite some violent and vitriolic confrontations, he had wanted to keep the relationship going 'for the sake of the kids', and tried to go back: 'I wanted to be with the kids but it just didn't work. I just couldn't forgive her for what she'd done'.

Nathan was married for nine years and he and his wife Donna had two children, the first of whom was born while he was in prison. Nathan always felt the relationship was a successful one, until the 'barny' (argument) that split them up, and believes they still have feelings for each other, though Nathan is not one for sentiment, which makes the following remarks all the more poignant:

> It was the first real barny we ever had. She went up her mother's, took the kids and said she wasn't coming home. I left it over a week and then I started performing. I kicked the door in of her mother's house: come on, they are my kids. And it blew from there really. It just blew out of proportion. Sad really, because I still love her in my little way and I think she still loves me.

Nathan feels there is 'something still there' but it has not been enough to bring them back together, though he still harbours some hope this may happen one day.

Infidelity by the Boys' partners features prominently in their accounts of the breakdown of many relationships. Vic came back from the north of England after trying his hand at professional rugby league, met and moved in with a girl from a nearby town, before having a child (who is now 18) and moving to a house in the city, where his partner left him for another man. Vic recounts this in a very matter-of-fact way and appears to have taken it in his stride, though for others, the discovery their women were seeing other men came as a considerable shock. Richard was devastated when his wife threw him out, for though he had felt their separation was 'coming' he had certainly not expected it to be for this reason. Married when he was 21, he had become 'bored and fed up . . . and you think things are going to be better on the other side, but it never is', and before he was thrown out he had already thought of walking out:

> But then I didn't actually walk out. It was my wife that . . . showed me the door one night. And I thought that she was just menstruating or whatever. You know, they go through these bloody weird phases. I thought she would come and get me in about two or three days but she never did. Two weeks later, when I went to pick my kids up, they told me that there was a man sleeping there. She had met somebody else before I left. I realize now that's the reason she asked me to leave.

Shaun had a similar experience, for shortly after the birth of his third child in 1990, his wife Sue met someone else. She had gone back to college because

> she'd not previously done anything before and she wanted to get some qualifications; she had some aspirations of getting a decent job. And she fell in love with someone in the college. She wanted to split up with me and set up home with this other chap.

Shaun was mortified:

> Well by that time we were living in a three-bedroomed house. We had a nice car, we had had the three kids. Sue had then had a sterilization done after Kirsty was born. So we were looking at things getting better. Sue was going to start work and we were hoping to move to a bigger house in a nicer area. Apparently Sue had been struggling with her feelings for this other chap for quite some time and I knew nothing about this. And so when she said she wanted to split up with me, it was a bolt out of the blue. My first reaction was that it was that time of the month – give her a couple of days, she'll change her mind.

However, Sue did not change her mind, and though Shaun appeared on the surface to be stoical and pragmatic about these events, he still succeeded in exacting some

measure of retribution by abandoning his own job and not maintaining the mortgage repayments, suggesting he was very cut up about the collapse of his marriage. Indeed, for a time, he sank into depression, but eventually picked himself up,
establishing a new relationship and coming to constructive arrangements with Sue
over access to the children.

Denny was 'tipped off' by Trevor that his second wife was having an affair,
though at first he chose not to believe it, until he deliberately came home early one
day to find the other man there. He also discovered Joan had been spending all the
rent money on clothes, pretending they had been purchased in the sales, though
there had been few other telltale signs – 'she was covering her tracks very good' –
and when he realized the allegations were true, he threw a 'complete wobbly':

> I had a fire out the back and I burnt every stitch of clothing that she had, every pair of
> shoes, every hair spray canister, nail polish ... when I left there all she had left was
> what she had on, what she was wearing.

Denny's despair tipped him into a drinking binge which lasted for the best part of
two years, and included an attempted suicide when he threw himself into the traffic
on a main road after staggering, completely drunk, out of a pub. He had worked
seven days a week, he explained, to look after Joan and their three children (the
oldest of whom had been a baby when they met and whom Denny had 'adopted'
as his own), and felt completely betrayed.

This was the second time Denny experienced the collapse of a relationship, for
his first marriage had also crumbled, though for completely different reasons. He
married a local girl, Vicky, when he was 21 and they had a daughter, but he left
when she was 3: 'there was just too much interference from her family. Vicky was
a mummy's girl; her mother was always right. You know, I didn't want to be
married to Vicky's mother, do you know what I mean'. Denny walked away and
soon afterwards lost all contact with his daughter, despite the fact she still lives in
Milltown.

Denny's observation about not wanting to be married to Vicky's mother is
telling, for bonds between mothers and daughters in Milltown were usually very
strong, and the establishment of a relationship with a Milltown girl meant, in
effect, 'marrying' into *her* family. Many of the Boys grudgingly accepted this,
though they often sought to escape to the pub or club when the 'mother-in-law'
was coming round. For the Boys' partners, however, their mothers were routinely
a source of material, emotional and practical support for the family, especially
when it came to childcare, and, indeed, often held families together when times
were hard, relationships strained, or the Boys were in prison. On the other hand,
their interventions, and what the Boys typically viewed as 'interference', represented a recurrent source of friction between the Boys and their partners, and

sometimes strained relationships to the limit. Derek's first relationship, for example, like Denny's, 'fell apart' because of what he considered to be his partner's 'obsessive' attachment to her mother.

Only one of the Boys has been permanently separated from a partner through death. Soon after going to London, Pete established a relationship with Daniel, a middle-aged man who was the owner of a haulage company, and they lived together for a couple of years in his flat, with Pete playing a stereotypical gay 'queen' and homemaker. Tragically Daniel died suddenly of a brain haemorrhage and Pete found himself homeless and companionless, even unable to attend the funeral because Daniel's parents had no idea he was gay.

The Boys rarely suggested the cause of irreversible relationship breakdown was their own infidelity, though a number admitted to having 'strayed' once in a while. Only Paul admitted the ending of his (parallel) relationships was the result of his trying to 'play the field': he lived for many years with one woman (with whom he had three children), but for six years had also been seeing someone else (with whom he had one child).

Not that the Boys did not play away from home, for indeed many did, though few had any long-term 'supplementary' relationships, and in most cases, they indulged in one-night stands, preferably a long way from home. One-night stands were considered to be just 'harmless fun', producing potential problems only if 'you go back for seconds', and quite separate and different from their mainstream relationships, for as Gary put it, the women they met in such encounters were 'just bits of fluff, that's all they are'.

Parallel, Concurrent Relationships

Both Matt and Paul have had complex, parallel relationships at different points in their lives. Throughout the 1980s Matt – who is of African Caribbean origin – alternated between a white Milltown 'Girl', Valerie, whom he had been courting since his teenage years, and another woman, Sarah, who was black, and he now has four adult children, two by each of these women. He started living on an occasional basis with Valerie, but then met Sarah when he moved briefly in the mid-1980s to live with relatives in a nearby town, where Sarah bore his first two children – two girls. Matt stayed at home to look after them because 'Sarah couldn't really cope, so I brought up my girls for the first couple of years', then Sarah took the children with her to London, and, for the next two years, Matt went back to Valerie, with whom he had two sons. However, Matt then moved to London to be with Sarah and their daughters, though this did not work out, for he 'hated the place', and after a year came back to Milltown. Sarah returned his remaining possessions six months later, but lost all contact with Matt soon afterwards, and he did not see his daughters for the next ten years. He stayed with Valerie until the end of the 1980s, though he was never a regular presence, for they were always arguing, and eventually he left for good. In 1990 he met Camilla who, at the time, was living with one of his friends, by whom she had three children, but she left him for Matt and they remain together.

At the time of the research Paul's domestic life was in turmoil and deteriorating rapidly. The research interview was conducted in two stages with a month in between, and that month was a critical time, for it was when both of Paul's long-standing relationships came to an end. He met his wife Pat when he was 18 and had three boys with her, but for the past six years had also been seeing Jenny, with whom he had a daughter, who is only four months younger than his youngest son. Paul met Jenny during a period when he and Pat had 'temporarily' split up, though Pat then wanted him back and he went home, 'but I carried on seeing this other girl [Jenny] behind her back for the next four years'. In 1999, he left Pat again, moving into Mack's mother's house and putting his name down for a council flat, before going abroad for a short while and then returning to an ultimatum from Jenny: 'it's either Pat or me, you either move in with me or it's over'. Paul 'opted' precipitously to stay with Pat, though he soon realized he had made the wrong choice and left, but in the intervening period Jenny had decided to deny Paul all access to his daughter:

> A couple of months after I chose Pat, I realized it wasn't Pat I wanted; it was the other one, but it was too late then. And since then I've been to court for threatening words and threatening behaviour against the girl who's got my daughter.

Both women have now rejected him and, for the first time in his life, he is on his own.

No Relationships – Loneliness, Sadness and Uninterest

Five of the Boys have had few or no serious relationships in their lives. Two (Marty and Eddie) have suffered from serious mental health problems, while two more (Spaceman and Nutter) have succumbed to heavy alcoholism, and Spaceman has also had serious bouts of depression.

In his mid-twenties, Spaceman did have a relationship for a couple of years, though he does not depict it as 'serious', despite having bought a flat together, for Fiona was also an alcoholic and their common ground was largely shared addictions: 'she was my drinking partner, my shoplifting partner, my drug-taking partner'. Spaceman asserted his true love was his art, admitting he had never been much good at relating to the opposite sex, though he spoke of a profound sense of loneliness, now more acute since he stopped drinking, despite his art providing some level of comfort and compensation:

I do get real bad loneliness. It can be fucking dreadful. I have been absolutely paralysed with fucking loneliness. But I can lose myself in my painting. It's therapy for me and it's something that I really fucking love. I've got paintings everywhere.

Oh yeah, I've had loads of girls. Well there've been a few. I mean, there've been a couple since I've been at university. But, uh, nothing big . . . I'm no good at relationships, if I was honest with myself. I'm good at being a friend to girls. Girls like my company. I've got loads of girl friends. But I'm a bit fucking immature in my attitude towards relationships. I have to admit that.

Marty, as a teenager, was arguably the most good-looking of all the Boys, and from the age of 14 he had a long-standing relationship with Jeanette, believing he would eventually 'settle down' with her. However, she finally lost patience with his drinking and his recurrent flings with other girls, and they split up. Before his schizophrenia took hold Marty had a series of casual relationships, the last towards the end of the 1980s during his last proper job at Butlins, but since then he has lived alone:

There's never been anyone really since Jeanette. The thing is, women have always been attracted to me. I've never sort of gone out looking for a girl. I never had to make any effort. They came to me.

I suppose there was the girl I met at Butlins. She was absolutely beautiful. But nothing ever came of it. And then I come back here and since then I've been ill. I'm isolated, I am. I never see nobody.

Mental illness was both the cause and consequence of Eddie's failed relationships as far as he was concerned, for on a number of occasions he completely misread or misinterpreted the signals, the first time during a works cricket match in Bath, where he met a girl at the hotel. They kept in touch and he went back to see her, only to discover she was living with a boyfriend, and shortly afterwards Eddie was admitted to a mental hospital:

I just felt she was somebody that I could spend the rest of my life with. And when I rang her to say that I had booked into the hotel again she said oh great. I was really excited about seeing her again. But when I got there it sort of all blew up in my face. The image I had built up was destroyed. It was just, I suppose, naivety on my part. But that's the way things go.

It was certainly the way things went for Eddie, for two years later in 1985 much the same thing happened again, when he met a young woman from Milltown whom he had known for some time: 'I got these sort of delusions about her. I didn't really know her that well but I got it into my head that she liked me'. Nothing came of that either, and Eddie had another breakdown exacerbated, in his view, by this second experience of 'rejection'. It happened on a third occasion, three years ago, when Eddie expressed his interest in a young woman at work with whom he had had a lot of 'pleasant' conversations, 'and I just sort of told her at the Christmas party that I liked her and whatever and then again, again she was with someone else'.

Neither Colin nor Nutter have experienced or endured such angst and anguish, for Colin lives at home with his mother and noted the last 'serious' relationship he had was 'when I was around 18 – apart from that it's been get 'em and drop 'em as far as I'm concerned', while Nutter, preoccupied with drinking and his fascist 'blood and honour' literature and music, simply commented 'nothing, nothing at all'. Both appear to be quite uninterested in relationships of any kind and reasonably content about living on their own.

Conclusion

The settled and sustained personal relationships established by over one-third of the Boys in their late teens and early twenties contrasts starkly with the volatile, erratic and impermanent partnerships formed by many of the others. The patterns of relationship formation and the reasons for their subsequent collapse are complex, for many factors influenced these processes, although some of the Boys worked more diligently at protecting their relationships than others. Whether or not their relationships were ultimately 'successful' (and, though four of the Boys have never had a serious adult relationships, the remaining twenty-six have had forty between them), many produced children (sixty in all), towards whom the Boys displayed very different levels of responsibility.

–10–

The Boys' Children

Introduction

The Boys have sixty children, though two are not their own but were very young when they met new partners, and were 'taken on' as their own. (Tommy and Suzanne had another child who was born with spina bifida and lived for only an hour.) Twenty-six are boys; thirty-four are girls; their pseudonyms and age at the time the Boys were interviewed are provided here:

Ted	**Andy (21) / Natasha (17), Jenna (16) / [Robbie (15)], Hayley (10)**
Danny	**Cathy (9)**
Gary	**Simone (9), Adrian (6)**
Matt	**Aysha (19), Zelda (19) / Zak (18), Aaron (17)**
Paul	**Tim (17), Luke (12), Josh (5) / Stephanie (5)**
Richard	**Dan (13), Terry (12)**
Denny	**Helen (19) / [Chris (16)], Lenny (12), Rod (9)**
Ryan	**Debbie (19), Carla (17)**
Tony	**Katy (15), Hanna (13)**
Alex	**Harriet (11), Chrissie (4)**
Mack	**Stuart (12), Andrea (10)**
Mark	**Eirlys (15), Colin (12)**
Jerry	**Rachael (17), Chloe (15)**
Nathan	**Martin (9), Lawrence (7)**
Shaun	**David (21), Carl (14), Kirsty (10) / Eve (8)**
Derek	**Ophelia (7)**
Jamie	**Jack (11), Roisin (9)**
Gordon	**Ianthe (3), Melissa (2)**
Kelvin	**Damien (15), Jack (12), Lucy (10)**
Trevor	**Roger (19), Cherie (17), Matthew (15)**
Tommy	**Raymond (20), Lorraine (16), Vanessa (14)**
Mal	**Natasha (17), Bethan (15)**
Vic	**Alice (18) / Jade (15), Jake (13), Jolene (8)**

/ = children from different relationships
[ ] = unofficially 'adopted' children – 'taken on' by the Boys as their own

Twenty are already over the age of 16, twenty-one are of secondary school age (11–16) and nineteen are below secondary school age, between 2 and 10 years old (see Table 10.1).

Table 10.1 The Children – Ages in Year 2000

Ted	21			17	16	(15)				10	
Danny										9	
Spaceman											
Marty											
Gary										9	6
Matt	19	19	18	17							
Paul				17					12		5 5
Richard								13	12		
Denny		19			(16)				12	9	
Ryan		19		17							
Tony						15		13			
Alex									11		4
Mack									12	10	
Mark						15			12		
Jerry				17		15					
Nathan										9	7
Shaun	21						14			10	8
Derek											7
Colin											
Jamie									11	9	
Gordon											3 2
Eddie											
Nick											
Kelvin						15			12	10	
Trevor		19		17		15					
Tommy	20				16		14				
Mal				17		15					
Pete											
Vic			18			15		13		8	
Nutter											

20 aged 16+ --------------------------------------- //21 aged 11–15 ------------- //19 aged 0–10

The Boys' observations about their children will be considered in relation to these age bands and in terms of whether or not the children are from 'stable' or 'fractured' family contexts (see Table 10.2), the former being those who have lived with both parents throughout their childhood, the latter those who have experienced the breakdown of their father's relationship with their mother.

What follows is, of course, the Boys' *perceptions* and description of 'how the children are doing', rather than any more objective assessment, though some more dispassionate commentary will be offered by way of conclusion to this chapter. It is worth noting immediately, however, that most of the children over the age of 16 have experienced 'fractured' family relationships (Table 10.2). Twelve of the twenty children concerned fall into this category; this does not include Trevor's two children aged over 16, who went through their parents' separation and divorce, then their reconciliation, but otherwise grew up in a 'stable' relationship.

Table 10.2 The Children – Ages and the 'Stability' of their Parents' Relationships

	'Stable'			'Fractured'					
	M	F	Total	M	F	Total	M	F	Total
16+	2	6	8	6	6	12	8	12	**20**
11–16	7	8	15	6	0	6	13	8	**21**
2–10	1	11	12	4	3	7	5	14	**19**
	10	**25**	**35**	**16**	**9**	**25**	**26**	**34**	**60**

Only one of the twenty children over the age of 16 – Mal's eldest daughter, from a 'stable' background – is in post-16 academic learning, with many of the others already apparently following in their fathers' footsteps in terms of casual relationships, erratic employment and involvement in crime. Many more of the younger children appear likely to do rather better than this, for they live in more 'stable' relationships and circumstances, which is partly to do with *time* (and they may yet experience the relationship breakdown of their parents), though it is also to do with *different* parental relationships and more clearly planned family formation, within a broader context of greater employment and housing stability.

The Older Children (Aged over 16)

There are twenty children in this group, of whom twelve experienced the breakdown of their fathers' relationship with their mothers while they were children, and seven lost touch with their fathers, though contact was sometimes renewed when they reached their mid to late teenage years. In contrast, eight of these children spent the whole of their childhood with both of their natural parents.

Of these eight children from 'stable' backgrounds, Tommy's two oldest children Raymond (20) and Lorraine (16) are, without a doubt, 'chips off the old block', for they both attended the local comprehensive school and left at the minimum school leaving age with few qualifications. However, Raymond has always worked regularly: 'he's a postman . . . straight into the cadets, Post Office, until he was 18, then full-time'; and so long as he got a 'decent' job as soon as he left school, Tommy 'wasn't bothered' whether or not Raymond got any qualifications. Raymond did, in fact, attain three low-level General Certificate of Secondary Education (GCSE) passes (in maths, english and geography), though he was always determined to leave school at the earliest opportunity, just like Lorraine, who had only just left school officially, though she had been excluded for aggressive behaviour some months before. She was hoping to do a hairdressing course at college and, at the time of the research, was awaiting a letter of confirmation. Tommy did not mince his words about his older daughter: 'Lorraine's like me, thick as shit. She never done exams, she got kicked out of school. She's like me, she hated school . . . couldn't wait to leave'.

Two of Trevor's three children are also over the age of 16. Like Tommy, Trevor has always taken pride in the fact he has 'always worked' (even if both, at times, have done so on the fiddle), so he is pleased that his children also appear to have absorbed this work ethic, for though both went to the local comprehensive school and left at the minimum age, they have both been in regular employment since, with Roger (19) working in a garage, and Cherie (17) on a training course in a shop.

The other four children aged 16 or more from stable backgrounds did not attend the local comprehensive school. Ryan's two daughters Debbie (19) and Carla (17) were quite intentionally sent to a school beyond the estate in order to try to give them a better chance, though according to Ryan, it hadn't made much difference, for Carla lives on social security caring for her 1-year-old daughter, while Debbie now works in a pub and 'just wants to enjoy herself'. She sublets part of a house from someone on benefits: 'that's how she can afford it, though she only works a few nights a week', which is an ironic twist on the Boys' exploitation of the housing market and Ryan's particular track record on this front.

Jerry and Sam's 17-year-old daughter Rachael is profoundly disabled and attends a special school. Though her disability was not evident when she was born, Rachael's condition progressively worsened:

> By the time she was 3 years of age they are saying she can't thread beads, there might be a problem here. Then her legs were starting to go. Her body started to deteriorate. We were young, we didn't know what was happening and then we found ourselves back and forth to the hospital for about ten years. She baffled them, they didn't know what was wrong. I suppose we hoped Rachael would improve. It's only in the last two or three years that we have finally thought, no, it's not going to happen. She's down as spastic paraplegic – just to give her a name. They don't really know what it is, it's just to put her into a category.

Rachael, wheelchair bound and unable to speak, is likely to continue attending a special school of some kind for some years to come.

Of all the Boys' children over 16, only Mal and Jane's daughter Natasha (17) has stayed on at school beyond the minimum leaving age. Mal and Jane are extremely proud of her, for they both recognize the importance of learning and sent both of their daughters to a church school beyond the estate, despite living virtually next door to the comprehensive school. Mal was adamant his children were not going there, for as far as he was concerned, the school had done nothing for him. Natasha was doing A levels in art, maths and sociology, and hoping to become a nursery teacher.

Given the mixed progress of these children from stable backgrounds, it is hardly surprising that the twelve children over 16 from 'fractured' family backgrounds have fared considerably worse. All four of Matt's children are over the age of 16 and none obtained any educational qualifications. His two daughters by his second relationship live in London, and he lost touch with them for many years and now has only casual contact with them. Aysha (19) works in a shoe shop and Zelda (also 19) works in a clothes shop, both in the West End. Matt's two sons by his first relationship (which he renewed after leaving the mother of his daughters and returning to Milltown) live locally. Zak (18) works in a bakery and Aaron (17) is unemployed, though he is hoping to become an artist.

Ted's oldest son Andy, from his first relationship, is now 21 and a heroin addict, with three children by two women, though he currently lives 'at home' with his mother. Ted saw him very briefly when he was a baby but not again until he was 16: 'I see him on birthdays and Christmas, he usually just wants a handout'. Ted's two daughters Natasha (17) and Jenna (16) by his second relationship live with their mother, and he rarely sees them; as far as he knows they are 'doing nothing'.

Paul's 17-year-old son Tim was recently released from prison. He has already served a previous custodial sentence, and both convictions were for offences of violence. Paul deplores his son's offending behaviour, not per se but because Tim robs houses and steals cars *in Milltown*: 'I mean, you don't shit on your own doorstep'. Almost perversely Paul argues that if Tim, who left school at the minimum age and has never worked, needs money he would prefer him to go shoplifting! Paul recognizes his son is, in so many ways, simply following in his footsteps, though he insists there is a critical difference:

> Yes I am disappointed. There was a time when I hated his guts. When I've had a go at him he says well what have I done with *my* life. And what *have* I done with my life? It's true what he says. When I was younger people used to say you're not going nowhere. Just what I says to him. And I haven't got nowhere but, unlike him, I still got respect for people.

Neither Denny nor Vic have any contact with their eldest children, Helen (19) and Alice (18) respectively, and they have no idea what they are doing now. Denny's eldest son Chris (16) from his second relationship, 'adopted' by him when he was just a few months old, is apparently doing 'OK', though he was unable to be more specific, for he has never asked him, despite seeing Chris quite regularly.

According to Shaun, his eldest son David (now 21) was deeply affected by the break-up of Shaun's relationship with Sue, for David was 11 at the time and making the critical transition to secondary education. Shaun was the only one of the Boys to leave the local comprehensive school with any qualifications at all and wanted his own children to do well, and for some time, therefore, had been disappointed in David's lack of educational progress, though he felt he knew the reasons for it:

> We had a bit of a rough time with him. He was back and forth between me and Sue up until the time he left school really. He had to change schools and this kind of knocked the stuffing out of him. In his new school he was nothing special whereas before, in Milltown, he'd been respected by the teachers for his effort and achievements. He had a few problems in the new school and came out with virtually nothing – a few exams, low grades. But he didn't achieve what he was capable of achieving.

On leaving school, David managed to get himself an apprenticeship (as his father had done), as a pattern maker, before joining the army, which he had always wanted to do, though it was not what he expected and he came out after six months. Shaun continued:

> But he was lucky enough to find himself another apprenticeship but by this time he had discovered sex and well, he got his girlfriend pregnant, started losing time from work and got the sack. He was out of work then for a while. He broke up with his girlfriend just before she had the baby. But then he met another girl, couldn't control himself and she got pregnant and had the baby, and within a couple of months she got pregnant again and had another baby. And then they got married and then she got pregnant again, so they are now expecting their third. And he's only 21!

Shaun felt relieved David was now starting to 'settle down', for he has found himself a regular job following a spell on a government training programme (probably the New Deal), and Shaun is 'reasonably happy', though he feels David has still not realized his true potential. Nevertheless, Shaun is proud David 'has never been in any kind of serious trouble, he's not been fighting, he's not been getting pissed and he's not been stealing cars or taking drugs'. All in all, Shaun was pleased David has turned out to be essentially a 'nice bloke': 'he's a really nice kid . . . he's a good-looking kid and all, but a bugger with them looks'!

The Children of Secondary School Age (Aged 11–16)

Of the twenty-one children in this age group, less than one-third (just six) – all boys – have experienced the breakdown of their parents' relationship, though in Mack's case, there continues to be daily contact with his two children (including his 12-year-old son Stuart), and both Denny and Shaun have regular contact with their young teenage sons. Only Paul and Richard now have limited contact with their boys in this age band. Paul's 12-year-old son Luke makes no effort to see him, and Paul will not go to Luke's mother's house, while Richard is occasionally visited by his older son Dan (his younger son Terry now lives with him), though Richard holds the view that Dan, who is 13, has 'found his feet' and no longer really 'needs' him.

Fifteen of the children in this age group still live with both of their natural parents. Only five of these children from 'stable' backgrounds, from just three families, go to the local comprehensive school. Trevor's youngest son Matthew (15) is doing some GCSEs, but Trevor does not expect him to stay in education, and just hopes Matthew will find himself a job, relieved that so far he has stayed out of trouble. Mark's oldest daughter Eirlys is also 15, but he has little idea what she is doing at school, though he knows she is 'in the fourth year now' and has done some work experience. His son Colin (12) is in his first year at the comprehensive, and according to Mark, 'he's a little bleeder, full of mouth, not interested . . . can't you see me in him?' Vic also has a 15-year-old daughter, Jade, who is doing her GCSEs and 'stands a chance of getting some', but it is his son Jake (13) who is causing him concern, for – just as Mark views his son Colin, though with less inherent pride – Vic can see in Jake too much of himself at the same age. Jake is currently excluded from school and attending a pupil referral unit:

He's not really doing very well. He's getting into trouble. He's disruptive. It bothers me, yeah, because I've been down that road. I tries to talk to him and make him listen to the teachers in school because they are all there for his benefit. Like they were for mine, it was just I didn't take that chance when it was given to me. I gets *very* angry with him, very angry. I tries different things. I grounds him, I threaten to put him into care, you know, I threaten to beat him up. I've tried everything.

Hopefully he will go back to school but I have to say that his behaviour at school has been diabolical. Terrible bad language to women teachers and that. I never done that at school and I didn't do it in the street either, but him . . . he's just terrible in school.

And he's already been in trouble with the law, for stupidness as much as anything. They tried to set fire to an empty house and then he was caught on the church roof, messing about. Then there was an assault. But he was only cautioned because the kid who was assaulted admitted annoying my boy so he was really defending himself more than anything else, so the police were happy with that.

Given these accounts and concerns around educational underachievement and emergent anti-social behaviour, it is no wonder four other parents who also still live in Milltown have found or taken opportunities to send their children to schools other than the local comprehensive. Jerry and Sam send their younger daughter Chloe (15) to a Welsh-medium school away from the estate, believing she receives a much better quality education there, and hoping she will remain in school to do her A levels. She is on course for this, currently studying for her GCSEs and doing reasonably well. Similarly, Mal and Jane have sent their two daughters to a church school, where Natasha (17) is doing A levels, and Bethan (15) is doing GCSEs with a view to staying on at school or going to college.

Kelvin has taken advantage of his notional Catholicism to ensure his children potentially benefit from a Catholic school education. He has two secondary school age children, Damien (15) and Jack (12), who both attend a Catholic secondary school in another part of the city, and are apparently doing well, though Kelvin does not want to inflate his expectations for their educational success (he is basically laid back and just wants the kids to be 'happy'), despite harbouring secret hopes they will continue with their studies and perhaps even go to university.

Tommy and Suzanne would never have planned for their youngest child Vanessa (14) to go anywhere other than the comprehensive, which their two older children attended, until they were called to Vanessa's junior school and told she had the potential to gain a scholarship to the city's elite public school for girls. Vanessa took the entrance examinations and got the scholarship (a 'free place'), to the obvious delight of her parents (though Tommy's attitude is somewhat more muted), who considered this to be a 'chance of a lifetime', though they are alert to the tensions and challenges facing a girl from Milltown going to such a school, which have indeed been prominent. (At this point in the research interview Suzanne stopped doing the ironing and joined in the conversation.)

Tommy: My baby goes to that private school in town, private school.

Suzanne: She passed a scholarship.

Tommy: She's as brainy as you!

Suzanne: We didn't decide for her to go there.

Tommy: The school did.

Suzanne: Her school, in the junior school. They decided that she was really clever, they told me, when she was in Standard Two, that if she keeps on the way she's going, she could get into that school. But I never said nothing to her at the time, because I wouldn't push her, do you know what I mean? And then, at the end of Standard Two, well in the March, we got called up there again and they said, we would like her to do the test for [the private school] and I said, well it's not up to me, it's up to her, she's got to go there, not me. And then we had a letter to go and look around there, didn't we?

Tommy: Yeah, what a fucking place.

Suzanne: He hasn't been there since! And then she passed the test. I sat her down and I told her, you are going to lose all your friends from your old school, 'cos they'll all be going up the road [to the local comprehensive], and you're going to have to make new friends. I told her it was not going to be easy. I have never pushed her into doing any of it. But she said, yes, I'll go then. Well the only thing I did tell her was that they are paying for your education there, six grand [£6,000] a year. You come out of there without any GCSEs or A levels and you'll be just the same as those from [local comprehensive]. You will have wasted an opportunity. But I didn't have too much to worry about – in her first report, she had ten A*s. I'm very proud of her.

Tommy: I'm proud of her too, but I don't show it so much.

Suzanne: Yeah, he just don't show it. I'm very, very proud of her, but then, in here, back home, you've got to be careful because of Lorraine . . . You know, like the day Vanessa passed the test to get into that school, Lorraine was on report up at [local comprehensive]. I bought both of them something. I said, right, that's for passing the test, and that's for having a good report this week. You've got to treat them both fair.

But it has been very hard for her, sometimes . . .

Tommy: Yeah, it gets to her sometimes.

Suzanne: We had trouble last year, didn't we . . . she was being picked on. She's always had some problems there, because she's from Milltown, like she's the 'rough' girl in the school. But there was one girl and it was just after Christmas and she was saying what she'd had for Christmas, and Vanessa had said that she thought that was wonderful. And then this girl said that she didn't think it was enough. And Vanessa said, you make me sick, people like you. She said her mind. She will say what she has got to say. That's how we've brought her up.

Tommy: She's got a wicked right hook on her now, by all accounts!!!

Suzanne: No, she should be able to say what she wants to say, but this girl hit her. Anyway, she come home and said this girl had hit her but she had turned her back, said don't hit me again, and turned her back. Of course, Tommy's having a fit – you never turn your back if you have been hit, what have I taught you . . . And then she said, the girl smacked her again, so she turned round, and this is the thing she said to us, she said she dropped her shoulder, and at that point I'm thinking oh my God . . . 'and I just busted her nose'. And I thought that she would've been expelled but no, Vanessa explained, the girl who'd hit her said that she deserved everything she'd got, because she'd hit her twice, and that went in Vanessa's favour. And then Vanessa said, and he [Tommy] loves this, she'd said to the headmistress, see the thing is, where I come from, I'm from Milltown and I'm proud of it, she said, and if you get hit you have got to hit back, if you can give you've got to be able to take. She'd said, my father taught me how to fight, and apparently the headmistress said, oh I've seen your father, he is a very big man.

But Vanessa won't have no one get one over on her – just like her father!

Tommy: Yeah, I was proud of her that day. But there's the other side to it as well. She haven't got many friends round here.

Suzanne: She have got no one.

Tommy: They don't want to know her, 'cos they think she's a snob. That's a laugh, isn't it, when you look at us.

Suzanne: She's made a few friends at school, but they are upper class, most of them, isn't it? She don't often go to their houses. It's like they're embarrassed about her. And only a couple of them comes here.

Tommy: Yeah, Kayleigh, and what's the other one, the half-caste one? The Pakistani one? But she hasn't got time most of the time, because when she is in school, you should see the homework they give them.

Suzanne: Yeah, she'll have five pieces of homework a night. None of the kids round here never does any homework.

Tommy: I never done any!

Suzanne: So most of the time, she's just doing her homework, or baby-sitting, to earn some money.

Tommy: Well *we* don't do her homework for her, that's a dead cert! Because we can't. But she gets on with it. She has to do it out here on the table. There's nowhere else for her to do it.

Suzanne: She used to do Lorraine's homework when she was like in the first form and Lorraine was in form five. Because she's just so far ahead. She's basically a year ahead of them in state schools anyway. But it's not been easy for her. And sometimes it has been very hard.

Tommy: Anyway, I hopes she does well, good luck to her. I hopes she does well, because she can look after me and her when we're old.

Suzanne: She's going in the army.

Tommy: She says she wants to go in the army as an officer. That's what she wants to do.

Suzanne: She's looked into it already.

Tommy: She said she don't want to be a doctor, and she don't want to be a lawyer or a solicitor because she'd have to look after perverts and all them bent bastards, and she said she couldn't handle that. And, uh, so she said she wanted to go in the army. I said, well if that's what you wants to do . . .

Suzanne: She said there's nothing here for me.

Tommy: So we said, carry on, get all your exams then and your qualifications and you'll fly in there. Saying that, she's only 14, she might change her mind, but I am pleased.

Vanessa's aspiration to become an army officer is illuminating, for it represents a combination of an acceptable and understood employment pathway for young people in Milltown with an appropriate occupational destination for someone with a formal education. It symbolizes, therefore, an effective amalgamation of background and experience for someone who otherwise might feel – as Vanessa certainly does on a regular basis – trapped between two worlds.

Four of the other Boys with secondary school age children live away from Milltown. Ted lives on a comparably rough council estate some fifteen miles away, where his 15-year-old son Robbie attends the local comprehensive school and is unlikely to achieve anything more than a few low-level GCSEs, though he excels at sport which, so far and to Ted's delight, has largely kept him out of trouble.

Harriet (11), the elder of Alex's two daughters, will shortly start secondary school. Alex describes her as 'nothing really, just an ordinary kid', and is perfectly happy for her to remain that way, though he hopes she may go on to succeed in education and perhaps even go to university, for they live in a respectable part of the city and Alex is confident the local secondary school will serve his daughter well.

Two of the Boys who attended the Catholic school in Milltown also have prospectively successful children. Jamie does not live far from Milltown, and his eldest child Jack (11) has just started at the local secondary school. According to Jamie, Jack is a 'trier', which is good enough for him: 'he doesn't have to be brilliant . . . so long as he makes the effort, that's what I care about'. Tony lives a long way from Milltown in an expensive bungalow in a rural village, where both his teenage daughters Katy (15) and Hanna (13) attend the secondary school just down the road and look destined to do well in their GCSEs. Like Alex, he would like to see them go to university, though unlike Alex, he is reasonably confident they will, for they already display considerable aptitude and potential, and he has the resources and motivation to support this taking place.

The prospects for the children from 'fractured' family backgrounds appear much less rosy, and most of the fathers expressed some anxiety their boys (for they are all boys in this group) were already showing signs of slipping down the 'wrong path'. Paul, however, still has some hopes for his 12-year-old son Luke, from his first relationship, despite the fact Luke's 17-year-old brother Tim already has a substantial criminal record. Paul suggests Luke is doing quite well at school – so far – but is aware that he was also doing 'OK' at the same age:

> He's in a high class but he's only in form one and so the same could happen to him like what happened to me. The first couple of years I did all right. When you start going into your teenage years, you go one way or another. I just hope he stays the way he is.

Richard is equally concerned about his two boys, Dan (13) and Terry (12), especially Dan, who, since Richard's marriage ended, has continued to live with his mother and sees Richard only occasionally. Dan is 'somewhere in the middle', Richard says, doing 'all right' at school and not getting into *too much* trouble, though only time will tell. Terry now lives with his father, and Richard has endeavoured to draw Terry's attention to the consequences of getting into trouble and the importance of learning, though he admits his own track record is far from exemplary.

Denny's middle son from his second relationship, Lenny (12), has already been in trouble with the police, and Denny says he seems to have a gritty determination to become the 'hard man' of his peer group. He sees Lenny on three weekends out of four, but is becoming increasingly frustrated about his inability to control or correct Lenny's wayward behaviour. However, Denny is fatalistic, maintaining there is not much he can do about it, and he will just have to let things run their course. Problems were also emerging with Carl (14), Shaun's middle child from his first relationship, and though Shaun attributes much of this to 'typical adolescence', he is concerned Carl cannot express his feelings, which Shaun feels may be a consequence of the break-up of his marriage:

> We've started having a few problems with Carl. He's a reasonably intelligent kid so I'm hoping he'll come through without too many problems. I've had a word with him about it and so has his mother. The big difficulty is he won't express his feelings. He just goes totally blank. It drives me bloody mad. It is so frustrating.
>
> I think a lot of it is more to do with adolescence than anything else. He has got his own circle of friends and he's kind of finding his feet on the street a bit. But I still worry for him. In school he's doing quite well but I've got to keep an eye on him now, because he has reached that kind of adolescent stage where things could go wrong.

Mack's son Stuart is 12 and is already something of an exception among the children of the Boys, for he *already* excels at something – as an under-18 speed pool champion. Mack claims Stuart is a bright kid who is doing 'fine' at school, though most of Mack's interest is focused on his son's prowess at pool. Not a lot of money is yet to be made from these talents, and the Boys in The Fountain have a whip-round to send Stuart and Mack off to tournaments and exhibitions, but Mack considers this to be the 'career' route Stuart should be taking – and he is already a very competent 'hustler' on the pool table in the pub!

The Youngest Children (Aged 2–10)

There are nineteen children in this age group, seven of whom have already experienced the breakdown of their parents' relationship, though all but two (Paul's two 5-year-olds, by different mothers) continue to be in regular contact with their fathers.

Twelve of these children have therefore grown up (so far) in 'stable' backgrounds with both of their natural parents. Danny dotes on his 9-year-old daughter Cathy, who is completely indulged through his ill-gotten gains, with a bedroom full of books, every conceivable video, and a horse at her disposal every evening. She is a bright girl and the headteacher of her junior school has already suggested she could be a candidate for a scholarship at the elite girls' public school (which Tommy and Suzanne's daughter, Vanessa, attends). Gary's two children, Simone (9) and Adrian (6), also appear to be bright, for both he and his wife Amelia are keen for the children to do well in their education, and he waxed lyrical about the significance of having a kitchen table over which to talk with the kids about their day at school (I found this fascinating as I had never been in a house *without* a kitchen table before I went to live in Milltown):

> We've had the kitchen table now for a few years, nothing special but a kitchen table. I'd never had a kitchen table before. We was always eating, watching the telly off trays and

just munching, munching, munching – ever since I was a kid, with my sister, my brother, my mother and my dad. But since we've had this table, honestly, everything goes across it. We all talks to each other more. We all eat together and it's fantastic. It's just fantastic and it's such a silly thing. But, you know, Simone comes home from school and everything starts flowing across that kitchen table. It's a weird stupid little thing and then again it's so bloody important. It's a big help. All the family are sat together and we are talking. You know, how's it going Adrian, what did you do in school today and he tells little stories about what he's done. Whereas before it wasn't happening, so it's a really important tool to have in the house I think. It's the proper way to do things. You've got to do those sort of things for your kids. We all eat together and we are all by the table and they've all got table manners. They're nice kids, you know, and I think that is a big learning process, you know, around the kitchen table.

Vic's youngest child Jolene (8) goes to the same junior school as Gary's kids, and he is hoping she will not go off the rails as her older brother Jake already appears to have done. While Gary's 'tool' to foment dialogue and encouragement is the kitchen table, Vic's is the fridge magnet:

Yeah, Jolene's great, she's doing all right. See all her certificates on the fridge. Not so many for Jake, but he's got one for music. We puts them all on the fridge. Well it's nice for the kids and it's a bit of a show off for me as well, and we can have a bit of banter with them about it. Like Jolene has got more than Jake and I says to him, look she's catching up with you and she's so much younger. And we buys them things when they get certificates. We try to encourage them. Yeah, Jolene is doing all right at school. She's doing what she should be doing.

Of the twelve children under the age of 10 from 'stable' backgrounds, only these four go to school in Milltown. Three others are below school age, while four are at school elsewhere in, or just outside the city, and one, Ted's youngest child, Hayley (10), goes to school on the estate where they live. She is completely indulged and highly temperamental, and Ted believes she is doing 'all right', though he has little idea about how she is really getting on, most of the time simply providing her with another cash handout or a present, with little further curiosity or communication.

Some of the other Boys, quite understandably, feel it is premature to pass 'judgement' on their younger children. Derek, for example, said his 7-year-old daughter Ophelia *seemed* to be getting on 'reasonably well', while Jamie observed his daughter Roisin (9) *seemed* to be doing 'well enough' at her local Catholic school and was excelling at the violin. Kelvin 'wangled' his youngest child Lucy (10) into a Catholic school in a small village beyond the city, for this would enable her to 'go on to the high school there which apparently is really well known for good exam passes', and so far Lucy was doing 'OK'. Alex has a 4-year-old daughter Chrissie who has not yet started school, and Gordon has two small daughters, Ianthe (3) and Melissa (2).

The bridge between the youngest children from 'stable' families to those from 'fractured' family backgrounds is embodied in Shaun, who has a 10-year-old daughter, Kirsty, from his previous relationship, and an 8-year-old daughter, Eve, from his current relationship. Both attend Welsh-medium schools (though different ones), which was a quite intentional decision, for Shaun is convinced such schooling provides a stronger foundation for learning and development, especially in relation to language skills and in literacy and numeracy. Kirsty and Eve were 'plodding along nicely' as far as he was concerned.

Apart from Kirsty, the other six youngest children from 'fractured' family backgrounds all go to junior schools in Milltown. Denny's youngest boy Rod (9), from his second relationship, is a mild-mannered, polite yet inquisitive individual, in striking contrast to his troublesome older brother Lenny. Mack's daughter, Andrea, is 10, and Nathan's two boys, Martin and Lawrence, are 9 and 7 respectively. All live with their mothers in Milltown, and all see their fathers on quite a regular basis both through planning and by chance, yet their fathers had little to say about their children in terms of either education or behaviour, one way or another. Only Paul, denied access to both of his 5-year-old children – Josh (by his first relationship) and Stephanie (by his second) – proffered some limited remarks. Josh, apparently, is 'crazy', throwing temper tantrums constantly, screaming and shouting: 'there's something wrong with him, but nothing has ever been done about it'. Paul has not seen Stephanie for over eighteen months but asserted she was 'good as gold', though he had heard more recently from others that Stephanie was now terrified of him, ever since he 'performed' outside her house threatening violence towards her mother.

Overall, then, the Boys have thirty-five children who have grown up with them in 'stable' relationships, and twenty-five children who have experienced the breakdown of their parents' relationship. Of the latter, the oldest children, born when the Boys were very young themselves and in already precarious or collapsing relationships, often lost all contact with their fathers. However, most of the children under 16 from 'fractured' relationships have continued to have reasonable levels of contact with their fathers, though this has sometimes taken time to agree and set in train.

What should be apparent, however, is that many more of the children from 'fractured' family backgrounds are already part of a cycle of reproduction of educational failure and anti-social behaviour patterns which the Boys themselves displayed. Those children already over the age of 16 are largely in menial and manual occupations, if they are working at all, some have themselves already become parents, one has already succumbed to drug addiction, and others have already acquired criminal records. Their younger siblings do not appear to be faring much better, presenting behavioural problems and having difficulties in school.

In contrast, many of the children from more 'stable' family backgrounds appear to be doing relatively well, though the Boys, *as fathers*, remain strikingly ill informed about the detail of their children's educational and social development, especially in relation to their daughters. Indeed, they are expressly more concerned about their sons, recognizing that the critical time of mid-adolescence will prove to be the acid test of whether they 'come through' with marketable educational resources, particularly those who still live in Milltown, where the competing, negative cultural pressures are considerable. However, nine of the fifteen children of secondary school age from 'stable' homes are girls, and the majority of these look as if they are destined for some form of post-16 learning. For the younger children it is certainly too early to say.

It is not, of course, just the stability of family life which is exerting an influence in one direction or another, for household location (and therefore schooling location), and active (or passive) decisions by the parents about the children's schooling are also clearly important. It is, indeed, the *combination* of these factors which is significant and which will be addressed, albeit somewhat speculatively, towards the end of this chapter (see Table 10.3).

No Children

Seven of the Boys – Spaceman, Marty, Colin, Eddie, Nick, Pete and Nutter – have no children. Four of these (Marty, Colin, Eddie and Nutter) have never been in a 'serious' adult relationship, by choice or through circumstance, Pete has only ever had gay relationships, and Spaceman's one 'serious' relationship was relatively short-lived. This does not mean they did not want to have children; indeed, four of them, including Pete, despite being gay, regret they have not had the opportunity to have children.

Only Nick, however, has been in a very long-term and stable relationship where the absence of children has been a source of deep and recurrent regret, for he and Karen are unable to have children, as a result of surgery Karen underwent as a young woman, though they did not become aware of this until after they were married. Nick talks powerfully and poignantly about the agonies they have suffered as a result, especially when they were told they would be unable to foster or adopt because of Nick's criminal convictions for violence:

I mean, we got married and then we found out seven weeks later that she couldn't have kids, which is something that we both wanted. I always wanted kids. So had Karen. She comes from a large family and they've all got loads of kids. I have to be honest with you, it's been difficult, very difficult. It's not no more, but it used to be. It always used

Table 10.3 The Children – A Hierarchy of Opportunity and Vulnerability

Family stability/orientation Housing location	Schooling	Parental contact when parents apart	Children
Stable positive Away from Milltown	Away from Milltown	N/A (parents together)	Tony 1/2 Jamie 1/2 Shaun 4 Gordon 1/2
Stable positive In Milltown	Away from Milltown	N/A (parents together)	Jerry 2 Kelvin 1/2/3 Mal 1/2 Tommy 3
Stable neutral Away from Milltown	Away from Milltown	N/A (parents together)	Alex 1/2
Stable positive In Milltown	Inside Milltown	N/A (parents together)	Gary 1 Gary 2
Fractured positive Away from Milltown	Away from Milltown	Regular (planned/agreed)	Shaun 1/2/3
Stable neutral In Milltown	Inside Milltown	N/A (parents together)	Tommy 1/2 Mark 1/2
Stable negative Away from Milltown	Away from Milltown	N/A (parents together)	Ted 4/5
Stable negative In Milltown	Inside Milltown	N/A (parents together)	Danny 1 Vic 2/3/4
Fractured positive In Milltown	In Milltown	Regular (*child with father)	Richard 2
Fractured neutral In Milltown	In Milltown	Regular (planned/agreed)	Denny 2/3/4
Fractured negative In Milltown	In Milltown	Regular (casual/ad hoc)	Nathan 1/2 Mack 1/2 Richard 1
Fractured negative In Milltown	In Milltown	Limited None	Paul 1/2//3 Paul 4

to be, when I saw my mates and they've all got little boys and little girls and what have you. But now I think, I look at them, and see how some of them are turning out, and think maybe I'm lucky in some ways. But it's not nice when somebody else says, you don't know how lucky you are and things like that. Sometimes that cuts a little bit, because they have got kids. It's easy to sit your side of the fence and say, oh look, they are little bastards, you don't know how lucky you are. And yet they're there cursing one side of the fence and they've got kids, and I'm here cursing the other side of the fence, without kids.

I mean Karen, it still cuts her as deep as it did from day one. One, because she keeps going on that she has this fear that one day I'm going to go out and shag willy nilly just to have kids, which I wouldn't do. I couldn't do. If I'm going to be a father, then it's got to be full-time, I don't want to be a weekend father. But that doesn't stop her fear.

My wife says, oh you should have done child work, everybody, even my mother, says you should have gone into youth work from day one and blah, blah, blah. I am good with kids. I knows that. I gets on well with kids.

But I had a nasty experience with the system. We had dealings with the system. We went to try to go through the adoption process. And we met with a fucking sledge-hammer, that's what it was like, that's how Karen felt, yeah. And then I had a guilt complex for two or three years. It kept playing on my mind that I should leave this woman, because if she gets a decent husband without a criminal past, then maybe she will have a chance of having a kid. Because they turned us down point blank because of my record. Especially because of the last one [Nick's conviction for Grievous Bodily Harm].

It was like probably a year after I come out from the GBH charge and I went to see somebody to do with fostering. We thought we won't go in for adoption first, we'll try fostering. Karen didn't really want to do fostering, which I can understand from a woman's point of view, because you're not going to want to give the kids back. And you're not going to want to form a bond with somebody and then have to be told, well they are gone now. So I can understand that.

But we decided to try to foster first, anyway. Yeah, and we were met with a brick fucking wall, a real brick wall, which was something we weren't expecting. We thought they were going to be quite open, give us some consideration. You know, those poor fucking kids out there, the biggest thing you can give them is love and attention and your time, you don't have to have any money. I mean, we were working at the time, we had our own burger vans. We could prove, at the time, some financial stability, so it wasn't anything to do with that. It was to do with the fact that I had a record for vio-lence. And I said, well what the fucking hell do you think I am going to do, beat the kids? I beat up an adult man, I said, that had fucking insulted my wife, if you read the judge's report, he deserved fucking beating up, and that's what the judge said on the day. But they wouldn't shift. I had a record for violence, and that was it. Fostering, adoption, no way.

When they said this, I was hurting, God I was hurting. It was our kind of last chance of having kids. And I was hurting more for Karen than for me. I don't know whether it's because she's a woman, and it's supposed to be every woman's dream, I suppose, to have kids, it's their function in life, or that's the way most women see it, anyway.

Nick claims he has now become reconciled to these circumstances, but his graphic account demonstrates quite clearly how much it still 'hurts', and perhaps more than any of the Boys, Nick has paid a heavy, and unexpected, price for his offending.

Conclusion

In this account of the circumstances of the Boys' children, a very clear 'pecking order' of chance and opportunity or, conversely, risk and vulnerability, emerges for the next generation. Family structures, geographical location and the nature of schooling combine in different but highly influential ways, and it is possible, speculatively, to draw these together into a 'hierarchy' of opportunity and possibility, mapping out those children who have the greatest prospects to those who have the least (Table 10.3).

There are, inevitably, exceptions which do not fit comfortably into this framework, such as Ryan and Laura's two daughters, who grew up in a stable household and were educated beyond the estate, yet one ended up in the casual labour market (bar work) and the other became a teenage mother. Nevertheless, the model is indicative of the kind of virtuous or vicious circles which prevail in the opportunity structures for the children.

There is an alternative way of conceptualizing the Boys' family relationships and their impact on the children, less in terms of the *organization* of family life and more in terms of its *orientation*. Once the Boys established more personal relationships, *some* shifted their focus almost exclusively towards their family responsibilities and to the futures of their children, while others remained primarily focused on the Boys (their peer group – see Chapter 12), and left family responsibilities, child-rearing and educational decisions largely to their partners. Such orientational differences were often integrally linked to unfolding 'careers' in the labour market and with crime, though they also appear to derive from the 'idea' of family emanating from their own schooling and family backgrounds. The Catholic school Boys were generally much more family oriented and concerned about their children's schooling than those who had attended the comprehensive school (see Table 10.4).

Whether or not it is the *organization* of family life and active decision-making about schooling, or an *orientation* towards actively supporting their children's learning and development – and it is almost certainly both (one feeds the other) – there is little doubt the Boys' children are destined for very different futures. Stable rather than chaotic family backgrounds do appear to have played a significant part in this, though rarely an exclusive one, and from this account of the Boys' children, one might surmise that some of them will build further on the relatively successful pathways forged by their parents (in cases such as Shaun or Mal, and certainly

Table 10.4 The Children – A Question of Orientation?

Family/education oriented	←————————→		*Not family/education oriented*	
Gary (2)	Richard (2)		Ted (5)	
Tony (2)	Denny (4)		Danny (1)	
Jerry (2)	Ryan (2)		Matt (4)	
Shaun (4)	Alex (2)		Paul (4)	
Jamie (2)	Mark (2)		*Mack* (2)	
Gordon (2)	*Derek* (1)		Nathan (2)	
Kelvin (3)	Trevor (3)			
Mal (2)	Tommy (3)			
	Vic (4)			
8 (19)	9 (23)		6 (18)	23 (60)

Catholic school Boys: *italics*
Number of children in parentheses

Tony and Gordon), while others will establish a legitimate but modest life course through regular work and desistance from crime (such as Tommy's two elder children and Trevor's kids). A third group, however, face a strong probability of cementing a position at the margins, often following in the footsteps of their fathers, but finding themselves even more distant from legitimate prospects in the labour market, yet at the same time more attracted and connected to broader prospects (especially around drugs) in terms of criminal activity. The eldest boys of Ted and Paul already bear witness to this, and the teenage sons of Denny, Vic and Richard appear to be treading a similar path.

In other words, there is likely to be a further *polarization* of the existing distinctions and divisions among the Boys, who themselves had been firmly clustered *together*, as teenagers, at the margins. During adulthood, their 'public' lives (in employment, crime and housing) have diverged, and this divergence is both reflected in, and reinforced by the course of their 'private' lives – their relationships and children. Table 10.5 seeks to capture, albeit speculatively, how such trends are likely to continue in the life course of their children.

Table 10.5 The Boys' Children – A Speculation on their Futures

Negative (crime and drugs)			'Respectable'				Positive (qualifications and choice)		
1	**2**	**3**	**4**	**5**	**6**	**7**	**8**	**9**	**10**
Paul 1		**Paul 2**			**Gary 2**		Gary 1		
Paul 3		Paul 4							
Ted 1	Ted 2/3		Ted 4				**Shaun 1/2**		*Tony 1/2*
	Ted 5						Shaun 3/4		
			Matt 1/2		Alex 1/2				
						Danny 1			
	Matt 3/4		Mark 1		***Jamie 1***			*Gordon 1/2*	
	Vic 1/2			**Tommy 1**			***Kelvin 1/2***		
		Richard 1		Richard 2			*Jamie 2*	*Kelvin 3*	
Vic 3			Denny 1		**Denny 2**				
	Denny 3		Vic 4				**Denny 4**		
		Ryan 1/2		**Trevor 1/3**				Tommy 3	
			Tommy 2		Trevor 2				
			Mack 1						Mal 1
		Mack 2		[Jerry 1]		Jerry 2			Mal 2
		Mark 2							
		Nathan 1/2		*Derek 1*					

Catholic school Boys: *italics*

Sons: **bold**

Numbers relate to the 'order' of children

–11–

Health – Drink, Drugs and Deterioration?

Introduction

Health issues affecting the Milltown Boys over their life course include, predictably, health risk behaviours such as smoking, drinking and drug-use, as well as
many other acute and chronic physical and mental health problems which have
from time to time, or more persistently, had an impact on their lives. In terms of
physical health, at the age of 40, the consequences of their casual attitude to health
are starting, but only *starting*, to show some deleterious effects, even though – in
a general sense – the Boys have arguably remained surprisingly healthy. This is,
indeed, what they themselves would claim, despite growing evidence to the contrary, for some have already suffered, and more are beginning to suffer, the consequences of social lives characterized by significant health risk behaviour and
occupational lives which often presented unavoidable health risk environments.
The Boys' saving grace has been, for many at least, their strong commitment to
active participation in sport, which is only now starting to decline, though it has
curtailed over the past few years. For a number of the Boys, golf is now their
favoured sporting pastime, though in the past many were regular football and
rugby players, which kept them 'fit', even if matches were routinely followed by
heavy bouts of drinking and smoking.

With some notable exceptions (such as Vic's respiratory disease or Marty's
schizophrenia), a more 'objective' assessment of the Boys' health is hard to deter-
mine and even more difficult to forecast, for theoretically it could still change
direction – for better or for worse – as a result of individual decisions or the impact
of wider circumstances, especially concerning relationships and jobs. Paul's
drinking, for example, has worsened dramatically since his relationships collapsed,
while Spaceman's recovery from addiction now offers him prospects for the future
no one would have anticipated a few years ago.

Others have had episodic encounters with poor health, especially mental health,
and with greater health risk behaviour (through, for example, drugs consumption),
but for most of the Boys the path is firmly set, underpinned by a cavalier attitude
to their health – the 'que sera, sera' philosophy which more generally informs their
lives. Despite some positive attention to certain acute health problems, many patterns of health behaviour are well established, in terms of declining physical

activity, a reluctance to address symptoms until they become unbearable, and the heavy consumption of alcohol and tobacco, all of which bode ill for the Boys' futures. Some health difficulties surfaced unexpectedly (literally, by accident), though many others are the rather predictable consequences of 'lifestyle' developments cemented early in their lives.

Teenage Years

The Boys started to take risks with their health as teenagers or even earlier, for most started smoking at 9 or 10, and not much later they were regularly drinking alcohol (usually cider), purchased for them by older youths – for a small consideration – and consumed over in the woods.

Illegal drugs rarely entered the picture in the Boys' early teenage years, though at least one-third of the Boys sniffed glue from around the age of 14, for glue was readily available, and large tins of Evostick were stolen from hardware shops in town. Glue-sniffing became a daily routine for some of the Boys (such as Jerry, Ryan, Alex, Gary and Paul), when they were 15 and 16, and in Paul's case continued into early adulthood. Cannabis, by contrast, was less accessible and was anyway, at the time, negatively associated with hippies and students, and therefore not a drug of choice among the Boys. The popular cocktail at teenage parties was cider mixed with aspirin, which got them drunk and made them crazy – crazy enough, as many later admitted, to display some confidence with the girls! As they approached their twenties, amphetamines came to be used increasingly by some of the Boys, for 'speed' not only was associated with the Mod revival culture of the late 1970s to which, post-punk, they expressed some affiliation, but also provided the energy to party (and fight) all night.

Thus, before the end of their teens, most of the Boys had become socialized into cultures of regular smoking (often between twenty and thirty cigarettes a day) and heavy alcohol use (ten to fifteen pints a night on 'weekends' which usually stretched from Thursday to Sunday). A few had started to experiment with illegal drugs, and most lived on a staple diet of pie and chips.

Fitness and General Health

Most of the Boys, however, look in remarkably good shape. Even those clearly overweight often claim they are 'fit', for they assert proudly that until fairly recently, if not still today, they have been able to run around a football or rugby field for the whole match. To the Boys, physical activity – both in sports and in their working lives – is invariably the weather-vane for judging their general *health*.

There are of course exceptions, especially those with chronic illnesses and those who experience mental illness, and those who have endured drug and alcohol dependency who, even if they now appear to have 'come through', are clearly far from 'fit'. Here it is important to remember those of the Boys who have not made it this far, for not one of them died of natural causes, but as a result of suicide, drug addiction or through being killed by drink- and drug-fuelled 'friends' or drunken drivers. The 'malaise' of the local environment has, therefore, already claimed its casualties, which is perhaps a benchmark against which the Boys are inclined to judge their own 'survival'.

Ted is a bull of a man who claims to have stayed 'pretty fit over the years' despite smoking, drinking heavily and using his fair share of illegal drugs, for until fairly recently he played rugby regularly at the local level. Danny played too when he was not in prison, and rather perversely Danny (who smokes cannabis, rarely drinks and can 'give or take' a cigarette) argues the time he has lost to date through imprisonment (some twelve years) will benefit him later in his life:

> Because when you are in jail you do training if only just to get out of the fucking cell. You go to the gym, any time you can. What I say is this. With jail, it's took twelve years off my life . . . But then on the back end – you know, in jail I have been on a strict diet, I haven't been drinking, I haven't been smoking so much, I've been training – so it has put about twenty years on the back end of my life.

Danny has always prided himself on keeping in shape, though he doesn't train so much these days, commenting 'It's only now that I've come up to 40 that I've laid off a bit'. Nevertheless, he still believes he could compete with the younger generation if need be – 'it's getting harder, but I can still do it'. Even Eddie can 'still do it', for despite suffering both from asthma and mental health problems, he turns out regularly for his local football team, though he concedes he drinks too much and is definitely overweight, 'but I must be reasonably fit . . . if I'm still running round the pitch for ninety minutes, I can't be doing that badly'. In contrast, Denny – who also played regular football until quite recently – acknowledges his heavy smoking is now taking its toll, for 'whereas before I could run up the bloody street, now I can barely trot and I'm still out of breath'.

Gary does little sporting exercise but points out his painting and decorating requires considerable physical exertion, and therefore he considers himself to be 'pretty fit, basically'. So does Trevor who, despite the ankle injury which ended his footballing 'career' and left him with one leg shorter than the other, which initially caused him back problems, and has also suffered from ulcers, still maintained 'I feel all right, not too bad honestly, I feel good'.

Even those of the Boys who clearly indulge in high-risk health behaviours (*very* heavy smoking, drinking or drug-use) often assert they are 'fit'. Nutter has reduced his alcohol consumption from an extraordinary twenty pints a day to around five pints a day, and he smokes around 100 grams of tobacco a week (which he thinks is 'not a lot'), yet he claims to be in 'good shape' on the grounds he rides his bicycle down to the woods (to drink!) every day and, apart from an acute injury, has never had any health problems. Jamie describes himself as a 'weekend alcoholic' but contends 'health wise, touch wood, I'm generally OK, yeah', despite a number of operations on a damaged knee. Mal also maintains he is 'generally fit, no problem', despite having high blood pressure from stress at work and smoking and drinking excessively.

Fitness and general health are often defined by the Boys in the context of never having had to visit the doctor. Derek's last visit was years ago, 'so, yeah, I must be pretty healthy, like', while Alex commented likewise: 'yeah, no problems, never go to the doctor'. Many of the Boys would argue, further, like Danny, that their preoccupations with 'training' and 'working out' has represented some protection against the health risks present in their social and working lives. Despite the bad back incurred while labouring on the fiddle, Ryan said he remained 'pretty fit' and went on to list the sequence of fitness activities he had followed during his life: boxing, football, weights, Thai boxing and now mountain biking. Richard had also done bodybuilding as a young man, then gave it up for a decade, but took it up again until the mid-1990s. However, he also used steroids to enhance his physique, and unlike Ryan does not believe he is either fit or healthy, despite his impressive physical appearance, for he has asthma, smokes and drinks too much, and suffers from depression. Working out, Richard noted, was always something of a compensatory mechanism, to fend off his wider health anxieties.

Vic has at least tried to continue playing rugby – which he had done briefly, professionally, as a young man – in spite of his chronic lung disease and permanent breathlessness. He knows he smokes and drinks too much, and often struggles to walk up and down the stairs, and therefore compliments himself on his ability to be still actively playing sport at his age, albeit only occasionally: 'I see a lot of guys my age and they don't do nothing any more. But I still have a run around. At least I still run around'.

Jerry no longer smokes and now drinks only moderately, but today suffers from arthritis, which limits his capacity for exercise. Until recently, however, he did a lot of running and swimming, 'but now I am sort of limited to walking the dog', and still views himself as being 'pretty fit', arguing that even in his heavier drinking days 'I could get totally pissed up the night before and still go running the next day'.

Gordon smokes 'very little', drinks (mainly wine) within 'sensible' levels, and uses cannabis occasionally. Like Richard he has always 'worked out' and continues to do so, maintaining he is 'one hundred per cent fit and healthy'.

Beyond the elision and alignment of 'fitness' with 'reasonably good health', through their references to physical activity, the Boys do little to address, more directly, their health risk behaviour and the avoidance of ill-health. For Pete, as a gay man in the early 1980s, this issue was particularly pronounced. None of the

Boys had seen him for many years, often assuming he might have died of AIDS, which Pete acknowledges could have been the case; that he had not was more down to luck than judgement:

> Well I was on the game for a while so I was quite lucky. It was right at the beginning of the AIDS thing. The first person in Britain had just died of it. But the gay community was more aware of the safe sex messages even before they started to advertise with that bloody huge monolith 'AIDS – don't die of ignorance'. And quite right too. But having said that, well I wasn't practising safe sex then, by and large, but I was practising safe sex by default. I was rarely buggered and if I was buggered, while I was on the game, it was always with a condom. But that wasn't very often. Because I've got a good reputation for my mouth, you see, so that saved me probably. My gob saved me, so there you are.

Pete may joke at his own expense, noting the risks he took were inadvertantly (marginally) less than they might have been, though he is now only too aware he did take risks and was lucky not to reap the consequences.

The Boys therefore argue they have, to date, maintained reasonable health and fitness, though a more dispassionate view suggests they have borne a disproportionate share of health problems, as well as engaging in excessive health risk activity (see Table 11.1).

The Boys conscientiously recounted the injuries, accidents and other health problems they have experienced, as well as reporting their often excessive consumption of both legal and illegal substances, though Tony, true to form, adopted his typically ironic stance:

> Touch wood, my health's been excellent. I mean, as you can see, my body is my temple! You know, a lot of people say, God I'm not as fit as I used to be. I don't think like that because I've never been fit, so I've nothing to compare it against! All I can say is that I'm quite fortunate. No operations, no nothing. So far, so good.

Mental Health

Seven (almost a quarter) of the Boys have suffered mental health problems at different points in their lives. Marty was formally diagnosed with paranoid schizophrenia in 1995, and his mental health problems are exacerbated because he often forgets to take his medication, continues to use 'speed' (amphetamine), and still drinks very heavily:

> Schizophrenia, yeah ... I got little voices in my head and all sorts of things. It was about five years ago when I was admitted to [psychiatric] hospital. It just come out in me all of a sudden. It's terrible. I had voices in my head telling me I'm dying all the

Table 11.1 An Overall Picture of the 'Health' of the Milltown Boys

| | General health/illness | | Current weekly substance consumption | | |
	Chronic	Acute	Smoking (cigarettes)	Drinking (units)	Illegal drugs
Ted	Broken wrist		140	60	Soft/regular Hard/occasional
Danny			50	40	Soft/regular Hard/occasional
Spaceman*	Ulcers/depression/ fractured skull		200	Alcoholic-nothing	Soft/regular
Marty*	Paranoid schizophrenia		200	140	Soft/regular
Gary		Hernia/ear infection	70	60	None now
Matt	Chest/headaches/arthritis		140	40	Soft/regular
Paul*		Depression	200	140	Soft/regular
Richard*	Asthma	Depression	100	60	Soft/occasional
Denny	Piles/broken leg/vasectomy		200	60	None now
Ryan	Bad back/stomach		None	40	None now
Tony			None	30	None now
Alex			20	20	None now
Mack			100	100	Soft/regular
Mark	Ulcers/appendix		250	60	None now
Jerry	Arthritis/stomach trouble		None	20	None now
Nathan			70	60	Soft/regular
Shaun*		Depression	200	10	Never
Derek			140	20	None now
Colin	Bad back/deafness		200	120	Never
Jamie	Knee operations/vasectomy		Never	50	None now
Gordon	[Car accident]		Very little	20	None now
Eddie*	Asthma/breakdowns/weight		Never	40	Never
Nick	Asthma		70	Alcoholic-nothing	Soft/regular
Kelvin	Varicose veins/bad back		100 gm tobacco	30	None now
Trevor	Shorter leg/hip	Ulcers	Never	20	Never
Tommy	Diabetic/overweight/tonsils		None	120	Never
Mal	Blood pressure/vasectomy		100	40	None now
Pete*	Bad back/depression/hip op		70	Limited	Soft/regular
Vic	Lung disease		200	40	Soft/occasional
Nutter	Double fractured skull		100 gm tobacco	80	None now

* Mental health problems (chronic and acute)

time. And I forget to take my medication. I'm always on medication now, of one sort or another.

Marty is routinely described by the Boys as having 'lost the plot', for he rarely ventures out, except to take his dog for a walk around the block and to buy his cans of lager from the local off-licence.

Eddie has also suffered regular and repeated mental health problems, having his first serious breakdown just before he left school in 1976, a second in 1983, and a further relapse in 1985. On the latter occasions he was admitted to hospital for a short period and, following the last episode, then to residential rehabilitation. Eddie attributes his breakdowns to pressures arising from changes at work, initially when he took on greater managerial responsibilities, together with various 'misunderstandings' in his unfulfilled relationships with women. More recently, workplace reorganization threatened yet another breakdown (his workplace had become a call centre and Eddie could not handle working 'on the phones'), but on this occasion he 'saw the danger signs coming'. Unable to face going into work, he went instead to see his doctor, who signed him off work for six months, though following an independent medical assessment which concluded he was not suited to call centre work, he underwent retraining for 'back of office' work on a reduced working week. Eddie is still far from happy in his job, but is confident he is no longer recurrently on the cusp of yet another mental breakdown, a prospect which continues to terrify him, in the light of his past experiences.

In a less pronounced way, Shaun has also suffered from stress 'if life's not going the way that I want it to', and admits to getting 'a bit depressed sometimes', though the only time he had sunk to some serious depths of depression was when his marriage collapsed. Paul also acknowledged he had been depressed following the death of his father, and 'the problems I had with different women and all that', which led to his increasingly heavy drinking:

> I think it was like a breakdown or something and the doctor said it was drink depression – you are drinking because you are depressed but the drink also makes you depressed, it don't make you happy.

Paul had initially 'played up' his drinking and 'mental health' problems as part of a scam to get a social security grant and in order to avoid possible imprisonment for breach of a community service order he was serving at the time. He did not think he was *really* depressed but ended up being prescribed valium for clinical depression: 'that scared me, I thought I was going crazy'.

Richard and Nathan had similar experiences following the collapse of their relationships. Nathan's depression was never formally diagnosed but he described the round of heavy drug-taking following his separation from his wife, the spiral of self-pity and self-abuse ending only when he went to prison. Richard has repeatedly suffered from clinical depression over many years, taking prescribed medication when the need arises.

Pete and Spaceman have also had periodic bouts of depression throughout their lives. In Pete's case, these have been triggered by moments of melancholic reflection about the tragedies in his life (the death of his first partner, the near-fatal injuries incurred by his second partner), while Spaceman's have been fuelled by his heavy drug and alcohol addiction, as well as his sense of profound loneliness.

Apart from Marty, whose illness is all too self-evident, none of these Boys talk much about their 'mental illness'. It is simply not something to be mentioned in routine conversation, and they put on a 'brave face' or find a cover, like Paul's drinking, to pass it off as something else.

Physical Injury and Illness

Many of the Boys have experienced specific problems, both acute and chronic, in relation to their physical health, which span a spectrum of ailments and injuries. Not surprisingly, many of their acute problems have arisen from their involvement in sport, and from the Boys' unrestrained enthusiasm for drinking and fighting. Both Nutter and Spaceman have incurred serious fractured skulls, the latter on two occasions while in his teens. Indeed, on one of those occasions, after being smashed over the head with a chair in pub brawl, Spaceman was not expected to live and was given the last rites. Nutter was matter of fact about his injury, sustained only a couple of years ago, and recounts the experience with some transparent sense of pride:

> I fight people. I always fight people. Always have. I had a *double* fractured skull. I had a fight in a pub and they took me to hospital but they sent me home. But I was feeling groggy so I went back, had some X-rays and they said there was nothing wrong with me and sent me home again. The next day they sent an ambulance for me, because they'd found I'd got a fractured skull. But I wasn't at home. I was in the pub, having a beer! Well I didn't know, did I? Anyway they did a brain scan on me and said I'd got to stay in. I said no way. They'd let me out yesterday. I'd let myself out today! So I walked out, yeah.

There had, however, been surprisingly few other broken bones, though Ted broke his wrist boxing, while Denny broke a leg playing football but made a full recovery. Trevor was not so fortunate, for after his ankle injury he was left with one leg shorter than the other and, for a while, suffered from 'terrible backaches' on account of his distorted posture. Discovering Sylvester Stallone had a similar problem and wore 'raisers' in one shoe, he got a friend working in an appliance department to make him some 'wedges': 'so I'm a bit taller now and it's stopped the backaches but, as a result, I've got to strap up all the time'. The injury, however, put paid to Trevor's ability to play club football ever again. Jamie's football playing, certainly at the more senior level to which he aspired, was also put in jeopardy, when at the age of 20 his knee was seriously injured in a fight. Despite two operations, however, he carried on playing parks football until 1997, when a cartilage operation finally ended his playing career. Pete, during a vicars and tarts party in the pub he ran with Barry (he was, predictably, dressed as a tart; Barry was Friar Tuck), had to have three pins in his hip after falling out of a window: 'I fell out, maybe I jumped out or was pushed out. I don't really know, it was the tequila that did it'.

Jamie and a couple of the other Boys have had vasectomies, which Mal described with incredulity:

> Into hospital and out again. Unbelievable experience. Weird, mate, I tell you. You can actually feel it – you can hear crunch, crunching. Like, what the fuck is going on? You're John Wayne for a couple of days!

Shortly after the birth of the third child in his second relationship, which broke down soon afterwards, Denny had his vasectomy, though when he met Annie he had it reversed: 'yeah, I'm hoping to put it to use again!' Apart from the 'snip' and his broken leg Denny had an operation for piles: 'yeah, I had an operation for the old metric miles, piles. I had them bad, like a golf ball, in fact a cluster, if you really want to know'.

Denny was also badly injured by a car, when he walked out into the road during his period of heavy alcohol abuse, though he cannot remember much about it, except to note 'I don't think I would have done it without the drink, I wasn't that mad, but when you're drunk, you know, sod it . . . you just don't care'. Gordon had a serious car crash while he was in the United States, though he recovered eventually from his multiple injuries. Of the Boys interviewed, these are the only two severe car-related accidents, which may be surprising, though it should be noted that two of the Boys were killed in motor vehicle accidents.

There have been few other *acute* problems, apart from Gary's recent hernia operation and 'a couple of ear infections', and Tommy's tonsilectomy in 1998.

Increasingly, however, the Boys have experienced *chronic* health problems. Matt, probably as a result of over well over a decade of drug misuse and the nighttime armed robberies which financed his habit, suffers not only from a serious breathing condition but also from pervasive arthritis:

> My chest, I am always bringing up shit. And I've suffered from headaches, bad, bad headaches. I've got arthritis going all through my body, all my joints are fucked . . . that's through raising, all them wet fucking nights looking at buildings and this and that. That's it, my bones, my bones are hurting me.

Jerry doesn't smoke these days and is now only a modest drinker, but he too suffers from arthritis and, though firmly opposed to illegal drugs, maintains cannabis should be legalized for medicinal purposes: 'I mean, I'm told it helps with arthritis and so it's no different than a doctor giving me pain killers'.

Spaceman, Mark and Trevor all suffer from ulcers. Trevor attributed his to 'constant worries' about his children: 'I was told that that was what was causing the acid build up in my gut. I've had a barium meal. I've had the tubes down there with the camera; that's why I don't drink tea or coffee any more. I only drink water – and beer at the weekend'. Spaceman's ulcers are almost certainly connected to years of alcohol and substance misuse, and he takes prescribed daily medication for these and other ailments, while Mark said his ulcers were also related to his heavy drinking and described in rather unpleasant graphic detail how he became aware of them:

> See I used to drink dark beer and I was shitting black but I thought it was just the beer. Never took no notice of it. Then I was up the club and I went all hot and giddy. I was sweating and shaking. Six months earlier I'd actually had a barium meal but they never found anything, so I never had an inkling. So anyway I went to have a go on the bandit . . . and the joke goes that because I won twenty pence I flaked out, like I flaked out *because* I'd won twenty pence! They took me to hospital. It turned out I had a bleeding ulcer and I'd lost a lot of blood. I was in for about ten days. They gave me some antibiotics and, touch wood, and now they've said your ulcer's gone. I still have a few stomach aches. I don't know whether that is down to the beer or what.

Mark *is* a heavy drinker, though his consumption is tempered by his shift work on the railways (where random tests for alcohol are in force). He is also a heavy smoker, though vehemently anti-drugs.

Like Matt, Colin – who shifts pallets all day long and spends every evening in the pub – has chest problems (as well as a bad back and lifelong hearing difficulties, for which he has had three operations), which he attributes to heavy smoking. Nick also smokes heavily (some cigarettes, but mainly cannabis), though he suffers from asthma, a condition which also affects Eddie, who does not smoke and still plays football regularly, while Richard continues to smoke heavily, despite using inhalers 'like they are going out of fashion'.

Vic has contracted a lung disease as a result of many years of industrial painting. This is another perverse twist in the Boys' lives, for as a young man Vic came closest to pursuing a career as a professional sportsman and continued playing amateur rugby on a regular basis until well into his thirties:

> Yeah up until a couple of years ago and then I got this disease and I've been put on the sick now. Obviously I was very fit when I was a teenager but I got to the stage where I couldn't hardly breathe. And Lisa kept nagging me to go to the doctor's so eventually

I went. That's when they found out I had this disease in my lung which is not going to go away. And since then, well the Boys will tell you, you heard me just coming down the stairs. I'm always gasping for breath.

This does not, however, stop Vic from smoking some twenty to thirty cigarettes a day, yet, somehow, he still manages to play the occasional game of rugby.

Given the heavy labouring work which many of the Boys have done throughout their working lives, both legitimately and on the fiddle, it is to be expected some now suffer from chronic back problems. Ryan had to give up labouring on the fiddle after incurring a back injury while carrying cement. Colin, as mentioned, has humped pallets for twenty years and has had treatment for a back problem, whereas Kelvin (who also has varicose veins) has so far resisted seeking treatment:

I've got two worn vertebrae in my spine that they want to pin, but they ain't going to pin them, so that plays me up now and again. But I live with it. That's why I sit like this. If I sit up straight for too long it just kills me. But I'll never have it pinned, no way.

Pete also has a back problem which he 'never dealt with for ages', though prior to an operation, his back had 'gone' three times. On the first occasion he tried to ignore it, on the second consulted a chiropractor, and on the third went to an osteopath, but the problem persisted and some years later he collapsed again and, following a CAT scan, required an operation: 'so in the end I had to be rushed into hospital because I couldn't get off the table'.

The Boys predictably have a miscellany of other chronic health problems. Tommy, for example, described himself as being not only unacceptably overweight but also 'borderline diabetic . . . my sugar level is too high, basically', and though Ryan has rarely had a day off work since returning to legitimate (factory) employment in the mid-1990s, he suffers constantly from a 'bad stomach', which he attributes to inhaling rubber fumes at his workplace. Jerry also admitted to suffering from 'stomach problems'.

Only six of the Boys, then, reported *no* significant health difficulties in their lives, which clearly runs counter to their broad assertions they are generally 'fit' and 'healthy'. The two positions are potentially reconciled both by their lay expectations of what constitutes 'good' health and by cultural expectations that they should not 'make a meal' of their health problems. Arguably, their health *is* remarkably 'good' when one takes more account of the health risk behaviours to which they have exposed themselves throughout their lives.

Smoking

Most of the Boys smoke at least twenty cigarettes a day, often considerably more, and only four have never smoked, though eight are now non-smokers or smoke only occasionally. The Boys who have 'never' smoked struggle to find reasons why they did *not* follow the crowd, explaining it largely by their more serious commitment to sport, for Jamie, Trevor and Eddie were all dedicated footballers in their teens and, indeed, well into their adult lives. Gordon also claims he has 'never really smoked', though he does have a very occasional cigarette.

Tony, Tommy and Ryan briefly (sometimes very briefly) smoked in their early teens but have never done so since. Tony, physically one of the smallest of the Boys, commented with his typical wry humour – 'stunts your growth, wouldn't touch them' – though he admitted to having once rolled his own, with his next-door-neighbour's father's nub-ends: 'I hated ever single second of it and fortunately I've never smoked since'. The only heavy teenage smoker to have completely stopped smoking as an adult is Jerry, who gave up smoking in 1986.

Those who do smoke often assert they do so 'moderately', though moderation is clearly a relative concept. Alex smokes only when out drinking: 'oh minimal, ten on a Friday, if I goes out'. Paradoxically, all the other 'moderate' tobacco smokers tend to be regular cannabis smokers. Danny doesn't 'do the fags like I used to', for he prefers a joint these days, as do Nick, Matt and Nathan, who smoke about ten cigarettes a day, and Pete, who smokes about ten joints a day and generally smokes cigarettes only 'if there's no dope left or if I'm in a social circle'. Kelvin rolls his own cigarettes, maintaining he also is a 'moderate' smoker because, though he smokes around twenty a day, 'I only smoke little roll-ups'.

If twenty cigarettes a day is the threshold between the Boys' conception of 'moderate' smoking and more 'serious' smoking, then the remaining half of the Boys are dangerously heavy smokers. Since he contracted his lung disease Vic had 'cut down on the fags' – 'I suppose it'd be around twenty fags a day, thirty easy' – saying he smoked most when he is 'doing nothing', and indeed many of the heaviest smokers are those who 'do nothing': Spaceman, Marty, Ted and Paul. Mack also does 'nothing', but says he smokes less than twenty a day.

All the other Boys smoke considerably more than twenty cigarettes a day (see Table 11.1) and this is often supplemented by regular cannabis smoking. Even the Boys who do 'something' (are in regular employment) rarely have their opportunities to smoke proscribed, for only six – Jamie, Eddie, Tony, Gordon, Ryan and Mal – are currently in jobs which restrict smoking, and none, except Mal, smoke anyway. Working conditions and regulations, therefore, do not put a brake on smoking and sometimes even serve to increase consumption. Mark does shift work on the railways:

> I goes through thirty a day easy, if not forty. And it's worse because I am on twelve-hour shifts. Like on the first night you are smoking all day and then I'm smoking all night as well. You smoke more because you are up more. So it's hard to put a figure on it. I smokes a hell of a lot, mind. I do smoke a hell of a lot.

Mark once gave up for five days, when he was in hospital being treated for his ulcer. However, other health (and perhaps smoking-related) problems rarely have much effect on the Boys' smoking, as Vic's circumstances demonstrate very clearly. Richard's asthma has never led him to contemplate giving up smoking: 'yeah I smoke a lot and my chest hurts as a result of it. I suppose I am a bit of an idiot. Definitely. But I never does anything about it'. Colin acknowledges he has a smoker's cough but continues to smoke 'twenty, thirty a day, more on weekends', and Derek, Denny, Shaun and Gary smoke a similar amount. Shaun commented, 'I'm always determined that I'm going to stop but I never seem to get round to it'. Nutter smokes roll-ups and uses about 100 grams of tobacco a week.

The only smoker who has his smoking restricted at work (in a factory) is Mal:

We're not allowed to smoke in work. So when I'm in work, six or seven a day, maybe a few more. When I'm not in work fifteen or twenty. More when I goes down the club.

The Boys almost certainly understate their tobacco consumption, for when they are out socially they virtually chain smoke. Some do curtail their smoking at home and one has his smoking curtailed at work, but most do not accept that their levels of smoking are sufficiently problematic to merit attention, even when they have self-evident reasons for 'cutting down' or stopping. As noted, only Jerry has given up as an adult, while the other seven non-smokers either never started or stopped in their early teens.

Alcohol

Virtually all the Boys used to be inordinately excessive and heavy drinkers, especially over (long) weekends, and many still are, especially when measured against official benchmarks for 'sensible' drinking (21–28 units, or 10–14 pints of beer, a week, with at least one day of abstinence). A number of the Boys have tempered their drinking as a result of their wider (personal and occupational) circumstances, though some, like Paul, have not. Their patterns of drinking, however, have become more diverse.

The reasons for a general reduction in alcohol consumption are varied, contingent upon economic, domestic, health and social reasons, as well as the fact of ageing. Danny readily acknowledges he simply cannot 'take' the quantities of drink he used to consume routinely:

I could sit in the pub and drink twenty, twenty-five bottles, from eleven in the morning to eleven at night, come home, have my tea. Oh I would be pissed but I know that I would wake up in the morning with no hangover. But now I have about eight bottles and I'm bollocksed.

Vic has been compelled to reduce his intake, for since the onset of his chronic illness, he is now living mainly on benefits: 'Now I'm not working no more I suppose I drink about twenty pints a week. Before it was every night of the week, ten pints a night, sometimes more'. Nutter has also curtailed his drinking largely for financial reasons, though he knows he has a drink problem but doesn't care, for he will not entertain the idea of professional counselling, and asserts his drinking is now more in hand, primarily because he cannot afford to drink the astronomical amounts he did before:

> I used to have a drink problem but . . . well I still has a drink every day but I don't drink so much as before. If I had more money it would go on beer. If I don't have money, I don't. That's the only reason.

Jerry has cut down not for financial reasons but because he now has 'stomach problems' and consequently limits his drinking to the weekends and social occasions: 'I used to have six or seven cans a night but now it's just the weekends. Sunday lunchtime I'll have six or seven pints of Guinness and on a Saturday night maybe a few glasses of wine and a couple of whiskies'. Shaun's second wife Gaynor is a non-drinker, who has influenced both how much he drinks and *how* he drinks, for they spend their social life together, whereas before he used to go to the pub on his own. Now he rarely drinks, and when he does usually has no more than three or four pints. Likewise, Alex is no longer a 'big drinker', indicating that these days it is 'one night a week maybe, eight or nine. I'm not a Thursday, Friday, Saturday, Sunday man no more. Been there, done that', though he conceded he had occasional binges, usually in the context of big sporting events 'like everyone else does'. Derek does the same, but apart from that hardly drinks at all, a far cry from the self-confessed excesses of his youth: 'it wasn't unusual then to have twenty pints a night but I don't really drink at all these days'.

Nutter and Paul may accept they have a 'drink problem' but have done nothing specific about it, whereas in contrast both Spaceman and Nick have admitted their 'alcoholism' and addressed it. Spaceman hit 'rock bottom' before he went to Alcoholics Anonymous:

> Nobody can believe the state of my life, what I was like. I was in fucking purgatory. I was constantly fucked, pissed, but the Boys would buy me pints. I'd go in The Fountain and the Boys would buy things off me, stuff I'd nicked, like a car battery, a fucking cassette recorder, things like that. I'd sell anything just to get booze, whatever the fuck I could lay my hands on. I was fucking pathetic.

Spaceman was lying on the settee at his sister's house in the summer of 1996, drinking a bottle of sherry, when two friends of his sister persuaded him to go to AA. He attended one meeting, drunk, but was then rushed into hospital, expecting, on discharge, his mother to look after him. To his surprise, she refused, which forced him to reflect further on his condition:

> She said that if she had had me back I would have stayed there for a couple of weeks, got fit, got some food down me and then gone out and done it all again. She said no and she was right. When she said no I was fucking shocked: no one loves me, no one wants me, I might as well be dead. That was my gut reaction; even my own mother wouldn't help me. It made me look at my life. It made me realize that I was completely on my own. You know, the buck stops here. I suppose it was that moment of clarity. I just woke up one morning and said this is it, I'm not drinking any more. Well I had this flagon of Stonehouse in the flat and I was shaking and rattling. I looked at it. That flagon will stop the shits, it'll stop the fucking blood coming up, it'll level me out. So I should drink it, get another couple, drink them and then go out thieving. That was my fucking routine at the time. I decided to drink it but said to myself it's my last drink. I drank it. The shakes stopped. And then I just stayed in my flat for about six days and, God, I really fucking went through it. Completely on my own.

This was the start of his 'final' concerted effort to stop drinking, for when he was in hospital, Spaceman had been warned that, if he continued, he would be dead within six months:

> I knew it was going to be hard. But in my head I'd been building up to this. I knew time was running out. I knew that if I didn't do something I would be dead soon. When they told me I'd got six months to live part of me just wanted to die. I wanted to pull the blankets over my head and die. I can't describe how I felt. I would like to describe how it is so you can picture it but it's almost impossible to picture it. It's not self-pity, it's just everything, you just can't handle it all no more. Well it's a kind of self-pity but it's something even worse than that, a kind of lack of hope in yourself as a human being, lack of anything in the world, lack of life. Lack of believing in life. You just want to fucking die. But that was the fucking start.

Spaceman graphically describes the process of self-detoxification he went through before he emerged from his flat:

> So I went through that horror . . . seeing things, hearing things and things crawling over me. It went on for ages, sweating and fucking kicking out all the shit off my system. And I had nothing to fall back on, no booze, no downers, no fucking nothing to level me out, no ganja, nothing . . . just me. After a couple of days I managed to get some soup down me and a couple of bananas, gradually I got some food into me. And then after a week or so I started to sleep, for a couple of hours. Because up till then I was awake. But gradually I slowed down. I was taking some drugs still; I was taking my ulcer tablets.

When he finally emerged from his flat, neighbours told him they thought he *had* died, like so many of Spaceman's drinking acquaintances who 'just died in their rooms and nobody cared'. He went to ninety AA meetings in ninety days, despite feeling at first that AA was 'fucking dodgy' and akin to brainwashing: 'and it is brain washing . . . they said your brain is fucking stinking, it needs a good fucking wash'. So he decided to 'give it a go', and once he got 'out of the gutter' he found a purpose in his drawing: 'I started to value myself because I am good at art'. By the time Spaceman told his probation officer he had always dreamed of going to art college, which she encouraged him to attempt, he had 'fucking piles of drawings, sketches of people, places, things . . . so I took them along and got accepted on this foundation course and now I'm doing a degree'.

Nick dealt with his alcoholism in a very different way, reflecting, during his final prison sentence, on the fact that so many of his convictions had been alcohol-related. Indeed, that prison sentence was the result of an alcohol-fuelled revenge attack when he had purposefully set out to 'teach the bastard a lesson'. He had escaped with a relatively light custodial sentence, for the original charge had been attempted murder, and while in prison a fellow inmate had lent him the AA 'bible': 'it was me to a fucking tee off'. On release, he attended a few AA meetings, but they did not resonate completely with his own philosophy about drinking:

> Every time I drank I got aggressive. I think I was looking for a buzz in alcohol that was never, ever there. At least I never recognized it. A lot of people get merry and then have the common sense to recognize they are happy there and stop. But with me I always wanted more. So of course I would have that extra pint – on top of the eight or nine I'd had already. It takes one pint for everybody to get pissed as far as I am concerned because you are not pissed until you drink that extra pint. Everybody has got a different tolerance level.

Nick's wife Karen had first alerted him to his 'drink problem' and he thought he should do something about it because 'I didn't want to lose her', though he did not at first anticipate the impact this would have on his social life:

> But it took me some time to really do something about it . . . See I didn't want to miss out on all these social occasions. I thought, if I don't drink I'm not going to feel the same. And I was a good darter [darts player] when I was a piss-head. I have probably played darts twice since I stopped drinking. And I was completely embarrassed by how shit I was. Once I stopped drinking, I couldn't throw a dart.

Nick realized that if he was going to succeed in tackling his drink problem he would have to take a 'clean break' from his social world:

Sobriety came to me in the hardest form, which was doing it by myself. Like I said, I tried to go back to darts. I'd sit there and my hands would be sweating, only because I was thinking that I'm missing out on a drink. And it was then that I realized that it was fucking hopeless trying to do that. I had to take a clean break. And after that I didn't go to a pub, function wise or other . . . I was invited to weddings, parties, engagements and I just wouldn't go because I wasn't sure of myself. I thought I would fuck it up if I went – I would have another drink. So I never went to anything like that for probably around three years close on, maybe even a little longer. I'm not even now 100 per cent in that kind of surroundings. I wouldn't say I miss a drink because I don't. It's not so much the drink itself, it's the sociability side of it that I miss.

Both Nick and Spaceman paid a heavy social price for their decision and determination to give up drinking, for they cut themselves off from their social worlds in order to extricate themselves from their dependency on alcohol. When Nick says he still does not feel 100 per cent in 'that kind of surroundings' (pubs and clubs), despite not having touched a drop of alcohol for a decade, he testifies to the major challenge for any of the Boys who wish to address their drink problems. The other Boys simply cannot understand, or elect to deny, the idea of alcohol *dependency*: 'surely a couple of pints won't do you any harm?' It is this latent and sometimes more explicit pressure which keeps Spaceman and Nick away from many of their old friends, but at least Nick has his wife for company and support, while Spaceman is often consumed by 'utter loneliness'.

Drinking is too much of an essential part of his daily round (no pun intended) for Paul to think of giving up, and the prospect of dealing with his alcohol dependency is too frightening for him to contemplate. Paul recognizes he has a serious drink problem, which has worsened considerably since both of his (concurrent) relationships broke down, but now his entire social world revolves around the Boys in The Fountain:

To stop drinking you've got to change your whole life, haven't you? Like it's not my mates who've got the problem, it's me who's got the problem. But then I look at the ones hanging round by the river or by the shops, you know, with their cans . . . I look at them people that *looks* alcoholic and then I don't see myself as an alcoholic. I know that I'm half way to one of those ones that hangs around and have got nowhere to live and I know that I'm not just drinking to socialize. I mean, Danny will come down here every day and he'll drink Coke, he'll only drink proper maybe once or twice a week. Mack will come down here, have a couple of pints and he's gone home teatime to have his meal. I'm not like that. I'll drink all day and I'm not even eating. You know, the last time I ate was, um, Friday, a bag of chips. That's me. And a packet of crisps when I goes out.

Now that Nick and Spaceman have stopped drinking, Paul (alongside Nutter) is certainly the heaviest drinker of all the Boys, though considerably more also consume 'unsafe' levels of alcohol. Their drinking patterns and practices are, however, organized in very different ways.

Many of the Boys have settled into domesticity during the working week and either drink very little at home or just have 'a few cans'. Gordon, for example, always has a few cans of Studleys in the fridge 'for friends who might come round' and will have a bottle of wine with a meal. Otherwise, though, home drinking is limited. The exception to moderate drinking in the home is Marty who, reluctant to venture out, drinks heavily in the isolation and loneliness of his one-bedroomed flat: 'I just gets up and starts drinking, like ten cans of beer a day, in here on my own. I've got nothing else to do'.

The most typical pattern is one of modest or no alcohol consumption in the domestic sphere during the week but heavy drinking in a social context over one or more days during the weekend or on specific social occasions. Gary typifies this pattern, contrasting it with the drinking behaviour of his youth:

> Well that's another story. All the Boys did that. Eighteen pints a night and all-day benders. But as you get older, you mellow out. I still enjoy a drink. But only a couple of cans in the house. Mind you, I do drink a lot when I go out. I have a blast. Sunday's my day for a good drink. I go to the pub to watch the football. Go up about four o'clock, meet up with a lot of the Boys, have a good chat, watch the football and stroll in about nine o'clock. I suppose I spend about forty quid – fifteen pints or so? So I have my quota on Sunday, maybe my double quota on Sunday!

Gary drinks about thirty pints of lager a week, though he believes his drinking habits are well under control. His hostility to illegal drugs is because he has seen too many friends become out of control and he recognizes this can also be the case with alcohol: 'some of the Boys can't stop. It's all about moderation. I still enjoy a pint but I don't go over the top like I used to. Just mellowed out, I suppose'.

Kelvin has also 'mellowed out', rarely drinking during the week but still drinking quite heavily on the weekends: 'when I do go out I have a good drink, eight or nine on Saturday and Sunday night'. Trevor *never* drinks at home and, despite excessive binge drinking from time to time, is among the third of the Boys who now just about comply with 'sensible' levels of alcohol use:

> I leave it to weekends now. I don't drink at all in the house, not at all. But give me a party and I'll go round there and drink all night. But it's usually just the weekends. And it depends. I'm 40 now; you have to pace yourself a bit more. Sometimes I'll just have a few, five or six. Then again it could be ten, eleven, easy. But sometimes I'll just drink squash. I'm not a heavy drinker, I never have been really.

Much of Trevor's current drinking revolves around his activities with a local rugby club, where he coaches a junior team. Sport may have been one reason why some of the Boys did not start or continue to *smoke* but, paradoxically, it provides the context for a great deal of heavy drinking, especially on the weekends. Eddie 'hardly ever' drinks during the week but still acknowledged that he drinks 'too much':

> On the weekends, usually on a Saturday, mainly. Maybe ten to fifteen pints. After football. Fridays and Saturdays I nearly always go out. Not so much on a Sunday now because of financial considerations. But occasionally I do go out on a Sunday and occasionally I'll train in the week and I'll have a couple of pints after training. The Friday and the Saturday is the one. Always the Saturday, with the football. Or maybe if there's not football but there'll be a rugby international or what have you. There's usually a reason. If not, you make one!

Mal does not drink at home either but goes out on two nights a week, on Sunday lunchtime and whichever day in the week 'skittles night' falls upon, and in each of these sessions drinks about ten pints. Jamie drinks about the same each time he goes out, describing himself as a 'weekend alcoholic': 'I like to have about ten pints on a Saturday and about the same on a Sunday, but in the week I hardly drink at all. Maybe a can of cider or a bottle of wine with a meal, you know, with the wife'. Denny follows a similar pattern now he has settled down with his third wife Annie and overcome the alcohol dependency which followed the break-up of his second marriage:

> I don't drink a great deal these days, although I still have a few beers. I still like my pint. On skittles night I might drink about a gallon. Saturday maybe another gallon. Friday night, say six pints. Thirty pints a week on average. Sometimes it's more.

Tony, who has moved geographically, occupationally and socially far away from Milltown, depicted his drinking habits as very different from the practices of Milltown's club and pub culture, while still confirming the social significance of alcohol in his life:

> Well it's very different from the society I grew up in which was, you know, 'beer swilling' – get it down your neck. Then when we got our first home we had no money to buy alcohol, so alcohol wasn't on the agenda. And then years later we started drinking again and now I drink every day of the week. Maybe just two glasses of wine or a couple of small bottles of beer – in the house. But on weekends the alcohol consumption is considerably higher. We socialize a lot. We go out, go to people's houses or they come here.
>
> I've been pissed many a time. It depends on the company. Quite often I drop in the pub for a couple of pints but it's not unusual to go out to friends' and it's harder to recognize how much you drink when you're having a great dinner party. You know, you might have half a dozen bottles of wine. Yeah, alcohol is a big important part of our lives.

By most standards the Boys' drinking continues to be relatively 'heavy' but, for many, it has at least come to be *structured* within the parameters of wider (competing or complementary) domestic, occupational and social commitments.

Seven of the Boys, however, remain immersed in regular, very heavy drinking. Whether at home in his lodgings, in the woods by the river (in the summer) or in a pub, Nutter is rarely far away from a drink, though he claims to drink far less than in the past 'when I'd have about two hundred quid a week, paid on Thursday and I'd have to borrow on Saturday'. He estimates he used to drink about twenty pints a day, but 'now it's about six, more on weekends', though heavier sessions involve having 'about twelve cans in the house, then I goes to the pub'. Paul also drinks a few cans, every day, before he goes to the pub: 'I just can't seem to get out of drinking, I can't see a way out; nothing's happening with my life and it's just drink, drink, drink – that's all I does'. Whereas many of the Boys have tempered their drinking to some extent at least, Paul's routine has become worse:

> I've just always been in the pub. Always. I used to go on a bender every weekend. Thursday, Friday, Saturday, Sunday, I'd take my drugs, I'd take my drink. You'd give your body a good beating and then you'd have a rest period. You'd lay off Monday, Tuesday, Wednesday, getting the body ready for the weekend again. But now I don't even give the body a rest. Now I'm just on the piss all the time.

The vacuum created by the breakdown of his relationships has, literally, been filled with alcohol, and Paul now has no respite from his excessive consumption. Nathan is in a similar position, saying he has routinely combined heavy drinking (eight to ten pints a day) with considerable illegal drug-use (notably amphetamine), though he claims to have curtailed his alcohol consumption in recent months: 'to tell you the truth, I'd rather have a spliff'.

Tommy works but readily admits to being a 'piss-head', drinking every day – five or six pints on weekdays, ten or twelve on weekends. Colin also reckons he drinks eight pints a day (every evening, after work) and spends all day Saturday in the pub, while Mack, who is unemployed, has five or six pints every day at lunchtime before he collects his children from school, though he rarely goes out in the evening.

Mark's drinking patterns are equally excessive, though rather different, for he works shifts on the railways where random tests for alcohol are frequently carried out. This means he has to remain constantly vigilant about the amount he drinks before days (and nights) at work, though when he is not working he drinks both at lunchtime and in the evening: 'at least forty pints a week, maybe more; if I've got the money, I'll go out'.

Such patterns of routine heavy drinking were compounded when relationships collapsed. Paul's circumstances provide the most graphic illustration of this, but Nathan and Denny also ended up drowning their sorrows in drink. Nathan's downward spiral into drug and alcohol misuse was stalled only when he was sent to prison, while Denny 'turned the corner' when he met Annie, though prior to that he had 'no outlook on life, I'll just go to the pub and have a drink, that'll solve it':

> I was a complete piss-head for a while. My favourite saying was, oh I'll drop in the club and have a couple of beers – and I'd finish at twelve o'clock. And I'd started at three o'clock. I'd have a pie from behind the bar. I was just drinking all the time, about fifteen pints a night. Looking back it was just a waste. But for a while I just didn't give a shit. As far as I was concerned, the world was against me. And my attitude was fuck off, don't fucking tell me what to do, just let me have another drink.

Substance Misuse

Only five of the Boys have never, at any point in their lives, purposefully taken illegal drugs, while three more have only ever sniffed glue. The rest have at least experimented with a range of different substances, though almost two-thirds of the Boys are no longer users in any way and indeed often express firm opposition to illegal drug use. In contrast, almost one-third continue to be recreational users, while four have succumbed, at different points in their lives, to serious drug dependency, though two (Matt and Spaceman) have recently sought to address their addictions (see Table 11.2).

Those who embraced second-generation Mod culture in the late 1970s experimented with most of the stimulants 'celebrated' by Mod youth culture in the 1960s, though many stopped long ago. The Fountain Boys routinely smoke cannabis, from lunchtime onwards, and some also deal in it. A few of the Boys are occasional users of harder drugs, such as cocaine.

Some of the Boys (like Spaceman and Matt) became firmly addicted (to heroin and crack cocaine respectively), and many believe that Marty's schizophrenia was triggered by his excessive use of 'speed', but most of the users have generally 'managed' their illegal drug use reasonably effectively.

A few of the Boys were never attracted to illegal drugs in the first place and others tried on just a few occasions, for many still favour alcohol over its (illegal) alternatives as their drug of choice. Of the five who have never knowingly used illegal drugs, two (Tommy and Colin – both of whom had 'always preferred a pint') have had their drinks spiked on occasions in the past, while the other three have never had any involvement whatsoever with the drugs culture. Trevor was simply 'not interested', Eddie said, 'I don't know why, but it's just never, never appealed to me', while Shaun commented, 'I can honestly say I've never touched an illegal substance, it really wasn't a normal thing to do when I was a kid', and as an adult had never mixed in circles where anyone used drugs.

Twelve of the Boys have tried various illegal drugs (usually cannabis), though for different reasons and at different times, and this was usually a relatively

Table 11.2 Illegal Drug-use – Past and Present

	Past	*Present*
Non-users		
Shaun	Never	None
Eddie	Never	None
Trevor	Never	None
Tommy	Never intentionally	None
Colin	Never intentionally	None
Experimental users		
Kelvin	Cannabis, speed	None
Mal	Cannabis	None
Denny	Cannabis	None
Ryan	Glue, hash-cakes, speed, mushrooms, cocaine	None
Nutter	Cannabis, speed, mushrooms	None
Tony	Speed	None
Alex	Glue	None
Gary	Glue, cannabis, speed	None
Derek	Cannabis, speed	None
Jamie	Speed	None
Gordon	Cannabis, mushrooms, LSD, ecstasy, speed, glue, cocaine	None
Mark	Cannabis	None
Jerry	Glue	None
Recreational users		
Ted	Speed	Cannabis, cocaine
Danny	Glue, speed	Cannabis, [cocaine]
Richard	Glue, speed	Cannabis
Mack	Glue, speed	Cannabis
Nathan	Glue	Speed, cannabis
Nick	Glue, speed	Cannabis
Pete	Speed	Cannabis
Vic	Glue, heroin	Cannabis
Problem users		
Spaceman	Speed, heroin, crack	Cannabis
Marty	Glue, cannabis	Speed, cannabis
Matt	Speed, crack cocaine	Cannabis
Paul	Glue, speed	Cannabis

fleeting episode in their lives. Kelvin smoked a 'bit of dope' and used speed as a young adult, though 'the only reason was because I was with the Boys; it was never something that really appealed to me'. Tony and Gary had taken pills as part of their skirmish with the Mod culture but they 'didn't really like it', while Gordon, Derek and Jamie were part of that same crowd and had similar experiences. Gordon, in particular, tried 'most things' as a teenager and during his time in the United States:

> Dope, mushrooms . . . some tabs [LSD], E's [ecstasy], but I wasn't so fussed on them and then cocaine obviously, speed, glue, you know . . . I'd be surprised to find people our age who haven't done most of that, at least tried it.

Nutter had also experimented with dope and speed, and with magic mushrooms, but always preferred alcohol: 'just blips here and there, I was never that interested, I'm a drinker, me'. Ryan had been a persistent glue-sniffer in his teens (when it was 'the business'), used some speed and mushrooms and eaten a few hash-cakes ('I've never smoked dope because I don't smoke'), though he too prefers a drink: 'I think the booze gives the best life'. Cannabis had had little effect on Mal and Denny, the latter asserting he 'got a better head rush from smoking a Hamlet cigar'. Both Alex and Jerry had been committed glue-sniffers for a while, though they maintained this had been 'just a passing phase', for both are now very hostile to the use of illegal substances, even if Jerry advocates the legalization of cannabis for medicinal purposes. Mark is equally opposed to illegal drugs, though he had 'smoked a bit of weed once, but all it done was make me sick', and like Nutter and Ryan, and Colin and Tommy, he prefers a pint.

Seven of the Boys had 'got on with it' at a recreational level. Ted, who also deals in cannabis and amphetamine, routinely smokes dope and occasionally dabbles with cocaine. Danny does much the same these days, doing 'a bit of coke once a month' and having 'a puff most days, in the afternoon', though he once also used quite a lot of speed. He was smoking a spliff during the research interview and I asked him why:

> What can I say? It's part of my life. In any interview – 'cause most of the interviews I've ever had are with the law or in the Job Centre – I am nervous. I have to get the stories right. And when I smoke a spliff it calms me down. I am nervous now although all I've got to tell you is the truth – like with the others I've got to lie. I've got to get my story right!

Nick confesses to being a heavy weekend cannabis user and has tried most illegal drugs at some point in his life but – having seen the corrosive effect of heavy drug-use among some of his friends – now limits his own use to marijuana. Like Ryan, however, he retains an almost nostalgic memory of the days he spent sniffing glue, 'which I swear to this day was the best buzz I had in my life, drug wise'. Pete is also a committed cannabis user, smoking some ten to twelve joints a day, while Vic's use of cannabis is less frequent, though he 'likes a smoke'. This is the only illegal substance he uses these days, though he admitted to sniffing glue and smoking heroin in the past, 'but I was really just dabbling in it'. Nathan, Richard and Mack all continue to smoke the 'wacky backy', and all were once also heavy users of speed, though only Nathan still uses amphetamine on a regular basis. Richard, however, is currently making a concerted effort to desist from *any* illegal drug-use, now that his younger son is living with him:

> because I know he looks at me and, well, I have got to give a good example. I don't want him looking at me and thinking his father is a druggee. I don't want my son to think it's normal for people to take drugs. I can't condemn it absolutely because I have done it myself. I don't condemn my friends who take stuff, but I just don't want my son involved with anything like that. So this has been a major step in my life. You know, I want him to grow up with a good clean life really.

Mack has only recently given up speed, which he had been using since 1988 – 'I don't know why, I'd just had enough of it' – and now just smokes cannabis: 'marijuana, that's all, at the moment'.

Four of the Boys have, however, succumbed to serious dependency on a variety of legal and illegal substances. For years, Marty has consumed vast amounts of speed (up to two grams a day), which hardly assists the management of his schizophrenia, especially as he often forgets to take his prescribed medication. Paul's regular 'benders' have always been fuelled by a combination of alcohol and other drugs, though alcohol is always the ascendant choice. Spaceman's and Matt's poly-drug addictions controlled their lives for well over a decade, though Spaceman now appears to have 'come through', abstaining from everything except cannabis since 1996, while Matt has also recently sought to address his crack cocaine addiction, though his circumstances are more in the balance.

Perspectives on the Drugs Culture

The Boys hold dramatically polarized views about illegal drugs, informed by very different perspectives on the causes and effect of use. Some differentiate between 'hard' and 'soft' drugs, while others are convinced of the slippery slope from 'having a little spliff' to dependency and addiction. Of most significance in their view, however, are issues of *control* and *personality*, for, while admitting to some loss of 'control' through alcohol, many of those who favour alcohol despise those who use drugs for getting completely out of control. Trevor felt he was in control because he could stop drinking, whereas 'it's not the same when you're on drugs . . . you can't stop taking drugs'. Denny, Ryan and Mark would agree, along with

Gordon, who observed he only ever 'dabbled', precisely because otherwise he would have lost 'that all-important edge' which was essential for his wheeling and dealing, and described how he had watched people, within six months, 'lose everything through cocaine'.

Gordon was also convinced 'the way you handle it is down to personality', arguing he was able to 'dabble' because he did not have 'an addictive kind of personality'. Richard certainly attributed his use of speed to being 'an obsessive sort of person' and never doing things by halves, maintaining this was consistent with his star sign Gemini: 'that's my personality again – all or nothing'. Trevor, however, was adamant that drug-use did not reflect people's personality but rather changed it: 'I had this neighbour and when he was sober he would look you in the face but when he got drugged up he became a fucking nightmare . . . it just changes people'. Spaceman would agree, maintaining he took his drugs to give him the courage and confidence to commit his crimes, for without them, he does not believe he 'would have had the bottle', and Matt feels much the same.

Some of the Boys, of course, were rather more pragmatic about the drugs culture, given that they were not only users of illegal drugs but also suppliers. Both Ted and Nathan defended their drug-dealing activities on the grounds they were simply providing a service and were not engaged in dealing at the hard end. Ted got visibly irritated during the research interview when he was asked whether or not he ever had any ethical dilemmas about selling drugs, asserting 'I'm the nicest drug-dealer anyone would ever want to meet'.

When asked how they would 'handle' the burgeoning drugs culture, the Boys' responses were equally diverse. Mark would lock all drug-dealers up for life, while Matt would legalize *all* illegal substances 'to fuck up the dealers and make the government some money'. Whatever they felt should be done about the drugs culture, the Boys concurred that drug-use had become dramatically more pervasive since their own youth and was a major contributor to the further corrosion of communities, not least their own. The 'new wave' of substances was more life threatening (in their view) and its more widespread use was a significant cause of the escalation of crime and violence. Matt said that when he started dealing crack cocaine he had 'just the one competitor', but as time went on, the market got 'crowded', producing turf wars. He discussed at length the ever increasing sophistication in the supply and distribution of illegal drugs, particularly heroin and crack cocaine:

There's loads of people dealing it these days. You can get it over the road – almost anywhere. It's as simple as that. They're just pushing it out to the estates – the brown [smokeable heroin], the crack. They don't use it. They smoke good weed! The buzz is wanting it, not smoking it. And the dealers know this. Once you want it, you'll always find the money to get it.

Even those of the Boys who expressed a more libertarian position on illegal drug-use articulated deep concerns about the impact of the drugs culture on the next generation. For the most part they believed *they* had handled the temptations of illegal drugs surprisingly well, but they were by no means convinced their children would be able to do the same.

Conclusion

Health has impacted on the Boys' wider circumstances just as their wider circumstances have affected their health. Marty's schizophrenia has overwhelmed him, Vic's lung disease (contracted through many years of industrial painting) means he can never work again, while Spaceman's drug and alcohol addictions have cut him off from social networks and left him isolated and lonely. Trevor's football injury changed the direction of his occupational life, and Ryan's back injury incurred while working on the fiddle 'forced' him back into factory work. The collapse of Paul's relationships drove him deeper into alcoholism. Since the company for which Mark works was privatized, things have become a 'lot stricter' in terms of testing for drugs and alcohol, and he no longer dares take the risks he once did: 'I've got a fair job that most of the Boys would give their left arm for'.

Time is catching up with the Boys. Throughout their lives most have adopted a macho, devil-may-care public image (though their private personas are rather different). Ostentatious smoking, heavy drinking and experimental drug misuse characterized their public lifestyles from an early age, though some have tempered this in their later years as a result of the disciplines of work and the structure of family relationships, as well as the responsibilities for children. Others have persisted with such lifestyles. Few, however, have desisted from relatively significant health risk behaviours, even if quite a number have ceased to use illegal drugs and some are now currently strongly opposed to them. Heavy alcohol consumption still typifies their lives, at least during the weekends, for what the Boys routinely describe as 'moderate' is still usually well in excess of normative health guidelines. Equally, though a few have never smoked, the majority still smoke heavily and only one who started smoking regularly during his teenage years has quit smoking completely during adulthood.

Those of the Boys who are still routinely involved in illegal drug-use (primarily cannabis smoking and, to a lesser extent, amphetamine use) have generally 'managed' that use, so far, without ill effect, though a few of the Boys have spiralled downwards into both legal and illegal substance dependency. For others, alcohol and illegal drugs have, from time to time, filled the space when other structures in their daily life, notably personal relationships, have fallen apart. Yet, with the exception of Paul, these individuals have been able to extricate themselves from such circumstances, through complete abstinence after treatment or self-detoxification (in the case of Spaceman and Nick), or through finding new purpose and structure to their lives (in Denny's case). Their futures once more appear to be more promising.

Mental health problems, however, are more intransigent. Some of the Boys (such as Marty and Eddie) have protracted and entrenched psychiatric conditions, while others (such as Spaceman, Pete, Richard and Paul) have suffered episodes of depression which seem likely to reoccur in the future.

The Boys have passed the age of 40, and given the physical abuse they have inflicted upon themselves, most have 'shaped up' surprisingly well. This they would attribute to having also been engaged in health-promoting physical activity as young men, largely through sport and occupations demanding physical exertion. Indeed, many played active sports until well into their thirties, and some are (just about) still playing. However, the heavy manual work many have done throughout their adult lives is now producing belated health problems and the cessation of active sporting involvement is compounding both latent and more explicit physical problems, especially to do with breathing, which continued heavy smoking and drinking do not assist.

What is abundantly clear, however, is that few of the Boys now engage in the kinds of physical activity which may support their fitness and good health in future years. Moreover, few appear to be taking any action to counteract the potentially negative health consequences arising from the drinking, smoking and drug-taking lifestyles which have characterized their lives to date and in which many of them persist.

–12–

The Peer Group and Leisure Activities

Introduction

The Milltown Boys were *not* a 'gang'. Though they hung around together, it was in loose and overlapping constellations, as Jerry recalled:

> We were all close in a sense, but . . . there were just so many of us when you think about that you obviously spent more time with some of the Boys than with others. You know, you are talking about something like twenty people at any one given time could be hanging around and you were all sort of friends, like.

Even now, the Boys look back and identify particular 'clusters' of mates within the overall group: the 'hard cases' (Ted, Danny, Vic, Nathan), a group from 'up the top' (Trevor, Ryan, Mal, Tommy), or some of those who had mainly attended the Catholic school (Tony, Spaceman, Jamie, Kelvin, Gordon). Derek was also part of this latter group for a while, as were Marty and Nutter, for there was considerable fluidity in these affiliations; they changed over time and for many different reasons. Gary, who went to the comprehensive school, ended up with the 'Catholic' Boys, while Mack, though he went to the Catholic school, was always more closely linked to Paul, Richard and Colin. Jerry knocked around for a while with Marty and Alex. Mark and Pete were the 'Little and Large' of the juvenile court, committing a long sequence of offences together, and they too were very close to Jerry, especially Mark, whose father was close friends with Jerry's dad; indeed, Mark and Jerry sometimes referred to each other as cousins. Jerry got quite heavily involved in glue-sniffing, along with Ryan, Gary, Alex, Danny and Paul. Mark shared with Nutter, Gary, Spaceman and Tony a fanaticism for the local professional football team. Trevor enjoyed going for a curry on Saturday evenings with Jerry, Shaun and Denny. Matt had always been close friends with Mark and Nick, but later also became attached to Paul and Pete, while Eddie played football and went drinking with Trevor, Mal and Denny.

The Boys, as teenagers, were therefore linked together by multiple strands: shared schooling, offending preferences, active and spectator sporting interests, musical tastes, gambling and drinking activity, glue-sniffing, and favoured pubs and clubs. Later on in their teens, employment was significant in cementing or fragmenting relationships, both through working together and through movement in and out of work. Those who had jobs had money for drinking and gambling, and would be found in one pub or another or, on the weekends, in a night-club in town, while those who were unemployed were more often on the street or over the woods, even into early adulthood. There were, of course, other ways of 'raising' money apart from work, but leisure and peer group practices were increasingly defined around employment status, for the *guarantee* of the requisite resources strengthened the probability of participation in more formal social activities. Conversely, those out of work often joined in when they could, but made contingency plans in the event of not having the money. Such 'contingencies', for some of the long-term unemployed, prevail to the present day, as Gary observed:

> The ones with the giros can't afford to drink in the pub so what they're doing still is buying the cans, the cheap cider and whatever, and getting charged up on that – just hanging around on the street.

It was in such circumstances that one of the Boys was accidentally kicked to death in a 'friendly' fight – a few weeks before he was due to be interviewed for this research. Few of the Boys were particularly shocked when this occurred, for as Gary once more commented, 'that's all they've ever done . . . arguing and fighting one minute, saying how much they loves each other the next'.

Many of the Boys, then, moved over time between different subgroups, a process captured by Alex, who depicted it as comprising different 'eras' in his contact with the Boys:

> from the rec [recreation ground] with Nick and Paul and Richard to The Fountain with Mack and Danny . . . and then to The Wayfarer into a Marty, Ryan and Trevor sort of era . . . and then I moved out, with Marty, and we went up The Centurion with Gary and Tony and them . . . and then we all sort of split up. You move on, don't you. But I still goes to the club now and again and I sees Mark and Mal. But some of them I haven't seen for donkey's years.

Alex has now lost contact with most of the Boys from his teenage years, which is not surprising, as he always occupied a rather marginal position on the edge of a number of subgroups. The strands linking him to the Boys were numerous but thin, for he was never much of an offender and, apart from his quite intensive spell on the glue, rarely an integral part of any particular 'crowd'.

Some of the strands connecting individuals were, indeed, tenuous – both singular and fragile – such as contact between Shaun and Ted, whose paths rarely crossed, apart from their shared participation in playing cards for money. Other links between individuals were multifaceted and robust, the most pervasive, shared almost without exception across the Boys, being the adulation of David Bowie.

Marty bought absolutely everything he released, including foreign language imports, and together with Gary and Pete, went to see Bowie at Earls' Court in 1978, much to the chagrin of many of the other Boys.

By their early twenties, however, the Boys were in less frequent contact with each other, as the strands connecting them (such as expressive delinquency, or glue-sniffing) dissolved, or individuals became 'detached' as they settled into 'permanent' relationships and parenthood. Some relationships among the Boys nevertheless remained strong, and even those which diminished were sometimes subsequently renewed.

Indeed, what is striking is that most of the Boys have continued to have *some* contact with each other, even though it may now often be infrequent and unplanned. Few have completely severed their connections (the only exceptions are Shaun and Derek and, until very recently, Pete), though the strands which keep them 'together' are now sometimes very thin. Such weak links between some of the Boys are, however, mirrored by remarkably and perhaps unexpectedly strong bonds between others. For example, Tony remains unconditionally loyal to Spaceman, though he has ascended to the heights of 'middle-class' respectability, while Spaceman plummeted to the depths of crime and drug addiction. Similarly, Gary (who is now a successful self-employed painter and decorator) keeps an eye out for Marty, who suffers from paranoid schizophrenia, and Richard maintains close links with Paul, as he has always done since the days when he checked he was 'safely' sniffing glue in the woods.

The Boys' friendships and peer networks were forged on the anvil of shared local life and schooling experiences from early childhood. Eddie noted how important his 'old' friends had been throughout his life, especially during his episodes of mental illness, commenting on the strength of the bonds between them 'because we go back such a long way, I guess'. He captured some core qualities, emphasizing the Boys are people on whom you can rely, whom you can trust, who care and who will be supportive even in times of adversity. These are the characteristics which routinely inform the Boys' comments about their peers, though some are more sanguine about their authenticity than others. They had, after all, been 'together' since they were 'knee high to a grasshopper', as Kelvin put it.

Friends, Mates and Acquaintances

The 'Boys' need to be conceptualized, therefore, as a constellation of overlapping circles of friendship groups. On the edge of more distant 'circles' were individuals who, to some, were little more than acquaintances, those whom you might chat to in the street or share a drink with, but with whom more active social pursuits were unlikely to take place. At the heart of each circle were cast-iron pairings of 'best *friends*' around whom other close *mates* were clustered.

Tony and Spaceman epitomized such a pair, despite going their very different ways in their adult lives. They met when they were 5. Spaceman recalls that when he reached the depths of his addictions many of the Boys abandoned him, crossing the road to avoid him, but Tony stayed loyal to him to the last, although geographical distance meant they saw each other only irregularly:

> I was probably the most loyal to Spaceman for the longest time because we had grown up together. Obviously I had gone away from Milltown but I always had a huge amount of time for Spaceman. I love Spaceman and it's great to see that he's doing well.

Jerry and Mark have a similar friendship, established through the close relationship between their fathers. Mark recalled the day his father died and when his brother committed suicide through drinking weedkiller, 'the only person I wanted to see was Jerry, we've always been close like that'. Eddie's best friend is Regan (who was not interviewed): 'yeah he's been a really good friend over the years, I've always been able to talk to him about anything'. Nick and Matt, Richard and Paul, Danny and Ted, Ryan and Trevor, Gary and Marty, and Tommy and Mal all have similar relationships. It is not stretching the point to assert they represent the kind of 'best friends' who confide their deepest thoughts and anxieties to each other, something they would be reluctant to do with any of their other 'mates'.

The Boys proclaimed to have 'loads of mates' but few real friends, and though the distinction may be hard to fathom, Matt endeavoured to capture the essence of friendship as he understood it:

> My friends are the ones who I know will always be there. Like with Nick I knows I don't have to ask him for anything. I'd just get it from him if I needed it. He'd feel the same.
>
> Others? I couldn't call them friends. I just call them mates. I've got loads of mates but only a couple of friends. I call a friend someone who can come knocking on your door.

Nick returned the compliment:

> There's a big difference for me between friends and mates. You only ever get very few friends, you can count them on one hand usually throughout your life. Mates can be a lot of people. If you need to socialize with them, then you would. But they wouldn't come round here. Whereas with Matt, if he's got something to say, he comes round here. We talk about everything together. We tell it how it is. I'm probably one of the few people that can actually tell Matt things to his face without him getting upset or wanting to punch your fucking head in. He might want to punch my head in but he never ever shows it. Matt is probably my closest soul mate, apart from Karen [Nick's wife].

The key defining characteristics of friends are therefore acceptance in the home and a willingness to give and take home truths about each other. It is an unconditional acceptance. Richard observed he hadn't really got any 'close, close friends' apart from Paul, and though he readily acknowledged Paul's faults, 'that doesn't change the way I think about him . . . I don't think anything bad of him, he's a friend'. Beyond acceptance and the exchange of home truths was the belief that help from friends, if needed, was *guaranteed*. Ted noted he could ask Danny to do anything for him, and 'if he had a problem I could help him with, then I would'. Nathan made a similar observation:

> I've got a lot of mates but there's only two important friends. They've always been there, since we were kids. If I've got a problem they would help me out. The same would happen if one of them was in trouble, I'd be there for them.

Mal had a broader conception of 'friendship', extending it to many of the Boys on the basis of their long association with each other. Not only would they help you out but also there was no scope for 'bullshit' precisely because they had known each other all their lives. For Mal, there was an *authenticity* in such relationships which did not prevail with those he had become acquainted with more recently:

> A lot of people give you bullshit. But with the Boys, they don't. They can't. Because we are all on the same wavelength, we've all been through a lot of the same things together. I've got a mate round the corner here, he's from London. He thinks he's my friend but he's not, he's a fucking acquaintance. He could never be a friend, like the Boys. I think he's narked that we stick so closely together. But that's what it means to be one of the Boys. I mean, I haven't really spoken to Danny for years, I can't remember the last time I spoke to him. But I know he'd help me if he could, if I went to see him.

Danny is renowned for his loyalty to the Boys and his generosity of spirit when it is required, and Vic, too, mentioned him when he was discussing 'friends and mates':

> The Boys have kept in touch all these years. I see a lot of them in the pub and we chat. But they are just sort of around. I wouldn't go out of my way to see them. That's the difference I suppose. I mean, Danny has been good to me over the years, same as Ted, when I needed them. That's what it is about really. You make them kind of friends only once in your life. You do things together when you are younger and so, when you are older, you know everything about each other. But with the other Boys you're not so sure. They are like a wider circle. They're mates really, but a mate is different from a friend.

Whether 'friends' or 'mates', however, the Boys have a deep sense of collective identity which derives from their common upbringing. It can accommodate immense diversity, so long as there is no betrayal or denial of those roots, which took Pete by surprise when he returned after nearly twenty years, but which Tony discovered only when it was too late. As a teenager, Pete believed his closet homosexuality had been a barrier to establishing deep friendships among the Boys, despite his relatively close association with Mark and Matt, and therefore his account of 'coming home' is both poignant and illuminating:

> I didn't realize that I had any friends until I came back. But there's all the Boys in Milltown – I'm not such an embarrassment after all! I'd missed them desperately for all those years. I cared about them but I never thought they cared for me. Because I always loved Matt, I love Jerry, I love Mark. They were brothers, they were friends. But I never really understood it at the time. When I left Milltown I just had to get away because it was such a homophobic place. I just didn't realize that the Boys could be so loyal to their mates. Really it was the cowardly thing to do to leave. But at the time I thought it would be too hard, even if I'd known my mates would stick by me. There was plenty to build on, but I thought it would be too difficult. And only now I've realized that I can come back and be accepted by the Boys even if they still hate queers generally.

Indeed, many of the Boys now express deep regret that Pete felt he *needed* to leave, for whatever his sexual orientation, he was one of 'their own' and, when he returned, Pete acknowledged this to the full. Thus he complied with the Boys' precondition for continued acceptance: as Spaceman put it, 'you can take the man out of Milltown but you can never take Milltown out of the man'. In striking contrast, Tony moved away and very explicitly set himself apart, which he now recalls with considerable regret:

> Yeah friendship means a lot to me. But there was a time where through my own behaviour I lost a lot of friends in Milltown, I mean the Boys. Basically I think I know why – now. We had moved away from home and, as I can remember it, I became a bit of a twat because I wanted them to think I was doing really well. In fact it was really tough for us, for a while at least. But on those occasions when I saw the Boys I think I became a bit of a snob. I used to pretend everything was great and that things were fantastic – that we were doing really well. I think I must have come over as a right pain in the arse and I think I alienated a lot of the Boys, definitely. I can understand that now. I can see why the Boys didn't like it. It was like I behaved as if I'd never come from Milltown.
>
> And I can remember, when I was a kid, we had a neighbour who had gone away and she came back in the same way I did later. You didn't have a conversation with her. It was just an opportunity for her to boast how well she'd done once she'd got out of Milltown. And it just puts you off. I think I fell into the same trap, to be honest. I was a victim of circumstances!

Once he moved away, Tony maintained contact only with Jamie, and to a lesser extent with Spaceman, though he has recently renewed contact with some of the other Catholic Boys who were his close friends during his teenage years. In The Fountain, however, where the 'criminal' Boys hang out, and in the working men's club, where Mark, Tommy, Mal and Denny tend to drink, Tony is talked about disparagingly as someone who tried to rise above his station (which, indeed, he did – very successfully). In itself, this is not a problem, for both Gary and Trevor have also done well for themselves, yet they are not subjected to the same vitriol; Tony's problem was that he tried, for a while at least, to deny where he had come from.

Although the Boys make great play of their shared history and mutual loyalty, there is also some recognition that the 'pull' of the Boys can be detrimental and destructive. Gary described the Boys who frequent The Fountain as 'a bunch of wasters . . . I know they are old mates but I tend to keep away from all that now'. Without the counterweight of domestic responsibilities (relationships and children), it was all too easy to end up back down the pub every lunchtime, as Richard recognized when his marriage broke up:

> I didn't want to get too mixed up again with that crowd because I was aware of what they're doing and where they're going. I did start going down the pub a lot at first, but I had this feeling that if I stayed with the crowd, then eventually I am going to end up like that without even realizing it. It would just happen.

There was a delicate balancing act to be effected between staying connected to the wider networks of the Boys and being sucked back into 'life on the street', which was still how about a third of the Boys were living. Richard commented that he knew Paul was envious of him because 'I made the break a long time ago' (when he trained as a bricklayer), for Paul himself has never really made the break, and when his relationships collapsed, saw no alternative but to re-engage completely with the Boys in the pub:

> My friends are all down there. I know everyone down there. Most of them I grew up with. It's like the same as it always was. It's the same people that used to hang about up the rec [recreation ground] all those years ago.

Despite the loosening and some fragmentation of bonds forged 'all those years ago', many of the Boys have made virtually no new friends (or mates) during their adult lives and remain closely and deeply attached to a small group with whom they became friends in childhood. Ryan ran through his current social network, noting 'yeah, it's all the old ones, the Boys are still the same now as they have always been', while Mal observed he had mainly 'all the same mates as I had before'. Only those who have permanently moved away from Milltown have, necessarily, established new networks of friends, while the rest have, by and large, stuck with (different) members of their teenage peer group, though this has been vulnerable to both active and passive attrition, as the strands linking the Boys together in different ways have become thinner (see Figure 1.1).

Gordon, once again, is the exception to both rules, combining – as he has done in all aspects of his life – the potential and reflection of a good education with the wisdom and opportunism acquired on the streets of Milltown. He has never 'abandoned' the Boys, who remain of great significance to him, but he has also established other groups of friends more in keeping with his intellectual and affluent lifestyle:

> I've got a broad spectrum of friends, more than enough. I don't want or need any more. I've got friends from work, friends from past work, friends in America, and I've got the Boys. I've got a lot of women friends. So I've got a broad spectrum of friends that covers all my needs and I just don't need any more friends.

The diversity of Gordon's life experience has produced this diversity of friendship networks, for he has consolidated old ones while simultaneously building new ones to the point, according to him, of 'saturation'. This contrasts starkly with the more restricted circle of friends maintained by most of the Boys, drawn primarily from within the orbit of 'mates' established during their childhood and adolescence. Where the life course has offered little change – geographically, occupationally, domestically and socially – it is perhaps hardly surprising there has been little incentive or opportunity to discover or forge new affiliations. Old friends and mates cement the daily round of routine and continuity, while the making of new ones is rarely considered, for the chance to do so does not arise and it is deemed to be 'unnecessary'.

They 'Went Missing'

The Boys do look back on 'the Boys' of their youth with great nostalgia and recount with regret the *dilution* of those networks, though never their complete disappearance. Marriage and children took their toll on the Boys: one by one, they 'went missing', as Jamie describes in some detail:

> I don't think I've changed that much. When I was courting and when I got married I still went to the pub and saw the Boys. But a lot of them got married and then you never seen them for years. We used to go up the pub and one by one the 'gang' was dwindling. It got to the point where there was no one left and I used to go in the lounge and have a pint with my dad instead. Gary might drop in for one, but once he was courting seriously nobody seen him for . . . well for a long, long time.
>
> They went missing and it just wasn't the same, although some would come out for a pint, like every four weeks or maybe more. I think you've always got to have your

friends. They are your roots. You can't just be a married man with kids and your wife and that. You've still got to be able to have your mates, be able to go back and talk about old times and that. You have got to have a little time away from family.

Kelvin, who had been one of the first to 'go missing', did not agree: 'when I got married my commitment was to my wife, not to my mates. We were round 23 and we were starting to go our separate ways'. Some of the Boys, like Kelvin, did retreat into family life, though many, like Jamie, tried to reconcile their family commitments with a continuing social life with the Boys. Those frequenting the working men's club epitomized this challenge, for, though often accompanied by their wives, they 'disappeared' to spend time with the Boys. Their wives played bingo while they watched football (in the 'men-only' room) or played skittles; though they proclaimed they put their families first, they still made plenty of time to be alone with their mates.

At the other end of the spectrum from Kelvin were those who never 'went missing'. The Fountain Boys were routinely criticized by the other Boys for never having got their 'priorities' right, for they were considered to have abdicated their responsibilities to their partners and families, as Trevor remarked:

> I have been in there sometimes and I've seen them hanging, from the drink and the drugs. And their missus could walk in and say 'get out of here' and they'd probably get 'fucking stupid cow' and all that.

Jerry also felt the Boys who frequented The Fountain had failed to grow up:

> I mean, I am still me but when you have got a family your priorities change. Your mates are always going to come second whereas before your mates were your family, so to speak. I mean some of those Boys [from The Fountain] do have families but they're a bit like Peter Pan, they've never grown up. Their way of life has never changed.

Matt was more measured in his view of the Fountain Boys, saying things were 'mixed up deep', and acknowledging they put their mates before their family which, in his view, was 'fucking stupid'. On the other hand, however, he suggested the Boys' network based around The Fountain was akin to a family, and the Fountain Boys themselves would certainly corroborate this contention. Indeed, Danny actually described them as 'like family' – their source of unconditional acceptance and support.

The domestic circumstances of the Fountain Boys – for those who had them – were certainly more distant, and their primary loyalty and commitment was to each other. Even those of the Boys who were often critical of the lifestyles and priorities of the Fountain Boys conceded this essential quality. Trevor, for example, having condemned them for their *selfishness*, went on to compliment their *selflessness*: 'They look after one another, they look after themselves, they are proud to be in Milltown, they love the place. And I love them for that'.

There is plenty of evidence of that selflessness and mutual self-help, even though it is supported largely through illegal enterprise. When the Fountain Boys have the resources (and, at any particular time, some usually do, though others may be 'skint'), they take pride in their generosity of spirit, ranging from buying rounds of drinks to more practical support for those 'in need'. For example, when Denny's first marriage failed, one of the Fountain Boys immediately found him a place to stay: 'The Boys are always there if you need them, they've always been there'. Similarly, when Mack and his son Stuart need to attend the pool tournaments in which Stuart excels, the Fountain Boys routinely have a whip-round to ensure they have enough for decent accommodation, meals and incidental spending money.

Women and work (the 'two Ws', as Trevor called them) may have contributed to the separation and fragmentation of the Boys' wider peer group, though rarely have these completely severed their connections. Gary and Marty (like Tony and Spaceman) now could not be more socially, domestically and economically polarized, for Gary is a gregarious man with a successful business, his own home, a stable relationship and two young children, while Marty suffers from schizophrenia, lives alone in a run-down flat and rarely sees any of the Boys. Gary provides Marty with emotional, practical and sometimes financial help, which Marty is in no position to reciprocate, but their bond of friendship appears to be unbreakable, which both acknowledge. As Marty observed:

I don't see many of the Boys any more. I sees Gary. He pops in here. He is a very, very good friend of mine. He has been superb, honestly. He took me to the hospital the other day. Apart from him, I'm really isolated. I'm desperately lonely.

Gary values his old friends enormously, especially Marty, to whom he continues to extend unconditional support:

He's not easy at all. Sometimes I do wonder why I've stuck by him. I don't know why. I think you've just got to accept people the way they are. I've known Marty all my life, I grew up with the guy ... When his head was together he was brilliant company. I really enjoyed having him as a friend. I won't have a bad word said about him. The Boys in the pub say his marbles have gone. I've said no, the guy is ill.

I didn't know any schizophrenics until Marty and I didn't know nothing about it. But since Marty have had it I've tried to read about it, in the magazines. I know a little bit, I don't know a great deal, but it goes back to this thing about friends. I love them all, I really love them all. That's why I look after Marty. I want to. I don't mind. I goes round to see him. I could be the only friend he's got left.

During their teenage years and often into their early twenties, the Boys' networks clustered in a myriad of ways. As they established adult relationships and families, however, and as their occupational trajectories took shape (within both the legitimate and less legitimate labour markets), different priorities took hold, though some of the Boys clung on to the peer groups of their youth. Others also continued to see their old mates, though more through chance encounters on account of still living nearby. Those who lived further afield inevitably had less contact, though (with the exception of Derek, Pete and Shaun), even they retained some level of contact with their closest friends from their teenage years.

The maintenance of this loose-knit peer network (within which there were some more solid sub-affiliations) has varied considerably among the Boys. The strong and overlapping connections forged during adolescence have, predictably, diminished, so the strands which once linked them are fewer today (see Figure 1.1). Nonetheless, though a few of the Boys have become 'disconnected', the resilience of these links is striking and occasionally surprising. Loyalties forged in childhood have often persisted despite the very different adult pathways of the individuals concerned. Beyond such personal loyalties, however, it is possible to project a crude map of the peer group affiliations which have been sustained. These are based on the extent to which 'the Boys' still 'come first' through to those who – for reasons of family, geography, health or something else – now have different priorities in their lives (Table 12.1).

Table 12.1 The Differential Maintenance of Contact with their Teenage Peer Group

Structured links		Casual links					Cut off	
The Fountain		*The club*					*Family/geography/health*	
Danny	[Ted]	Denny					(Spaceman)	
Paul	Richard	Mark	Gary	Jerry			Marty	
Mack		Tommy	Matt	Nick	[Tony]		Nutter	
Nathan		Mal	Ryan	Kelvin		(Alex)		
Colin			(Jamie)	Trevor			**(Shaun)**	
Vic			(Gordon)				**(Derek)**	
							Eddie	
							[**Pete**]	

[ ] = Live outside city; ( ) = live outside Milltown
bold = Completely cut-off (though Pete returned to Milltown in November 2000)

Despite their criticisms of each other, there is an unequivocally profound sense of loyalty among the Boys. Their deepest commitment remains to a close circle of friends, though there are still threads of obligation to a wider group of mates, based on the longevity of their relationships. There is a sustained sense of solidarity among the Boys even though, not surprisingly, a variety of domestic, personal, occupational and geographical circumstances have fractured the deeper relationships which prevailed during their teenage years.

The Boys go back a long way, often to early childhood, and they have shared many different experiences. As a result, the pulls and ties of Milltown are powerful, even between those of the Boys who have *never* really had a great deal of contact with each other, certainly not 'friendship'. This cultural legacy, which defines the peer group solidarity of the Milltown Boys against the 'other', was fluently captured by Gordon when he described an encounter with one of the Fountain Boys while he was working on security in a night-club in the city:

It had a profound effect on me. Patrick Wilkie was in town with some other boys I didn't know. I said to one of them, are you with Pat? And Pat said, oh they are just some friends, they are not us, but they are friends. And he had had a drink, and I was sober of course, because I was working and I said, what do you mean 'us'? Because, as you know, Pat is somebody who takes pride in his depth of shallowness! And he says, well us, you know, he's not one of us, he's not, you know, us. And I thought I knew what he meant, but I just wanted to make sure that I was, you know, getting what he was trying to say. So I said to him again, what do you mean? And he said, Gordon, they are my friends but they are not one of us, you know.

And he went on, you know, I used to smack you when you were a kid – because he lived two doors down from me – and your brother used to hit me on the school bus. My older brother used to hit him on the school bus, and I used to hang out with his younger brother . . . and, you know, he said, you know, us. And then it was like, yeah, I know what you mean, and he just verified exactly what I thought he meant. I was a bit surprised, because I didn't think he was one of those who would have those emotions.

But he did have those emotions. It was just, exactly, he's not one of us. Their lives had not been meshed together, linked together through family, school, friends, events, history, the whole nine yards. And it was just, like, damn, yeah, I know what he means. It was so true, and it was so important. It was about a feeling of belonging, a feeling of belonging because, from being kids, we'd known each other. And you know, I look now, and it's great when I go to The Wheatsheaf or The Centurion, and there is Gary and his brother, and everybody is there.

And I've taken friends, you know, that are from outside, and I have sat down and it's like, I say to my friends, you'll not believe that in this room I know most of these people, and I've known them since I was 6 years old. And that is so important. Especially when I think of America, where it's so transient, it's just people passing through. Whereas in Milltown I'm sitting in a bar and 70 per cent of them I've known since I was 6 years old. It's amazing. That was one of the reasons, especially up The Centurion, one of the reasons why I left to do what I did, and it's one of the reasons why I still go up there and feel great when I do. You know, it made me leave and I suppose in a way it made me come back. It wasn't suffocating, but I can remember thinking when I was young, I don't mind being here in fifty years' time, you know, but I want to do things in between, so that when somebody comes up to me and says ... Because when I was working in that pub, I can always remember these two guys being there forever. And somebody once said to them, what have you done in your life, and they said, oh we had a great party once and, you know, there was this wedding we went to and that was fun, and I thought no, I don't want to end up like that. And this is honest to God, I thought that when somebody asks me that, because I knew I'd end up back here, and it was like when somebody asks me well what have you done, then, you know, I've done this.

But Pat was right. There's us, the Boys, and there's everybody else.

Unlike Gordon, however, many of the Boys have never forged new peer relationships as adults. They have, as a result, clung on to their 'roots' either actively or by default – connecting time and again, or from time to time, to the Boys whenever the chance has arisen, in the pubs and clubs, through sport, at birthday parties, weddings and festive celebrations. This interpretation alone, however, would be insulting to them, for the Boys would celebrate the fact that their formative years shaped their world, entangling them in this complex spider's web of long-standing relationships and experiences. Rarely has this web been dismantled completely and the renewal of some of those connections as they have reached the age of 40 is a testament to the persisting bonds among the Boys, irrespective of the differential courses their lives have taken.

Social Life

As Denny observed, 'life is not a dress rehearsal, you are only here once, enjoy it', and whatever adversities the Boys may have experienced, they have always been adept at getting the most out of life. Their use of leisure time encapsulates both strong continuities and significant change. Sport, for example, though always a central feature of their leisure time, has shifted in recent years from active participation to passive consumption, as the Boys have given up physical exertion in favour of sitting in front of the TV. Only Eddie and Vic continue to play in (football and rugby) teams, which is quite remarkable in view of their respective mental and physical ill-health. Jamie and Trevor, both very talented footballers in their younger days, had their playing careers curtailed by injury but remain involved through supporting their sons' teams. Spaceman has occupied his leisure time since dealing with his addictions by working voluntarily in schools, assisting with the teaching of art, while Gary links together a family camping trip and a camping holiday for 'underprivileged' kids.

These are but examples of the burgeoning diversity of the Boys' leisure. Sport in some form may remain paramount, but four of the Boys mentioned reading books as one of their main hobbies. Music, surprisingly, now has a low profile, despite its pivotal place in their lives when they were teenagers, though two of the

Boys (Derek and Richard) play the guitar, while two more (Danny and Nutter) maintain an active interest in the music of their teens.

Much of the Boys' social life continues to revolve around local social space and the activities to hand in the pubs and clubs they frequent, such as skittles, darts, snooker and pool, which are commonplace interests. However, the Boys have also lived through a time which heralded the increasing availability of cheap package holidays abroad and a number have taken advantage, some reluctantly at first, of such possibilities, though, in contrast, others have remained attached to working-class holiday traditions of day trips to the seaside or a week or two in a holiday camp.

Golf has become surprising popular, though it carries very different meanings for those who participate in it. For a number of the Fountain Boys who make a living 'on the street', it fills the day – a crowd of them take a trip to the local municipal golf course, whereas for Tony, it is closely linked to business relationships and corporate hospitality. Indeed, he doesn't like it very much, but it is something that has to be done.

Rugby, inevitably, assumes a prominence given its position as the national sport of Wales, and it certainly would not command the same position among a similar group of men in England. Many of the Boys not only watch, with a passionate nationalism, the 'internationals' on TV (usually in the pub), but also make a weekend tour to the match if it is in England, Ireland or Scotland (they are less interested in going to Italy or France).

While some of the Boys' leisure and social activities are clearly detached from their families, others fully involve them, which reflects the differential relationships the Boys have to their families and to their mates. Some, indeed, like Vic, provide the material support for family holidays but do not actually go on them!

When asked about their leisure and social activities, the Boys invariably started talking about the things they used to do, with recurrent references to sport. At least half a dozen (Denny, Derek, Jamie, Eddie, Trevor and Mal) played regular football for local league teams, while many more joined in a casual kick-around every Sunday afternoon. Ted, Danny and Vic played rugby for proper teams, as did Nathan until the team at The Fountain folded.

Nowadays, however, for most of the Boys 'it's mainly on the telly', though it is not just age, injury and loss of fitness which has contributed to the decline in their physical activity. In Shaun's case, his family responsibilities took precedence, while for Nathan, Eddie and Nick, who used to play competitive darts, it was the fact 'there are not so many teams around now, darts is dying off'. Mark used to play competitive skittles and cards, but shift work and the death of his brother, who was his partner in cards, put an end to that. Alex was once 'fishing mad' and used to go out on the boats every week, but family activities and watching his beloved Arsenal have now taken over. Thus, over the years, both personal preferences and circumstances, and extraneous influences and developments have altered the

Table 12.2 Leisure and Social Life – A Summary of Current Activities

	Sports		Pubs/clubs	Holidays	Other
	Active	*Spectator*			
Ted	Golf	Football/rugby			Computer golf/ cards/gambling
Danny	Golf		The pub		Music
Spaceman		Football			'Teaching'
Marty					Drinking (home)
Gary		Football	The pub	Camping/ abroad	Eating out
Matt	Table tennis				
Paul			The pub		
Richard			[The pub]		Guitar/rabbiting
Denny	Golf		The club/skittles		
Ryan	Mountain biking/ canoeing/fishing				DIY
Tony	Golf	Football		Abroad	Dinner parties/ radio
Alex	Fishing	Football	The club/ skittles	Camping	
Mack	Snooker/pool		The pub		
Mark		Horse racing	The club	Butlins/abroad	Gambling
Jerry		Football/ rugby	[The club]	Abroad	Reading
Nathan	Snooker	Football/rugby	The pub		
Shaun		Football/other			Walking/family
Derek		Football		Butlins	Guitar
Colin	Darts/pool		The pub		Bowling/ gambling
Jamie	Cricket	Football			Skittles
Gordon	Weights				Wine club/ reading
Eddie	Football	Football			
Nick	Table tennis/ snooker	Rugby		Abroad	Swimming
Kelvin	Snooker			Abroad	Photography/ clubbing
Trevor		Rugby		[Family]	Coaching football
Tommy	Snooker		The club/ skittles		Cards/ budgies
Mal		Football	The club/ skittles	Abroad	Gardening
Pete					Dope/reading
Vic	Rugby	Rugby	The pub	Butlins	
Nutter		[no TV]	Any pub!		Birdwatching/ reading/ gambling/music

patterns of the Boys' use of their leisure time, culminating in the activities in which they now engage (Table 12.2).

Sport continues to dominate the Boys' social lives, though only Eddie and Vic remain active team players. Golf has become very popular among the Fountain Boys, but Tony and Denny also play regularly. Matt and Nick often still play table tennis together at the local leisure centre, while Gordon and Richard still 'work out'.

Surprisingly, however, Ryan is the only one who regularly makes use of the countryside which was so significant in the Boys' youth, when, 'over the woods', they spent their time rabbiting, collecting birds' eggs, climbing trees, lighting fires, or just hanging around, and for many during their mid-teens, sniffing glue. Ryan goes mountain biking and fishing, or just walks the dog:

> I know a lot of the Boys spend their time in the pub but I couldn't do that. I'm stuck indoors all day at work. No, give me bright light, sunny days and I'll be there every time. That's why I like Milltown. You can get into the country in no time at all. I'll be gone for four, five hours – just me and the dog.

Football remains, however, the key focal point of the Boys' leisure. In their teenage years, many were part of a 'crew' who supported their local football league team, home and away, though they never paid to attend the home games, for they knew a way of getting in free by going 'over the wall'. Spaceman, Gary and Jamie are still regulars 'down the City'.

The Boys may not play much any more, but Tony has access to corporate hospitality tickets at Anfield (Liverpool) and Mal would not dream of missing a televised Manchester United game and goes to their ground at Old Trafford 'a lot', while Alex has followed Arsenal since he was a child, and being self-employed can take days off to travel to London for midweek matches 'quite a few times a year'. He rarely misses a 'live' match on Sky TV: 'it takes up a lot of time, especially when there are championships all the bloody time these days'.

Beyond watching professional football live or on the TV, many of the Boys go to watch their sons playing for school or weekend teams, like Jamie, who gave up playing only a few years ago and whose weekends are now organized around the pub and his son's matches:

> I'm football mad. I played parks football for twenty years. I take my boy Jack down the City and I take him to football; he plays for a local team on Saturday mornings. And in the summer I play cricket with my football team. See my football team have got a cricket team, if you know what I mean. And I teaches Jack how to play football. He has never seen me play and, even if I must say it myself, I was a good footballer, very good. Really good when I was 16, 17. I should have went for a higher standard. And – don't laugh – well I play skittles as well for the football team. I plays in the winter league. The football club's got a mid-week skittles team.

The Boys' varied approaches to holidays divide into two groups, with some continuing to follow traditional working-class patterns of day trips, holiday camps and camping, while others, with the expansion of cheap package holidays in the sun, have increasingly taken their holidays abroad. Moreover, some of the Boys seek to have family holidays, whereas others take their breaks alone or with their partners (without the children).

Alex is 'not fussed on abroad', though his wife Honora would like to try a foreign holiday, but until now they have tended to go camping in Cornwall. Mal was at first resistant to going abroad, largely because of his fear of flying, but his wife Jane eventually persuaded him, and now they go to Turkey or Spain every year. Mark went to Benidorm one year, but hated the heat, and he and his family have now reverted to an annual holiday at Butlins, or somewhere similar. Tommy has also usually gone to Butlins 'with all of Suzanne's family', though unlike Mal and Alex, he would like to go abroad, but Suzanne is scared of flying. He is, however, determined to do so in the future, particularly as he feels Butlins 'is crap there now' and the kids have grown up, and he wants some 'guaranteed sunshine'.

Holiday camps like Butlins clearly have their place but they also have their time. They served some of the Boys well when the kids were younger, with the plethora of facilities and activities available on site, but as the kids have got older, their appeal has diminished. Furthermore, the guaranteed sunshine in a package holiday has become more of a financial possibility, which has sharpened awareness of the decaying drabness of holiday camp life, particularly when contrasted with the more attractive alternatives available. Derek used to go to Butlins:

> I would never go back to a dump like that again . . . we only went there for the kids, but it is such a rip-off these days. My mother's got the better idea – go abroad. She's taking my daughter to Kos this year.

Indeed, holidays are not always taken as a family 'unit', and even though Vic said 'we've always had an annual family holiday', it turned out that the kids and his wife Lisa went ('oh, all over the place, Butlins, all them holiday places'), while Vic spent a couple of weeks in The Fountain! Kelvin, likewise, admitted that 'we don't really do a great deal as a family', recounting foreign holidays with his wife Julie (her fortieth birthday in Ibiza, his in Portugal) when they left the kids at home. Their older son had a skiing holiday in France and there had been a footballing holiday for his other son in Ireland, while his daughter had a trip to Disneyland Paris. They have, admittedly, had a few camping trips as a family, but more often than not their holidays have been taken separately.

For many years Nick and Karen, who have no children, took no holidays or just local trips, until, in 1994, he got the 'holiday bug', since when, even if work has been thin, they have always put 'holiday money' aside to ensure they will spend a fortnight in Turkey. Nick fell in love with Turkey, and has never been anywhere else, for he equates the spirit and camaraderie he discovered among the Turks with the solidarity of the Boys in Milltown. They had first gone to Turkey quite by chance, for neither had ever been abroad until Karen's friend won a holiday to Lanzarote, and rather reluctantly Karen went with her, telling Nick when she returned she hadn't really enjoyed it, though Nick recalls 'she never shut up about it':

> and I started to think I should have a look too. It was basic curiosity. Turkey was just a pin on a map. Well not completely. First we couldn't afford to go anywhere. I couldn't go to Australia because of my criminal record. America has never interested me; I'd prefer to see some of Canada. I'd never been that interested in Spain. Anyway, we ended up going to Turkey and we had the time of our lives. It was only two weeks but I never wanted to come home. I felt I could live there forever.
>
> It's like home from home. The people there are as close as Milltown people. Some wide boys, of course, which is part of every society in the world. But they made us feel so welcome.

Unlike Nick, who has his heart set on spending time *only* in Turkey whenever he can, Jerry is keen to explore different parts of the world and venture well beyond typical package holiday destinations. Of all the Boys (with the exception of Gordon, who has done it rather differently), Jerry has travelled most widely, having got the taste for travel as a young soldier on tours of Germany and Northern Ireland. Since then, he and his family have tried to have at least one foreign holiday a year – 'a big holiday every three or four years and then a bit more routine, if we can'. Last year they went to Majorca, Greece and Turkey, and in previous years have been to South Africa and America, while next year they are hoping to go to India. This year they have been to Benidorm, and Jerry has also been 'to Ireland for the rugby'.

The different approaches taken by the Boys to their 'holidays' captures much of their wider orientation to their leisure, in terms of whether it is integrated with, or isolated from their family life, and, correspondingly, integrated with or isolated from the Boys. Even though many continue to find their 'personal space' in social activities with the Boys, their leisure is also framed and constrained by family pressures and expectations, which may sometimes be resisted but is largely accepted, even desired. Mal has 'always spent a lot of time with the kids', and though he is certainly not cut off from the Boys, he knows quite clearly where his priorities lie. More 'privatized' leisure time is spent not just with their immediate family, but also with the Boys' extended families – sometimes on holidays, but also in a more mundane social round of birthdays, weddings, parties and other family celebrations, a scenario captured by Trevor:

A lot of my time is with the family. We do a lot of things together. Not just with my kids but with their cousins. It's a close family. This weekend it's my sister's party, her birthday. And one of my *cousins* is 40 soon, so another party. We stick together as a family, on my father's side and on my mother's side and on my wife's side. So all my social events are really, since I have got married, family things. If it's a nice Sunday, we all go down the beach. Thirty or forty of us – have a game of baseball and a barbecue. Twenty-seven of us went on holiday together last year and the year before it was about thirty-two of us went. It was Ibiza the first year and then last year we went to Majorca. Honestly, you wouldn't believe it. Rent-a-crowd! We just enjoy life.

With this strong commitment to family-oriented leisure, Trevor is certainly on one extreme of the spectrum, for others juggle family and friends more expeditiously, in view of the competing attractions of spending time with the Boys. Gary, who tends to work extremely long hours, divides his precious leisure time between his 'own time' in the pub (*not* The Fountain) with some of the Boys, and a desire for 'good quality' family life:

For me it's basically up The Roundhead or down the City with the Boys and then hope-fully quality time with the kids when I am home. That's it. It sounds pretty boring and I guess it is. But we do try to have a family holiday. Camping with the kids. Simone's been to Spain this year, but that was with her mother. We had a caravan in Tenby last year as a family. When work goes a bit quiet – and it's a hundred miles an hour at the moment – then it's prime time to have a family holiday.

Even though Mack, who has not had a job since his early twenties, spends every lunchtime in The Fountain with the Boys, he dedicates much of his 'leisure' to his children, leaving the pub, without fail, in good time to meet his two children from school and 'take them out every tea time for a game of snooker and pool'.

Four of the Boys specifically mentioned reading as one of their leisure pursuits, though their reading material could not be more different. Gordon is an avid con-sumer of novels, his favourite book of all time being *Love in the Time of Cholera*, whereas Jerry favours 'true stories' of adventure and derring-do. Pete gets through 'a lot of biographies and some historical stuff', while Nutter, who does not possess a TV, consumes books closely connected to his neo-Nazi leanings: 'horror mainly, and military things . . . like all that stuff from the Second World War about Panzers and the Nazis and that'. Spaceman has also read, spasmodically, throughout his life, starting in his youth with Camus and Sartre, though now he reads less, mainly semi-autobiographical accounts of sport and music, preferring to concentrate on his drawing and painting. His old schoolfriend Tony is self-critical about the fact he does *not* read, though he was at pains to stress that some of his leisure time is spent keeping up with current affairs: 'I'm a bit of a philistine really but I do read the newspapers on the weekend and I listen to Radio 4 a lot'.

The Boys are surprisingly quiet about the place of music in their lives today, given that it occupied such a central position in their youth. Danny, however, remains a specialist in trivia, especially concerning The Beatles and Bowie, while Nutter remains preoccupied with the punk and neo-Nazi 'blood and honour' music of the late 1970s and early 1980s. Only Derek and Richard are musicians, both playing the guitar (though 'nothing serious'), and Richard is also a mean harmonica player, specializing in the genre of 'freight train' blues and occasionally giving a spontaneous rendition at functions held in the social club.

The leisure activities of the Milltown Boys have diversified so much that they now encapsulate both the traditional pastimes of the working class and the routine social habits of the middle class. Gordon, for example, is a member of a wine club, and Tony spends a lot of time at dinner parties. In contrast, others go fishing and rabbiting and many enjoy card games for money. Many of them play pool and snooker, and half a dozen play regular skittles for, or at, the working men's club. Tommy keeps budgies, and apart from enjoying a round of real golf, Ted enjoys computer golf: 'I play golf on the computer and so I have a once a week regular on Tiger Woods!'

Small-change card games were the Boys' introduction to gambling, when fifty pence was enough for an evening's entertainment, though these days, in contrast, according to Ted, they are more likely to need 'fifty quid'. Many of the Boys also have a regular flutter (and often more than a 'flutter') on the horses, though the big gamblers on horse racing are Mark, Colin and Nutter. Mark goes to the races and won't go 'with less than two hundred quid in my pocket'. He takes his gambling very seriously, though sometimes he takes his partner and their children along: 'they'll have their pound bet, I'll have my tenner or twenty pound bet . . . they enjoy it, it's a day out and a bit of fun for the kids'. Colin bets both on the horses and on the football: 'I wouldn't say I'm a heavy gambler but I do like a bet . . . sometimes I puts a hundred on, sometimes just a tenner'. Nutter spends 'fifty quid here and fifty quid there', apparently unconcerned whether or not he has a chance of winning, for he acknowledged he throws his money away one way or the other: 'either I give it to the bookies or I spend it in the pub'.

When Nutter is neither gambling nor drinking he can be found wandering around the woods pursuing his childhood interest in bird watching ('ornithology, it's called', he told me). Mal's solitary diversion is gardening, while Kelvin's is photography which, for a time, he did semi-professionally, though he is completely self-taught. However, with these exceptions (and Ryan's preference for the open air), the Boys' leisure is very rarely a solitary pursuit, and is firmly located either around family or around the pubs and the clubs of Milltown. Those pubs (The Fountain, The Wayfarer, The Centurion and The Roundhead) and clubs (notably the working men's club which many of the Boys frequent, though there are others they attend less often) serve the Boys' interests in different ways – within and beyond their leisure.

The Fountain, where the Boys who work 'on the street' routinely hang out, is clearly a space and place where (illegal) business mixes seamlessly with pleasure, for the Boys do their scheming and trading over a friendly drink, and gamble in the bookies over the road. Landlords at The Fountain have changed over the years, which has influenced the extent of interest in, and support for the repertoire of social activities available (as well as tolerance of more clandestine activity). As Nathan noted, the pub did sustain a rugby team for a number of years. More recently, with a new landlord who is related to one of the Boys and well known to all, it has started to put on karaoke evenings and special events on various festive occasions throughout the year. This may make it a more conducive environment for wives, partners and older children (should the Boys wish to involve them), for The Fountain has traditionally been a somewhat intimidating place, for men only, and then only men whose 'faces fit'.

The working men's club is much more of a social and sociable milieu, to which those Boys who favour it can always go with a certainty that some of their mates will also be there. Their wives, mothers and mothers-in-law and older children can also come along, and do so regularly for bingo sessions and special functions such as birthday and wedding parties. The club offers a range of routine in-house activities (from bingo to bands), cheap beer and (still) a men-only room to which the Boys can escape from 'their' women, watch the football, and swear without inhibition. It also has teams affiliated to various leagues, including darts, skittles and golf. Many of the Boys attached to the club attend like clockwork, especially at weekends, and pass many hours there, for it is, more than metaphorically, their second home, where they can drink with their mates to oblivion before staggering home. Denny, a lifelong regular, captures the spirit of the club:

> I likes the club . . . I like socializing. Like I'll go on trips with the teams and join in the competitions, but really it's just about socializing with people. Just going out, up the club. Everyone knows us. It's a laugh, it's a drink, sometimes with this group of people, sometimes with that. We gets on well with most people up the club. I like to enjoy myself. Life's too short. I try not to worry too much about things. I could have plenty of things to worry about but when I get up the club my outlook is that I just want to enjoy myself.

Other pubs also provide a place of respite and refuge between work and family life but for most of the Boys, if they go anywhere at all, it is typically either to The Fountain or up the club.

Voluntary Work

A few of the Boys do what might be considered as 'voluntary work' in their leisure time, though they seldom depict it as that, for it smacks of 'do-gooding', which they despise for its connotations of social work, or resonates with 'community work', which, to many, is synonymous with compulsory 'community service'. Nevertheless, some do give time as volunteers on behalf of others. As he was recovering from his addictions, Spaceman self-excluded himself from the typical social arenas frequented by the Boys, essentially because they invariably involved drinking, and instead became an 'extra pair of hands' teaching art in schools. Not only has this filled his social time, but also it has enabled him to rebuild some of his personal self-worth and a positive social reputation:

> I had to do something so I asked about helping in schools. I get a lot of ideas from the kids. And people look at me different now. It's like a metamorphosis. The kids think I'm a wicked artist. They see me as a *proper artist*. Sometimes I can't believe they are talking about *me*. And I'm proud of that. I've noticed that people have started to say hello to me in the street, because they just walked past me before or crossed the road to get away from this crazy cunt. It's fucking funny really, the way things change.

Gary has a mate involved in social work and has helped with camping holidays for 'disadvantaged' children, taking his own two children along:

> It was basically make your own fun. Four adults, eleven kids. They haven't got a lot but they are buzzing. And my two kids mix in well. They all got on like a house on fire. And I mean, there's nothing down there, except the beach. No big fun fairs, nothing like that. You just get the footballs out, or the frisbee and that was it. But it was . . . quality time. And I just wish I had so much more time I could spend to do things like that.

Closer to home, Trevor spends some of his leisure time coaching junior rugby and football teams, which he sees as an opportunity to instil some 'respect' in some of the 'rougher' kids who are involved. He was asked to take on these responsibilities because 'they know that I can get a little bit of respect out of them... I mean, they won't mess with me... firm but fair, that's me'.

Conclusion

Though the Boys' peer group networks have inevitably fragmented as they got older, weakened by their different trajectories in employment and family lives, many of the connections forged during their teenage years have remained remarkably robust. Old loyalties still prevail, especially between distinct 'pairings' of the Boys and within the different leisure sites of The Fountain and the social club. While some 'went missing', giving priority to their families and children, few have completely abandoned their links with the Boys, for they continue to place enormous value on specific friendships in particular and, more generally, their shared history with a wider group of 'mates'. Only three of the Boys have severed their links almost completely, while in contrast, a striking number remain in touch with each other, both purposefully and more casually, on a regular basis.

The Boys engage in a wide range of leisure activities, which can be further distinguished by the ways in which they pursue the *same* leisure interests and pastimes, for these are woven together in a myriad of ways – with different priorities attached to the family, to the Boys and to 'time out' for themselves. Sport remains of paramount importance, though the mainstay of much of the Boys' leisure is either the pub or the club. Despite their shared leisure preferences and priorities, however, lie highly individualized practices, based both on cultural continuities and new opportunities which have arisen during the Boys' lives.

–13–

Looking Forward, Looking Back

Introduction

The Milltown Boys are now over 40, somewhere in the middle of the life course, and it is evident they have had mixed fortunes. From a broadly common starting base in a classically 'disadvantaged' council estate, their pathways in life have diverged. Their 'careers' in employment, crime, housing, family life, health and leisure have taken shape in different ways at different points for different reasons.

Though many were unaccustomed to either looking back or looking forward, the research interviews concluded by 'taking stock': the Boys were asked to consider where they might be going in the future and reflect on where they had been in the past. Looking forward entailed some assessment of not only their own prospective futures but also, significantly, those of their children, while looking back involved an exploration of any regrets they may have, though many were transparently reluctant to engage in such reflection.

Looking Forward

The Boys were less focused on their own future than on those of their children. They themselves had grown up in poverty and disadvantage, and they wanted something more for their children. Resonating with a view expressed by many of the Boys, Alex commented, 'you want more for your kids than you had, don't you?'

Aspirations for their children centred on education and achievement, though this was considered to be more a platform of protection against failure, rather any guaranteed passport to success. The Boys tried to assist this outcome, indulging their children with the 'gadgetry of competence' – computers, educational videos, books and magazines, the best sportsgear – though they had little idea how to assist their children's learning and development in more interpersonal ways. Gary said his kids 'don't want for nothing', while Danny ensured his daughter had everything she wanted, and her designer bedroom, with books, TV and computer, would grace the pages of a promotional magazine.

Despite the scathing condemnation of their own schooling, the Boys sought to encourage their own children *not* to follow in their footsteps, though, like Richard, they acknowledged the apparent hypocrisy of doing so. Referring to his 12-year-old son, who lives with him, he outlined what he wants for Terry:

> To stay away from drugs. I want him to have a good job. I encourage him as much as I can with school. I've taken him to town and pointed out the dossers and told him that's what happens if you don't work hard at school. He understands now that school is important. So I do try to point out the rights and wrongs. Of course when he's about 17 he's going to realize what a bullshitter I was but by then he'll be on the right path, I hope.

Precisely because they want education to make a difference for their kids, many of the Boys have made proactive decisions to send their children to secondary schools beyond the estate. Sometimes they have taken some 'stick' from the other Boys for doing so, but they don't care. Mal's two daughters go to a church school:

> some of the Boys have a pop at me but the only thing for me is that they have a better chance over there than they would have had over here . . . Education gets you a long way in the world, they won't have to struggle the way I have.

Mal's decision seems to have paid off, for his older daughter is the only one of the Boys' children over the age of 16 who has gone on to post-16 academic learning. Ryan had adopted the same strategy for his two daughters, sending them to a girls-only school in the belief that single-sex education would assist their learning ('no boys, no distractions'), though, in his case, it hadn't worked. His elder daughter was expelled for fighting, while the younger one got pregnant, which had disappointed Ryan at the time, though he has now come to terms with this on the grounds that 'you can't live their lives for them for ever'.

A good education not only conferred the prospect of qualifications, but also engendered good manners, which the Boys have always felt to be important, deploring the lack of 'respect' among the younger generation, and not wanting their children turning out to be 'cheeky bastards' or 'chopsing cows'. Whatever wayward characteristics they displayed in their youth, they are convinced that, unlike their successors today, they were never rude or impolite to others simply 'for the hell of it'; as Ryan observed, 'we may have been little bastards, but we were little bastards with manners'.

On the other hand, however, the Boys did not want their children, notably their sons, ending up as 'ear'oles', for they wanted *their* boys to be able to 'handle themselves' and have at least *some* of the 'street-wise' aptitude which they themselves had acquired on the streets of Milltown. Jamie described his 11-year-old son Jack as 'naive', worrying that 'he doesn't know the streets, he doesn't go out like

I used to', and though Gary was already concerned his 6-year-old son 'could get out of control', given the neighbourhood in which they live, he was equally anxious about not 'turning him into a nancy boy'.

For some of the children, at least, such hopes and aspirations have already been dashed. The Boys had a number of explanations for this to hand, of which none pointed the finger at them! If history was repeating itself, it was a consequence of other things – family, school and community. In many cases, contact with the children had diminished or been lost completely, after they had split up from their children's mothers. The *Boys'* influence on their children's lives had therefore been limited, so if the kids had turned out 'bad', it was not their fault. Blame was also placed squarely on the standard of education at the local comprehensive school (a school which has now twice failed an inspection), for the Boys' own experience of schooling there was a poor one, and they suggested that little may have changed. Even if active decisions had been made to educate their children elsewhere, the Boys pointed to the negative 'neighbourhood effect' of growing up in Milltown. Indeed, a key reason for three of the Boys moving out of Milltown was to avoid the detrimental environmental influence on their children, and even Gary is now seriously contemplating doing so for the same reason, albeit only to a house not so far 'down the road'. As Mark observed:

> I hope they turn out decent enough . . . I mean, I am doing my best to bring them up properly but it's hard in Milltown, with the crime and drugs and violence and everything like that. I love Milltown, I'll probably never, ever move away but . . . well bringing them up round here, in a bad culture in a way . . . it's been hard and it's going to be hard.

The Boys all claim they are 'doing their best', or have tried to do their best when they have had the chance, though the evidence to date suggests their aspirations for their children have been dashed, for only three (all girls) of the twenty children over 16 are in any form of learning, and only one of these acquired any formal educational qualifications. However, the prognosis looks rather better for at least some of the younger children, whose home life has been more stable, and whose parents are both more likely and more able to take an active interest in their education.

The Boys see their own futures as consisting of little more than consolidating where they are now (wherever that may be). Only four anticipate any significant change. The spirited teenagers of the 1970s have settled into routine middle age, albeit in very different kinds of routines. They do not see anything getting much *better* and are well aware of the possibility of things taking a turn for the worse, for they have seen people's lives collapse all around them: death, redundancy, divorce, repossession and addiction. The modest success of those who have achieved it is fragile, and holding on to what they have got, or retrieving a little of what they have lost, is far more the challenge for the future than working towards further improvement. They are, anyway, reluctant to be 'Mystic Meg' (the stargazer in the National Lottery) and thereby tempt fate, and their comments on the future are typically cast in terms of dreams and hopes rather than any active plans.

Seventeen of the Boys were convinced their lives were unlikely to change much, with well over half asserting they were ploughing a comfortable, if not necessarily confident, furrow, though the others conceded they were probably stuck in a rut. Either way, they had established their own particular way of life and felt this would probably continue. The Boys who worked 'on the street' acknowledged there was always the risk in the future of another term of imprisonment, though they tried not to think about this too much, for they would carry on 'earning' in the only way they knew how. Others recognized they were trapped in low-level employment which they could do little about, while those a little higher on the occupational ladder knew they were 'never going to be millionaires', but were happy enough they had bought their houses and were in a position to afford a regular holiday.

Eight of the Boys felt the future offered the prospect and possibility (but nowhere near the promise) of something slightly different, though they did not anticipate anything would radically change. The grounds for expecting some change were, however, very different. Ryan, for example, believes his regular (legitimate) employment presents some prospect of buying his house, which he still often considers. Eddie is confident his mental health problems have stabilized, which may allow him to move beyond the low-level administrative job he is currently doing and secure a more senior position (after all, he was once a production manager). Shaun thinks about moving out of the city to a house in the country, while Derek would like to go to university when his daughter is older.

For most of the Boys the future is vested in their children, for so long as 'the kids are all right', they expressed little concern about themselves. Those whose relationships with their children have been through difficulties hope things will improve, and Denny, now with his third partner, contemplates having more children of his own.

Only four of the Boys indicated the possibility of any dramatic transformation to their lives, the kind of significant change which Jamie experienced in the late 1990s, when he abandoned twenty years of building site work in favour of an office job. Pete has a realistic prospect of becoming a millionaire, for there is currently a 'class action' in the US courts concerning the Atlanta bombing at the 1996 Olympics, in which Pete's partner Barry was almost fatally injured. This is likely to take years, though should the final judgment be in their favour, 'we'll get a huge settlement and I can be rich and do all the things I've dreamed of doing'. If not, or at least until that time, Pete will continue to care for Barry, who is still undergoing physiotherapy for his horrendous injuries. Marty, in contrast, believes he has *no* future, convinced his schizophrenia is the wrath of God wreaked on him for his past misdemeanours, and stating bluntly, when asked about his future, 'I'd just like to die, simple as that'.

Both Matt and Spaceman have come through years of heavy drug addiction. Matt extricated himself from his crack habit in the late 1990s and is now 'trying to do something positive with my life', which has included a course on the New Deal, though 'it didn't work out'. He admitted he was struggling – physically, psychologically and financially – though his relationship with his partner Camilla had improved considerably, and he was looking to the future:

> It's all been a massive change. Like I'm poor now but I've got a life. Although I suppose I was always poor, even then when I was doing the crack, because I wasted my cash. But I did have cash, whether I wasted it or not, I did have it. I've just got to get a job. But something will come up. I've done a few fiddles but I want something regular. I've got the rest of my life to live now so I'd better start living it and having something to think about, because I realize now I've never had much of a life. I've done jack shit with my life, all these last ten or twenty years. It's quite sad.

Spaceman also has cause for some renewed optimism about the future, for, having dealt with his alcohol and drug addictions, he is studying for an art degree:

> I want peace of mind, be happy with whatever I fucking do. I've got plans – I plan to get a degree. I want to have some options. For too long in my fucking life I never had no options. Anything could happen. I have got an option to go to teacher training college, which I will probably take up. I'm sort of poacher turned gamekeeper! I've been doing it [teaching] a bit for something to do, just volunteering but it's fucking great because when I was a kid, teaching was prestigious, out of my fucking boundaries. And I love it. Getting the kids interested. I can do that. That's what I'm going to do.

Spaceman has 'plans' for the future, unlike the vast majority of the Boys, though many made reference to the National Lottery, for they too had plans if their numbers ever came up.

Most of the Boys spent a few pounds each week on Lottery tickets and scratch cards, and it was not inconceivable they might win something, though of course they were not likely to win much. (A mate of Paul's had won £60,000 on a scratch card, giving Paul £6,000, which he spent in less than two months.) If, however, they *did* win the Lottery, Mal, Mark and Trevor were still insistent they would never leave Milltown, and would give some of their winnings to the community: 'the kids definitely need something up here'. Colin, Tommy and Derek would move away (as Tommy said, 'I couldn't be worth ten million and still live here, could I?'), though not too far; Derek would 'base myself quite close'. Alex would buy a boat to indulge in his love of fishing and a house in London, which 'would be handy for the football' and 'save messing around driving to Highbury every other week'. Jerry would buy a place in Spain and follow major sporting events around the world. Unlike those who said they would *stay* in and around Milltown, Nick was certain he would move away, asserting the neighbourhood had declined below the threshold which had formerly commanded his complete loyalty, while in contrast, Pete said he would move back 'to do something for *my* people', speculating he would buy one of the churches and turn it into a voluntary organization serving the community.

The Boys' lives have been characterized by numerous risks and relatively few opportunities. Some have made the best of the limited opportunities which came their way, though very few have endeavoured to *create* opportunity in their life. They have invariably adopted a 'que sera, sera' philosophy, believing the forces shaping the long-term direction of their lives lay beyond their control. In the short term, however, they snatched at opportunity where they could, and by doing so, most of the Boys have managed to establish some kind of stability and direction in their lives through a variety of legitimate, illegitimate and opportunistic means. Their own sense of the future is very much about consolidation rather than development, with most suggesting they would be happy enough if things 'stayed the same', though it might be argued this is yet another of the Boys' 'vocabularies of motive', a way of justifying their rather humdrum existence. The majority did, however, appear to be happy enough: they have worked regularly (on and off the books and on the street), they have raised their children and some have bought their own homes. In their circumstances and considering their starting point, they *have* 'done well' and are justifiably proud of it. The Boys *hoped* things would continue in much the same way and invested greater hopes in the futures of their children, but whatever happened, they maintained, there was not much they could do about it now.

Regrets and Self-reflection

The Boys were not accustomed to doing too much *thinking* about their lives. For some it would be too painful, while for most, there was a culture of acceptance that life unfolded unpredictably and not much could have been done to change its course: 'que sera, sera' or, as Ted put it, 'at the end of the day you can't change your life'. The Boys had always tended to 'take each day as it comes', rarely planning for the medium or longer term, preferring pragmatically to deal with the challenges and opportunities which life presented on a short-term basis. This was hardly surprising, since employment was often erratic and uncertain, relationships were often fragile and, for those trying to make a living at the sharp end 'on the street', there was always the prospect of a sudden turn for the worse through arrest and imprisonment. Their outlook was therefore in keeping with objective probabilities in their lives, yet precisely because of such chequered histories, one might have expected a raft of regrets, but instead, the reflection compelled by the research interviews usually produced an emphatic *denial* that they would change a thing. True to form, they routinely diverted some serious appraisal of their past and launched instead into various renditions of 'My Way' ('Regrets . . . I've had a few . . .'), debating the relative merits of Sid (Vicious) and Frank (Sinatra). However tough their lives have been (and, for some, still were), serious issues were invariably converted into repartee drawn from their tried and tested stock of jokes and embellished anecdotes. This was, arguably, a way of distancing themselves from the pain which some certainly felt about their lives, when this was subsequently explored.

The Boys' regrets were sometimes firmly interconnected (for example, more regular employment and income might have been forthcoming had they done better at school, which in turn would have enabled them to travel more), sometimes just islands of self-reproach in relation to very specific moments and episodes in their lives, though even when pushed on the matter of regrets, one-quarter of the Boys still insisted they had none at all. Nick acknowledged the misdemeanours (and more) earlier in his life, but asserted it was 'all part of my life, so you either accept it or you commit suicide; you just have to try to learn from the things you've done. Nobody can go through life blameless or perfect'. The past was gone, the present was here to be dealt with as best they could, and who knew what the future held, for life was a roller-coaster, as Jamie observed, 'No regrets, I'm a happy go lucky guy. Who knows what's round the corner . . . I've always been the same, don't worry about what's happened in the past and don't think too much about the future'. Vic was equally matter of fact: 'No complaints. I've had some good times, I've had some bad times, but then don't we all'.

Two-thirds of the Boys admitted to having at least some regrets, which clustered around four distinct themes, though different weight and importance was attached to each of them, and, moreover, their reasons for regret were often very different. Not surprisingly, given the pervasiveness of their teenage delinquency, many reflections revolved around crime, violence and substance misuse, though some simply regretted having been caught! Nathan rued the fact his second child was born when he was inside, while Danny wished he had not carved crude tattoos on his arms and hands when he was in Borstal, which he has, very obviously, failed to cover later in his life with more professional tattoos. More significantly, Marty, Mark and Jerry were ashamed they had once burgled *private* dwellings, recognizing now that they had been 'stealing off your own'. In their remarks, they distinguished carefully between domestic burglaries in Milltown and theft from more anonymous, unknown and often 'corporate' targets, for the latter were still considered to have been 'fair game'. Their deepest regrets on this front related to the direct and indirect pain they had caused to those they knew – their neighbours and their own families, for not only had they sometimes stolen directly from them, but also their offending behaviour, frequent arrests and regular court appearances had caused 'grief and upset' to those who loved and cared for them. However, though they might now regret some aspects of their instrumental offending, only Tony referred to the Boys' expressive offending, deploring the level of 'gratuitous violence' in which they had indulged. Even Tony argued it had been 'par for the course' at the time, and he wasn't going to 'lose any sleep over it'. Indeed, apart from Matt, who said the biggest regret of his life had been his involvement with crack cocaine (as both dealer and user), few of the Boys lost any sleep over most of the criminal behaviour in which they had participated in the past.

It was a different story in relation to education and employment. As Mal said, 'well I think I could have done a lot better, but don't we all', while Matt was sad he did not get 'a decent enough education', and Denny simply observed he had been 'too bloody lazy', wishing he had been pushed more, and pushed himself 'in the right direction, because I knew I had it in me', but instead he had just 'gone with the flow'. The Boys regretted their lack of personal effort, though they also apportioned blame to the absence of encouragement from their families and the school. Ryan commented caustically that 'if you'd had to stay on till you got some qualifications I might have still been there now!', recalling how he had just 'plodded along' until it was time to leave, though he felt the school could, and should, have made more effort to help him to become *something*, because 'without certificates, you're nothing, it don't matter how good you are'. Education was now perceived by the Boys as an essential foundation for progress in the labour market and many felt they could have achieved more. Mal talked poignantly about his struggle to get through the work-based training courses he had done, because he had never 'learnt to learn':

> I just wish I had got some qualifications. When you haven't got them, you've always got to prove yourself – every fucking day of your life. It's one long struggle. And the courses I had to do in work, they were really difficult for me. I really had to knuckle down. My concentration was shit, I used to drift away. I had to work twice as hard as everybody else, so when they used to go out on the night on the piss I used to sit and read the frigging stuff over and over again.' Cos I never learnt to learn, that's it, I had no capability of logging things into my brain and it staying there.

Trevor felt he could have 'done a bit more in the way of education', especially in technical drawing, which he had enjoyed and felt might have got him a better job, though at the time he had ignored the teachers, noting with irony how the cycle had repeated itself with his own children: 'obviously I wish I had known what I know now back then, which is why you try to pass it on to the kids . . . and they ignore it as well, just the same as I did'. Mark resented as well as regretted the fact his lack of qualifications confined him to his job as a fitter's mate, for had he done more at school he could have been a fitter 'on fifty, sixty pound a week more than I get', though, in his view, they basically did the same job. Mark observed he had 'had to learn the hard way', just as Jerry, observing that his lack of education blocked any possibility of him ever becoming a manager at the Post Office, said, 'and so I've basically got to take my punishment'.

Regrets expressed by the Boys about not having done better in education were not solely related to better labour market prospects. They were also, and possibly surprisingly, firmly about some sense of personal fulfilment. Pete almost cried out, 'give me just one fucking GCSE – just to prove I'm not thick'. At the other end of the academic spectrum, Shaun now has a university degree, acquired in his thirties, though he has never used it for work, and indeed, occupies a relatively humble occupational position (in a job he loves) but, privately, he conveys a deep sense of pride now he is 'just as good as anyone else'.

Given the erratic and sometimes traumatic track records of their personal relationships, the Boys did not express as many regrets as might be expected. Where regret was expressed, however, the feelings were profound. Most regrets, inevitably, though not exclusively, related to the women in the Boys' lives (or lack of them). Nathan's external 'Jack the lad' persona was exposed when he commented that his biggest regret by far is 'not having my wife no more', while Eddie expressed sadness that he had 'never found a partner'. Two of the Boys, one now on his third serious relationship, the other still married to his childhood sweetheart, regret having got married so young. Denny had 'jumped in at the deep end and wish I would have waited', for they had a child but, after an acrimonious divorce, he had no further contact with his daughter. Tommy had always expected to marry Suzanne but, looking back, 'it was too early', and with the characteristic fatalism of the Boys, he commented, 'but she got pregnant and you just make the most of what happens, don't you'.

Regrets in the context of personal relationships extended beyond those concerning their adult partners. Richard, for example, despised the way he had often reacted to his younger brother, who suffers from schizophrenia, and admitted to having 'shunned him a lot'. Shaun was saddened by the fact he had failed to establish a physical closeness with his eldest son David (now 21 and a father of three), which he had achieved with his three other children:

> he was about 6 years old and he used to come up and kiss me and cuddle me and I remember saying you're a man now David, you don't kiss now, we shake hands. That was the biggest mistake I ever made. It's like I damaged him. That's the way I feel. I mean, my dad was never kind of close to me in terms of cuddling and holding me, but that's no excuse for me not being that way.

One of Pete's major regrets was that he had never known his father: 'I would have loved to have known what it was like to have a father . . . I often try to imagine how a father should be'. Fathers, indeed, were immensely important to the Boys, despite incessant rows between them. Richard was mortified he and his father had had a major argument just before his father died, and 'never had time to make amends'. Other relatives who had died had left the Boys feeling some sense of guilt, like Jamie, who is convinced he could have done more for his mother during the last year of her life. Ted's brother collapsed and died, in his early forties, of a brain haemorrhage, apparently the result of a head injury incurred while doing building work on the fiddle, and although there was no connection, Ted still regrets hitting his brother over the head with a bottle shortly before his death.

Relationships with friends were rarely a source of regret, although both Tony and Shaun (two of the more successful of the Boys) were now sorry that their 'cockiness' had alienated them from many of the Boys. Tony admitted he had been 'so fucking cocky with my mates . . . you know, I was a bit like Harry Enfield "I've got considerably more money than you" . . . I wish I hadn't been such a prick'.

The self-professed arrogance of Tony and Shaun was simply an exaggerated characteristic of virtually all the Boys, for most of them projected self-confidence and witty repartee at all times, whatever inner struggles and dilemmas were concealed. Many of their disclosures are unlikely to have been revealed to anyone else, because – in the Boys' world – they reek of vulnerability and expose those concerned to ridicule and mockery, for being a soft touch or an 'old woman', when the Boys felt inclined to stick the knife in. Privately, however, many had craved some guidance and external support when they were younger, though it had rarely been forthcoming and when it was, the Boys' public image and premature independence precluded them from taking it. Derek regretted that the 'guidance' offered by his grandmother – about both education, respect in relationships and 'sticking together' – had not been reinforced elsewhere in his life, while Nathan bemoaned the fact he had been so 'fucking stubborn' about the support he had received from a local youth project:

> I done them wrong. They were trying to do something for me. It was good advice but I never listened and I ended up in the shit. I've paid the price for that ever since.

The Boys were a bunch of 'hard men' from an early age, living on their wits and on the streets, and discouraged from revealing or discussing their deeper feelings. This trait has persisted into their adult lives, and indeed during the research interview, when they were transparently hesitant about reflecting on 'relationships', although when pressed, they divulged a range of regrets in relation to partners, family and friends which displays a sensitive underbelly and exposes the veneer of their 'hardness'. Some, nevertheless, still refused to dwell on things which had 'gone wrong' in the past, especially if they believed they had been the cause of it, and others tried to skim over the hurt and blame they obviously felt, although many were eventually open and forthright about such regrets, which, understandably, are often painful to discuss.

It was much easier to discuss subjects which appeared to be lifted from Trivial Pursuits, such as sport and leisure, which featured prominently in the Boys' regrets. Vic was sorry about 'not sticking to the rugby when I had the chance . . . I could have been retired now with a couple of quid in the bank'; instead, he is living on incapacity benefit with a chronic chest complaint. Eddie, Jamie and Denny had passed up possibilities of becoming professional footballers, having failed to pursue the opportunity after being offered trials with league clubs. Others regretted not having travelled. Alex, for example, wished he had toured the world on a 'thousand pound ticket', while Trevor had always wanted to see the Grand Canyon. Such regrets had become more pronounced as these Boys witnessed some of their mates taking opportunities to see more of the world (if only the Costa Brava and Gran Canaria), while, for various reasons, they were not in a position to do so.

Some of the most tragic or troublesome episodes in the Boys' lives were apparently not a source of regret. Pete's first (gay) partner died unexpectedly and his second was nearly fatally injured in the carnage of the 1996 Atlanta bombing, but Pete still maintains he has been 'lucky' in his life, for the most part 'in the right place at the right time'. His homosexuality led him to 'escape' from Milltown, which paved the way, in London, for his first love affair, while his second serious lover (with whom he has now been for seventeen years) provided the resources for him to fulfil his dreams to travel. Indeed, their visit to Atlanta was the first stop on a world tour, where, exceptionally in Pete's view, they were just unlucky to be 'in the wrong place at the wrong time . . . it was a one in a billion chance, one in six billion actually'. None of this, however, is a source of regret, for had things not unfolded in this way, Pete might otherwise have remained in Milltown and stagnated all his life.

Less dramatically, Jerry acknowledges that many of the Boys did a 'lot of silly things', though he argued (conveniently), 'I don't think they really mount up to much'. Alex was dismissive of his days on the glue, asserting he grew out of it and 'it didn't really count as taking drugs'. Indeed, many of the Boys maintained most of their transgressions were a 'passing phase', invoking vocabularies of motive which enable them to explain away any personal responsibility for blame or regret.

Talking about regrets in life is rarely easy for anyone, for it represents an admission of failure, weakness, inaction, missed chances, lost opportunities and lack of direction. It is not surprising, therefore, that when regrets are discussed, those who admit to them seek to distance themselves from personal 'culpability' and agency. So, though the Boys did talk about their regrets with, arguably, a surprising degree of candour, inevitably they also sought to explain, and thereby justify, the episodes causing regret in positive and 'contextual' ways. For example, Denny's lack of application at school was essentially a product of the environment in which he lived (rather than laziness on his part), while Tony's involvement in violence was simply to do with the (punk) culture of the time (rather than any desire to prove himself). Therefore, though some of the Boys 'owned up' bluntly to regretted incidents in their errant past, many others who acknowledged regrets located them, correctly, within the wider circumstances and trajectories of their lives. Moreover, their reference points were, by and large, downwards – things could be, or have been, worse. Wherever they are, or have been, in the scheme of things, the Boys usually saw their glass as still half-full (rather than half-empty), which invariably prompted them to point to what they had, not what they had failed to achieve. Hence their limited regrets, for, on each rung of the hierarchy of 'fortune', the Boys could see those who had had a worse time of it – they were in daily contact with them. Mark might not have much of a job (and could have had a better one had he sustained his education), but at least he had a job. Mack might be unemployed, but at least he wasn't in jail. Paul might be facing a custodial sentence, but at least he wasn't dead. When one of the Boys has been kicked to death by some of *his* mates in the daily round of alcohol-fuelled 'play fighting' which had been *his* existence for twenty years, there is certainly less cause to regret some of the weaknesses and 'deficits' in your own life. It was easy, the Boys argued, to think of what might have been, but it hadn't happened, so there was not much point dwelling on it. After all, you could regret almost anything, with hindsight, as Jamie noted:

> Of course if you think about it now you are wiser. You know, if only I'd done a bit more, if only I hadn't done this or that. You just end up as doom and gloom merchants. But it's done and gone; there's not really much point in thinking about it.

Looking in the Mirror: Self-reflection

Ryan made a telling statement: 'Everyone's the same round here, whoever you are talking to, like, they have got to be the same as me. We are all the same, we are all from the same thing'. Asking the Boys to consider their regrets was hard enough, but getting them to reflect on their own character, motivations, orientations and personality was even tougher, though their responses provide a fascinating glimpse into the ways in which they see themselves.

Despite their common heritage and early parallel pathways through childhood and adolescence, the life course of the Boys diverged quite dramatically as they approached adulthood and subsequently unfolded very differently in terms of jobs, crime, relationships, housing and leisure. These tended to cluster in particular ways, producing three broad categories among the Boys in their adult lives. First, there are those who, somewhat against the odds, found regular employment, desisted from crime, broke ranks with their teenage peer group, formed stable relationships, bought their own houses and actively sought educational success for their children. Second, there are those who remain rather precariously attached to the legitimate labour market, are on the periphery of illegal activity, continue to socialize with their old peers in the context of the 'respectable' working men's club, have steady but separate personal relationships, live in social housing and send their children, without much interest, to the local comprehensive school. Third, there are are those who have stayed largely outside of legitimate employment, who remain involved in criminal activity, spend more time with their old mates than with their changing partners, live in social housing, and see relatively little of the children they have had by different relationships.

Inevitably the Boys within these different groups have different perceptions about themselves and their lives. The Boys are clearly *not* all the same, despite Ryan's contention, neither in the objective pathways they have travelled nor in the ways they have thought about and approached those journeys. Some have taken a 'passive' stance, doing their own thing in response to presenting circumstances. Others have developed a more active approach to 'life management' (see Table 13.1). There are, of course, overlaps between these two positions, and changes over time.

Table 13.1 Tossed Around or Life Management? How the Boys See Themselves

	Tossed around							*Life management*		
				Ted						Tony
				Danny					Trevor	
	Marty		Nutter		Tommy					Gary
		Matt		Nick					Jerry	
	Mack		Vic		Ryan				Kelvin	
						Alex	Mal			
Paul	Nathan			Spaceman						Shaun
			Richard			Pete	Denny			Derek
		Colin		Mark		Jamie				Gordon
		Eddie								

Note: The Boys may be positioned in similar places, but this may be for very different reasons

It is difficult for anybody to admit to themselves, let alone others, that their lives have largely been vulnerable to or victims of external forces beyond their control. Such an admission would be to concede no personal agency, and though structural determinants have clearly been powerful in shaping the direction of many of the Boys' lives, most have endeavoured to hold on to *some* sense of autonomy and self-determination, even when this has patently been absent. Apart from Paul through his alcoholism, and Marty on account of his schizophrenia, there is a poignant undercurrent of missed opportunities and 'what might have been', had they responded to circumstances more positively. Their 'que sera, sera' mentality conceals a view that things *might* have been done differently, though many of the Boys argued they had been trapped and 'tossed around' by the expectations of their culture and community. Nathan captures this position succinctly, for his life story is one of routine unemployment, imprisonment and broken relationships, yet as a teenager he was one of the major beneficiaries of various youth work experiences offered by a local project, and at one point looked as if he might become a youth worker himself:

> It showed me what was out there, if you want it basically. It wasn't that I didn't want it. I suppose, looking back, that I was too stuck up in the head, too much of an arsehole to go for it.

Vic is essentially a sensitive and considerate individual, but maintained he had always had to subordinate this side of his character to a tougher exterior, for the latter dominated his public image, led to a criminal record and custodial experience at an early age, and confirmed him as one of Milltown's 'hard men'. His mixed race ethnic background (white mother, black father) and large physique compounded his 'thuggish' appearance and disabled him from ever projecting or developing his deeper attributes:

> You do things as a kid and you don't realize then how they will affect you as an adult. People look at me and they think that's Vic, criminal record, hard case, he's a thief. A lot of what I did was just stupidness, but you get known for being a thief and for being a fighter and it stays with you. Most people don't really know who I am. They see a big bloke with a loud voice. You know me – I'm quite a sensitive, considerate bloke. That's down to my grandmother and my uncle. That's how I'd like to be, but it's not what people expect. I don't want to come across in the way I do to people, but that's the way it's been. It's hard, it is hard, honest.

Another of the 'hard men' among the Milltown Boys echoed similar thoughts. Ted was part of a family with considerable local notoriety, and from an early age had a 'reputation' to maintain: 'but you know that there's another side to me. I can be a vicious bastard when I want to be but that's not the only fucking side to me. The thing is I've had to be hard. What else could I do?' Danny, who has spent around twelve years of his life in custody, said he had never really wanted to be a criminal, but asked what other choices had been open to him. Exploited in the casual labour market for a few years, he had then felt a more risky criminal lifestyle gave him more freedom and self-control, though this was hardly a 'choice'; it was his only alternative. Indeed, though it is easy to suggest that these Boys at the tough end of the spectrum could always find useful post-hoc rationalizations, it is also important to accede the very limited 'choices' they have ever had for authentic and effective life management. At least Vic, Ted and Danny have sought to make the best of the very constrained choices they felt were open to them. In contrast, Mack, Paul and Marty have just 'tagged along', taking 'each day as it comes', opportunistically seizing the pickings of criminal enterprise, with any sense they were actively shaping the direction of their lives conspicuously lacking. Likewise, Matt became a hostage to his crack cocaine addiction, which at first held the promise of a lucrative income:

> What a fucking waste of life I've had for the last thirteen years. The crack completely fucks you up, but you just don't see it. No one could get me off it. Loads of people tried to get me off. And now I'm off it, I stays in the house most of the time. As soon as I am in control of my life I might start thinking about going out again. I've got to be more positive. I have got to state what I am going to do in life and let people know that I am doing something different now. But anything could happen to put me back on it. Before I can take that test I have got to find another mission in my life.
>
> See when I was on the crack I never thought about anything else. Because when you are part of that system you can't see outside it.

On just the other side of the criminal divide, Colin, Richard and Nutter have largely let life take its course with little active decision-making. At least they have stayed mainly in legitimate employment, and Richard did make the active decision to train as a bricklayer in his early twenties. Like Vic, he is easily stereotyped as a result of his appearance, for he is a huge, imposing man of mixed race, with a well-honed physique from years of bodybuilding and weight-training, an image which conceals, however, a more internal fragility and lack of confidence in his own identity:

> I have always wanted to be an upright citizen – clean living. I don't want people to look at me and ask me if I've got any ganja to sell. But that's what happens. There is a lot of conflict in my head. I know what I have been like, but I don't like to think that I have been like that. I would really have liked to be a different sort of person. But with the Boys, what else can you do?

Nutter is adamant that planning for the future is pointless: 'tomorrow comes or it doesn't come. And if it comes I'll go for a drink. Live for today. I never plan anything in advance. Except for tonight. If I wants to go out, I go'. Colin has held down regular work all his life, following a daily routine from which he has almost never deviated. Change, for the likes of Nutter and Colin, is inconceivable – their life ticks on, day by day, and the mantra of 'que sera, sera' fits them like a glove.

In contrast, about half of the Boys testified to having at least tried to impose some shape, structure and direction to their lives. Gordon, of course, was uniquely 'qualified' to do so, with his street wisdom and academic achievements, proclaiming 'I could have done anything . . . well, you can do whatever you want to'. In Gordon's case, it is relatively easy to see the reasons why he displayed greater confidence about personal self-determination, but explanations for the greater 'life management' of some of the other Boys, compared to those who were 'tossed around' are more elusive, though the Boys themselves advanced some views.

Family and schooling were considered to be critical factors. Alex attributed his relative desistance from offending as a teenager, and the values and boundaries which have informed his life as an adult, to having a much older father; for him, it was a matter of generations. His father was 42 when he was born:

> So he was fifties when I was in school whereas everyone else's father would have been thirties – different generation. My father had different standards, he was particular about right and wrong. He believed in manners. He used to ram that sort of thing down my throat.

Derek supported this contention, for he had spent a lot of his childhood with his grandmother, arguing that *her* wartime upbringing had instilled in *him* values of thrift and the importance of hard work: 'I like to think I've got a lot of her in me, in the ways I show respect for people and don't take anything for granted'.

Both Shaun and Pete suggested their capacity for debate and argument derived firmly from their family backgrounds, though these were very different. Shaun attributed it to his large family, believing his ensuing 'competitiveness' had prepared him well for his subsequent occupational career and educational success:

> Well I wouldn't say my life is a portfolio of achievement. But I do like studying. And I like to win an argument! It's competitiveness. I come from a family of eight. I can always get my opinion across and that's because of training as a kid . . . you had to raise your voice to get heard. And later it became a challenge for me to try to climb out of, away from, my circle of friends. Because I knew I could do better than that. I always wanted to prove myself, just like I had to when I was a kid.

Shaun's family may have been large, but at least it was 'functional', whereas Pete came from a completely 'dysfunctional' family riddled with potentially damaging experiences, but out of this he distilled elements which had given him confidence and self-assurance, including the courage to assert his homosexuality. He has had to deal with significant trauma in his life but has proved resilient. He now speaks with a clipped, virtually middle-class accent and is transparently gay, shedding almost all vestiges of his roots as a 'Milltown Boy'. The following is a very short extract from his lengthy reflection on his life:

My childhood? Well it wasn't working class, it was underclass. Nine kids, different fathers. My mother was just ahead of her time!

Seriously though, it's very hard to talk about. But in fact we did talk about a lot of things. See, we never had a television, so you had to talk. There was always conversation in our house. It gave me the confidence to speak that I have always had. And it was that that probably helped me to come out when I was about 17.

I've always been lucky, but I'm only now beginning to realize just how lucky I was. I could have been a closet queer in Milltown all my life!

Yeah, I've had a good life and I've done more than I ever dreamed, more than any kid I know. And largely that was being gay because it forced my hand. If I hadn't been gay I might never have got out of Milltown. And I might never have come out as gay if I hadn't got such a big gob. I've always had the confidence to speak out when I've needed to.

The perverse, or reverse, effects of a tough family background emerged in other accounts. Tony grew up just round the corner from Pete, and is now a successful businessman, yet his mother was a single parent and most of his siblings have had unsuccessful marriages. He believes the stability in his adult life derives from his wife's side of the family, certainly not his own:

I am proud of the stability I have achieved. I have definitely worked at it. I don't like the idea of failure. That's a key thing about me and I have to say that my whole family is, in many ways, a history of failures. My mum's marriage failed and every other member of my family's marriages failed. Some of them were a complete disaster. But me and Angie have stayed together and I think that's partly to do with her side. Her mum and dad are still together. And families have histories, don't they. We have values about what a family should be and I think that comes from her. I've learned a lot from her side of the family.

Adverse family experiences have certainly produced in some of the Boys a gritty determination that the patterns would not be repeated in their own family life. Mal said he had had 'the worst upbringing anyone could ever have in their life', for his father was a violent bully, resorting to lashing him with a knotted rope whenever the whim took him to do so:

All I learned from my father was the discipline and his violent temper. He would have you sitting like in court. He was everything, the prosecution, the judge, the fucking lot, the solicitor. And he would sentence you. You couldn't win. All you were worried about was how many lashes you were going to get. When he said ten you were happy with that – sometimes you had forty. You daren't fucking move or turn away or you'd get more.

Mal was resolute in ensuring his own children did not grow up in fear of him, and had never smacked either of his daughters: 'I have never wanted to end up behaving like him. I think we have made a good life for our kids and I have made a better life for myself'. Similarly, although Denny's first two relationships were unsuccessful, he has always tried to forge the family life he wanted, free from risk and fear, for as a child, he was regularly locked all night in the electric cupboard and whipped with electric cable: 'I don't ever want my own kids to be scared of me'.

Both negative and positive family experiences, then, engendered in at least some of the Boys attributes and attitudes which enabled them to assert particular proactive orientations towards their lives. This permitted them to engage in some level of 'life management' in personal, domestic and occupational arenas, rather than simply succumbing to the often negative and stereotypical expectations of the neighbourhood.

Schooling also played its part in contributing to a capacity for such 'life management', for it is fairly clear that the Catholic school Boys have generally done rather better in their lives than those who attended the comprehensive school. This applies to virtually all aspects of their lives (education, employment, housing and relationships), yet many grew up cheek by jowl with the other Boys, in exactly the same social milieu and from very similar families. Jamie suggested forcefully it was their schooling that made the difference:

> I think we were more intelligent . . . well the school made us more intelligent! It was a better school. The Boys at the comp used to go to school in jeans and T-shirts and we used to have to wear uniform. It was more strict. It set a different standard, I think. I mean, it didn't make us goody two-shoes but we were never big-time thieves, like Ted's gang were. I done stealing as well, but more for a laugh than anything else. We never screwed old ladies' houses or went robbing gas meters. And it wasn't because we had more money. I mean, my parents weren't rich. We were just the same as the other Boys in that way. Yeah, I think it was something to do with the school.

Eddie concurred with the view that the Catholic school had been more effective in engendering boundaries: 'there was more discipline, yeah, we did learn the difference between right and wrong although we didn't always keep to it'. Mack and Marty had certainly *not* 'kept to it', aligning themselves to the comprehensive Boys from around the age of 12, while Spaceman subsequently also spiralled out of control. The nine Boys from the Catholic school did, however, acknowledge it had been more effective in setting moral and behavioural boundaries through its approach to school uniform and attendance, and its emphasis on 'discipline'.

Such 'discipline' and an emergent self-discipline served many of the Catholic Boys well, though they usually attributed their greater success both to better judgement and more luck. Gordon felt he had been 'lucky' in his life, but also asserted he had 'always been able to take everything absolutely in my stride . . . no events, nothing ever startles me . . . I've always been able to deal with whoever, whatever'. Kelvin also felt he had had good luck 'but I also make things happen, I don't just wait for them . . . if you waited, you might end up waiting for ever'. In a somewhat more sophisticated analysis, Tony suggested luck was, at least in part, a product of making the effort:

> I feel for people like Marty and Spaceman and I try to be understanding. But I also think people need to help themselves. I mean, if you look at a place like Milltown, with the poverty and that, then you've got to expect the crime. You would expect to have some Marty's and Danny's. But if you look at the people I grew up with, well there's maybe one or two who've gone right down and maybe one or two who've made it. Life's about breaks, isn't it, and some people get them and some people don't. But it's also about effort. Although I know some people put in the effort but they still don't get the breaks. And perhaps that makes them give up. But maybe I am just being too kind. In a way, if you make the effort, you also make the breaks for yourself.

A number of the Boys from the comprehensive school eventually achieved similar levels of legitimate success to many of the Catholic Boys, and they, too, maintained their achievements were a product of both application and good fortune, though they were less clear about where such self-direction and self-determination had come from. Nevertheless, they distinguished themselves from many of the other Boys in terms of the personal effort they had invested in making 'something' for themselves. Gary, for example, who perhaps acquired some of his 'life management' ethos from an early association with the Catholic Boys, said things had been 'hard' for many years but had eventually worked out:

> I have been lucky, but it hasn't always been bloody rosy, although it's comfortable now. I haven't got to worry. If the telly went, or the washing machine I could replace it. But I will always remember that I have been in that position where I never had that. It's bleeding hard out there and I've been there. I've been on the dole, but I've always worked hard. Some of the Boys think it's come easy for me – they see me now in the Range Rover and think 'oh he's got a bit of poke' – but I just tells them that you get out of life what you put in, don't you.

Jerry held a similar perspective, advancing his typically quirky style of argument, which is nevertheless persuasive:

> It all depends on what you want out of life. I am a great believer that there is nothing out there a working man cannot have. Whether he want to go on a cruise or go on Concorde he can afford it if he saves. I am not saying he can afford a jumbo jet but he can still have the pleasure of a thirty-minute flight for a couple of hundred quid. You can have a *taste* of anything. There is nothing out there that's not within my grasp if I

want it. If you work for it, you can get it. We've done what we wanted to do. It might take me eighteen months but once we have set our stall out we go for it. I've been good in that sense, you know.

Jerry maintained he had always 'followed my own mind', a position also taken by the likes of Trevor, Shaun, Denny and Mal. This had required some dislocation from the Boys, though it had not demanded a complete fracturing of those relationships, but inevitably they had set themselves somewhat apart as they had pursued different aspirations in the labour market, family life and leisure.

These Boys from both the Catholic and comprehensive schools largely established an *incremental* approach to their life management, which has proved to be self-reinforcing and self-confirming over time. Others established or cemented such an approach only after some rather more dramatic, or at least, transforming, moments in their lives – what the Boys refer to as 'wake-up time' – which have occurred relatively early in some lives, much later in others. Jerry's hard drinking, free-spending life as a young adult came to an end when his daughter was born and evidence of her profound disabilities started to emerge, while Gary started to take more responsibility for his life when his father died when he was 25. Trevor had 'walked away' from a stolen car, in which he and two mates had been driving, when he thought about his aunt who was visiting from the United States:

> I thought, I can't get caught with these now, imagine her, you know, the humiliation, she has come all that way to see us and I'm in prison . . . little things like that. I started to think.

In his late twenties, after a sequence of prison sentences fuelled by alcohol, Nick gave up drinking and became 'a better person', reverting to the character he says he had always wanted to be:

> After I lost my job on the windows and I was just hanging round with Danny and the Boys my father used to say I was a three-time loser . . . I was. People used to say what a nice guy when he's sober but fucking keep away from him when he's drunk. And then I raised my hand to Karen, which is something I'd promised myself I'd never do. It was something my father did to my mother and I thought what a hypocritical twat I'd turned out to be. So, for that and other reasons [the prison sentence for violence], I stopped the booze. And I'm proud of a lot of the things that I've achieved since, even though the kids thing [their inability to adopt children because of his criminal record] is a terrible cross to bear. But I've worked hard, we've had good holidays, I give proper respect to Karen . . . You know, when I was a child I didn't see myself as turning into the kind of person I became – you know, hard man, big drinker, the good fighter. But that's what I was and I'm glad I'm not that sort of person any more. I'm glad I've finally become the person I am, maybe the person I've always really wanted to be.

Ryan also commented on the cultural pressures to be a 'hard, tough man', observing 'if you haven't got no brains you've got to live another way'. For many years, he lived by his wits in the public sphere, doing housing scams and labouring on the fiddle, until his back injury 'forced' a return to factory work. Though he detests the job, it has provided him with an opportunity to retreat more into a domestic sphere, since he now has the financial stability to follow his leisure interests and contemplate purchasing his house. Moreover, he no longer has to be the hard man: 'yeah, for all that time I was a big tough man but it wasn't really what I wanted to be. Now I've got a regular job, I don't have to be like that no more'.

There has been a lot of personal tragedy in and around the Boys' lives. Beyond the seven of the Boys who have died, Mark's older brother, an alcoholic, committed suicide, while Danny's older brother, who had learning difficulties, died of a brain haemorrhage. These inevitably provided moments for reflection and *sometimes* produced 'wake-up time'. Matt tackled his crack cocaine addiction only when, a few years ago, his father turned up at his house with two suitcases, homeless after his house had been repossessed:

> Yeah, he was losing his house and there was me wasting my money on crack. I think that was the start of me fucking thinking about it . . . like when you wake up in life and you see all the things you could have done and the things you fucking done instead. I mean, I could have bought the fucking house. Yeah, that was when I started to think that I should be doing something different.

Matt has since made a concerted effort to stay clean from drugs, though he has hovered on the edge of the labour market, noting he had 'even' cleaned public toilets – a humbling activity for a proud black man – to earn some (quasi-)legitimate money, for the first time in fifteen years, in order to pay for one of his sons to go on a football trip abroad.

Wake-up time came belatedly to Spaceman, in his late thirties, until when he had, in his words, lived 'existentially', exploring 'every corner of life's rich tapestry'. Always the yobbish intellectual among the Boys, he had done everything to the extreme and paid a heavy price for it in terms of drug and alcohol dependency, and imprisonment, though his only real regret was that once he had joined some of the other Boys in the burglary of a private house. Thieving and robbing and fighting had otherwise been his life – for good and for bad. Throughout his twenties and thirties he descended rapidly into 'a world of pissheads and druggies and fucking robbers and working class yobos', until wake-up time came in 1996. What follows are some extracts from his lengthy and profound self-reflection around the moment when he averted the trajectory of his life which almost certainly would otherwise have killed him prematurely:

I was back in the nick for assaulting a security guard. I got twelve months. And that was when my father was taken ill with cancer. He was dying. It is only when something like that happens that you realize how helpless you are.

Spaceman secured a sympathy visit to see his father, though this was largely a pretext to get some drugs, which he arranged to be delivered to the hospital. To his own surprise, however, he refused to accept them:

It was a confusing thing, because every time before I'd have snapped the opportunity. *But my old man dying was a turning point*, although he didn't die when I was in prison. He lived for another few months. I got out and I was still pissed up all the time. I was just full of self-pity but I think the turning point was still my father dying. I was fucking stinking. I was addicted to everything but mainly the booze, although I'd take anything else that came my way. And then my father died and in the next six, seven weeks I was rushed into hospital about five times. I was completely fucked. I'd lost contact with all my friends. I'd just bummed off them. I didn't see them as friends any more; they were just people that had money that could get me booze. It was fucking dreadful times. It was June 1996 and I was on my rock bottom. I was drinking as soon as my eyes were open. I had bottles of vodka, bottles of port, sherry, cider, cheap and nasty fucking stolen booze – you name it and I would just fucking whack it down me.

These are Spaceman's explanations for why he finally started to turn his life around, and he also reflected on why he embarked on his self-destructive trajectory in the first place, pointing to a sense of being trapped between two worlds:

I never felt like I was fucking normal, even when I was in school. I always felt like I was one of the Boys in a way but I always felt outside being one of the Boys as well. I did everything the Boys did but deep in my head I always had my own fucking rules, which was nothing like theirs. You know, it wasn't just football, clubbing and fucking. I was always interested in books. I'd fucking eat books for breakfast, do you know what I mean? But you can't imagine talking to Danny or someone like Mack about nature or fucking existentialism, stuff like that, the great poets – you just can't. They wouldn't know, would they? It wouldn't mean anything to them. They've never read a book in their lives. Well maybe they have but if they have, it'd be about the Kray twins or something like that. But you don't expect them to either. I mean, I am not dissing them guys at all. I am just saying that when I was a kid growing up they diss'd me for that. They'd say what are you reading that fucking bollocks, poofy bollocks, like, and that's the kind of attitude I had when I was growing up. *So basically I was too rough to be with the toffs and I was too poncy to be really part of one of the Boys*. It was, like, 'poncy art – who wants to do that?'

Rediscovering his art, and being recognized and valued for his inventiveness and talent, has transformed Spaceman's identity and sense of self. He has finally become the person he wanted to be:

This is my third year of studying and I fucking love it. I wouldn't change it for the world. And the great thing about it is that people just see me for what I fucking am, you know, a nice fucking bloke and a good artist. I'm good at it and I know what I am talking about and I can fucking stand my ground. Look at that painting over there [a self-portrait of a face in agony behind bars]. Some of them ask me what that is about. And I tell them it is me when I was in a fucking prison cell knowing that my father was dying of cancer and I couldn't fucking get out. That picture sums up everything, chained, not knowing what the fuck was going on, I couldn't do anything. And asking myself, why am I here? What has got me here? See, my painting is passionate because I've got my life to base it on. That's why it's so good. With other students, they've got to use their imagination. I can fucking use what's happened to me.

The extent to which the Boys exercised, and were able to exercise, control over their lives undulated over time, sometimes growing incrementally, sometimes dipping and resurfacing again, sometimes rarely evident at all. Whether or not their capacity for life management was, from their perspective, rooted in specific family and schooling experiences, it is very clear it was *personal* moments in the life course, rather than any structural or policy-related interventions, which engendered potential for change in this direction. The collapse of Shaun's first marriage was the catalyst for a reappraisal of his life course. The loyalty displayed by his employer when Mark was remanded in custody cemented his commitment to a workplace despite the appalling wages he received. Richard reassessed his use of cannabis and socializing with the Boys when his younger son chose to come and live with him. These were rarely the dramatic wake-up calls experienced by the likes of Matt or Spaceman, but they constituted some impetus for considering the direction of their lives, which otherwise simply ticked on day to day in routines established over many years.

Conclusion

Myriad influences have come to bear on the life course of the Boys in different ways and at different times, sometimes to positive effect, sometimes not. The judgement of what is 'positive' is, however, open to interpretation, for external perspectives may fail to acknowledge more 'internal' positions. This chapter has been very much about the Boys' own anticipations about their own futures and those of their children, and their reflections on their past. Their hopes for the future are very much vested in their children, while, for themselves, most hope for little more than the consolidation of their current circumstances. They have mixed regrets, often wishing they had paid more attention to their educational opportunities, but equally asserting that life has taken its course and there was not so much they could have done about it. This conveys the general sense of fatalism within the Boys, yet their own self-reflection indicates some have made more concerted efforts to shape the direction of their lives than others, with their family and schooling backgrounds considered to be significant in providing a foundation for doing so, alongside those personal moments which prompted some reappraisal of direction, or more profound experiences which represented wake-up time.

The Boys may all have grown up in the same area and been broadly exposed to the same influences but contrary to Ryan's assertion, they were certainly not 'all the same'. On both sides of the criminal divide, some made efforts to maximize moments of possibility and, through doing so, have created their own luck, while others have just been lucky and availed themselves of the breaks which have come their way. Some of the Boys, however, have had few breaks and made little effort, passively accepting the circumstances which constrained their options and opportunities, and a small minority have succumbed completely to the disadvantages which initially affected them all.

-14-

Conclusions – Did the Boys Keep Swinging?

Introduction

The Boys, collectively, had a sustaining love of David Bowie. Indeed, only Jerry dissented from this perspective, preferring Elvis Presley. In the original account of their teenage lives (1973–78), the book was framed by Bowie's songs, with the conclusion to the opening chapter headed 'Boys Keep Swinging?', for this is what they had sought to do, still congregating occasionally on the weekends, into their early twenties, for a night on the town (see Introduction). Even then, however, their lives were already moving in very different directions. Their lives since the early 1980s have been characterized by both continuities and change, and revisiting the Boys provided an opportunity to plumb the depths of that life course, through attention to both their public and private worlds. Judgements as to whether or not the Boys kept 'swinging', even on the basis of the impressive breadth and depth of the information they provided, remain subjective, though I am convinced their story should lead us to celebrate resilience and relative success, as much as to commiserate with risk and abject failure. Others, no doubt, may interpret this material rather differently.

Divergent Paths

It would have been possible to write even more about the Milltown Boys, for though the picture portrayed is, I hope, illuminating in providing coverage of key aspects of their lives, it is by no means complete. During the research interviews, perspectives and experiences were gathered on many other issues and themes, such as the Boys' political and religious beliefs, their 'community involvement' and ideas about neighbourhood renewal, and their attitudes to those professionals (social workers, police officers, solicitors and so on) who have sought to influence their lives.

The Boys did not believe in 'false prophets' – either politicians or priests. They had rarely voted and felt that politicians were unlikely to do anything for them. Most said that they did not believe in God, though, as in most aspects of their lives, they kept their options open – just in case! Few did much for their local community, though some played a part in organizing sporting activities in which their children were involved. Their analysis of 'community decline' resonated strongly with that of public policy, though their 'solutions' were more extreme, one way or the other, with some arguing for greater social provision, especially for young people, while others advocated more punitive responses. When Colin seemed to be suggesting some version of Islamic justice for young thieves and was asked for clarification, he said 'oh no, I wouldn't cut off their hands, just their fingers first'. The majority of professionals (from prison officers to employment advisers) were viewed with suspicion, for it was alleged they lacked any proper understanding of the Boys' circumstances, both past and present, and were routinely depicted as 'hard bastards to be avoided or soft touches to be exploited'.

The Boys' worlds have been made for themselves by themselves. They have endeavoured to make the best of the situations they encountered, and generally feel they have done pretty well in the circumstances. In view of the starting points in their lives, most believe they have 'battled' reasonably successfully against the odds. Indeed, given the prevailing social and economic circumstances they experienced as children, most *have* done reasonably well, for, whether legitimately or illegally, or on the borders, they have found ways of 'getting by'. Some, however, have succumbed to adversity, though many, quite justifiably, maintain that at least they have survived, while a few have patently done rather more than that. In broad terms, the Milltown Boys fall into three categories in terms of their life course trajectories (Table 14.1).

These are, of course, 'ideal types', for there is overlap between these categories, with few of the Boys falling completely and unequivocally into one category or another. Indeed, some fall *too* far outside any of these categories to be included in any of them. Moreover, Table 14.1 suggests on first reading that Group 1 reflects the success story, Group 3 the unsuccessful of the Boys, while Group 2 lies somewhere in the middle.

There have certainly been more 'casualities' in Group 3, though both Ted and Danny would contend that their lives have been reasonably successful, even if they have had to 'make it' on the wrong side of the tracks. In contrast, though Mark has ticked along in the middle, he would say that life has been a struggle. Colin, still living at home with his mother, has never married and has no children, though, as a result, his modest income is sufficient to finance a mundane lifestyle down the pub; in other circumstances, he also would be struggling. Spaceman's history presents a *prima facie* picture, at least until the late 1990s, of despair and desperation, yet he would be the first to challenge this, maintaining that until the drugs and alcohol really took hold, he had lived his life to the full. Matt, conversely, states that he has 'wasted' his life as a result of his drug addiction, hardly knowing where the last twenty years have gone.

Tony, prominent among the apparently 'successful' Boys, admits to still being riddled with insecurity, unsure he deserves his success and uncertain about his real

Table 14.1 A Classification of the Boys – Three Clusterings within the Life Course

Group 1: *Tony*, *Gordon*, Gary, Shaun, *Kelvin*, *Jamie*, Jerry, Mal, **Trevor**

Successful legitimate employment
Owner-occupation
Desistance from crime
Stable long-standing personal relationships
Active attention to children's education
More private and family-oriented leisure
Better health/less health risk behaviour

Group 2: Ryan, Derek, Alex, Mark, Denny, Tommy, **Richard**, Colin

Regular but often changing employment on the margins of the labour market
Social housing
Passive contact with crime (i.e. receiving stolen goods)
Relatively stable but 'separate' personal relationships
Passive acceptance of children's education
Social life within the orbit of the 'respectable' working men's club
Moderate health/greater health risk behaviour (drinking and smoking)

Group 3: **Vic**, Danny, Ted, *Mack*, **Matt**, **Nathan**, **Paul**

Very erratic employment (if any); making a living 'on the street'
Social housing
Active criminality and experience of imprisonment
Multiple and 'separate' personal relationships
Limited contact or loss of contact with children
Social life bound up with criminal enterprise around the pub
Increasingly poor health/greater health risk behaviour (drugs, drinking and smoking)

Beyond this classification: Nick, *Eddie*, *Spaceman*, Nutter, Pete, *Marty*

Catholic school Boys: *italics*
Black or mixed race: **bold**

competence, which is the reason he has never applied for other jobs beyond the company he has remained with all his life. In contrast, Shaun, another of the most successful of the Boys, does possess such certainty in his abilities, to the point where he has stayed working as a 'humble' electrician, despite holding an honours degree in electrical engineering.

Caution must therefore be exercised in passing judgement on the Boys on the basis of some extraneous measures of success (or failure), for the most significant finding from this study is the complex interaction between the life-course trajectories in the public domain and those within more private spheres. These have knitted together in multiple ways for the Boys, both positively and negatively, shedding light on the urgent need to *relate* trajectories in, for example, the labour market to those in, for example, family life, and casting doubt on the credence of analyses which do not do so. It would be so simple to portray the lives of the Boys as delinquents, drug addicts and dropouts, invoking appropriate theories of deviance and exclusion, but the issues and explanations underpinning such processes are integrally tied to the lives of the Boys as fathers, family men and friends. These latter roles influenced, and were influenced by, the former – sometimes propelling or sustaining the Boys' criminality, substance misuse, and economic activity on the edge, though equally, sometimes causing them to refrain and desist from such activity, and move in a different direction. Similar arguments can and should be applied to relationships between the housing and labour markets and, indeed, health behaviours and leisure. It is a complex spider's web (Figure 14.1), within which cause and effect is often difficult to ascertain, but where the interaction is absolutely evident, though invariably suppressed when attention is given solely to one 'strand' or another.

Illustrations from the Boys' accounts of their lives of this rather self-evident observation are legion. Ryan's bad back forced him to alter his employment trajectory, just as Vic's respiratory illness put paid to his regular enjoyment of rugby. The break-up of Paul's relationships gave him no respite from his heavy drinking. Neither Ted nor Danny have been able to purchase their own houses because their resources derived from their criminal enterprise. Trevor reverted briefly to offending (credit card fraud) during a spell of unemployment, in the 'interests' of his family. Nick's love for Karen was the catalyst for his abstinence from drinking

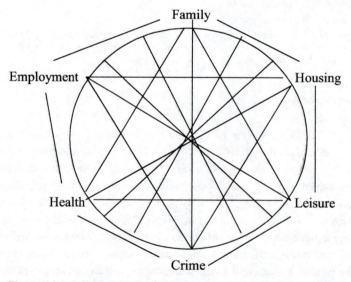

Figure 14.1 A Spider's Web of Relationships that Influence the Life Course

(and thereby also his offending). Marty's schizophrenia and Spaceman's drug addiction cut them off from their friends. Eddie's fragile mental health limited his capacities in the labour market, while Pete's homosexuality broadened his horizons. The disability of Jerry's daughter accelerated his move into private housing ownership, though he could hardly afford it. Alex's poorly remunerated self-employment was unlikely to change because it gave him the freedom to follow his beloved Arsenal.

The Boys had multiple identities across these different 'life domains', each of which was influenced or constrained by others, though it was their public face by which they were best known – their hard personas which, as some bravely admitted, had not always been entirely of their own choosing. It is this public face which so often, arguably too often, informs accounts of men and boys who are living at the edge. Infrequently, if ever, are more private layers underneath probed sufficiently, something which, in 1980, McRobbie (1980) argued still needed to be explored.

Beyond these elementary though critical observations, I cannot offer any significant advance on theoretical formulations concerning social exclusion, risk and the life course. What this study does, however, is to raise important questions about the validity and persuasiveness of a range of contemporary 'established' theories within youth research and within broader social theory. Perhaps others will make use of this comprehensive empirical account to further such considerations. Sociological explanations for the lives of the Milltown Boys seem at times hard to sustain, and there is a strong temptation to lean towards more psychological perspectives on why some of the Boys 'escaped' from their apparently predestined socio-structural condition and why others did not. Even within the different levels of success and achievement, some have made more of their presenting and past circumstances than others.

Conclusion

Times move on and so have the Boys. At the time of writing, it is well over three years since the fieldwork was conducted. In an *ad-hoc* way, however, I have kept in touch with the Boys, whose lives and those of their children continue to unfold in both anticipated and unexpected ways. You will still find Denny in the club and Danny down the pub. Mack's son continues to excel at pool. In the summer you can be sure to find Nutter having a drink by the river in the woods, while Marty is still sitting purposelessly in his run-down flat.

Few of the Boys have changed their economic activities, with the exception of Mal, who has given up his factory job and become a taxi driver. Spaceman got his degree and has displayed his art at a national exhibition; although he is still unemployed, he is no longer so lonely, for he is once again socializing (without drinking) with some of the Boys. Pete has also cemented his renewed relationships with the Boys, visiting Milltown regularly and even putting in an appearance in The Fountain, something he would have thought impossible a few years ago.

Mark married Veronica in August 2001, commenting somewhat caustically that he wanted to get married before his (16-year-old) daughter did. Matt has left Camilla, and now rents a room from an old friend. Nathan has also split up with his partner, so he is no longer even an owner-occupier 'by proxy', living once more in private rented accommodation.

Nick and Karen have moved off the estate to a slightly better rented flat not far away. Gary has also moved, to a large four-bedroomed house in a new private housing development on the other side of the estate, though he has kept his old house (the one in which he was born and brought up) and rents it out.

Marty is more diligent about taking his medication and also has a professional carer, who takes him out occasionally. His highspot in 2003 was when he went to see Bowie at the National Exhibition Centre in Birmingham. Around the same time, Ted was sentenced to twenty-one months in prison for 'intent to supply', writing to me that this was the 'last time', because he was getting 'too old for this game'. Paul has also done another spell in prison.

Meanwhile, Danny became a father for the second time, while both Tommy and Trevor became grandfathers, as their 16-year-old daughters abandoned low-level vocational courses in favour of motherhood.

Danny also passed his driving test (though he has been driving all his life!) with a view to possibly getting a legitimate job, now that his daughter has gained a scholarship to the elite girls' public school which Tommy's youngest daughter had attended. 'Had' because, just before taking her GCSEs, Vanessa dropped out. She had set her hopes on becoming an army officer but her middle-class schoolmates condemned the war in Iraq, questioning its legitimacy, in the process undermining Vanessa's confidence to go on. She left school with no qualifications to the chagrin of her mother and the manifest annoyance of her father, who had always quietly recognized the golden educational opportunity Vanessa's scholarship conferred. Now it has been lost, Vanessa is living with her boyfriend and working in a shop.

Jerry and Sam's younger daughter Chloe also left school, to their great disappointment, after completing her GCSEs, for they had pressed her to continue with her A levels. She left home and moved into a flat with her boyfriend, a lad Jerry describes, in his anger and frustration, as a 'complete waster'.

Their older daughter, Rachael, continues to receive special care and education. A charming, smiling young woman, she is always fully included in local social events, and on her eighteenth birthday was made an honorary life member of the local working men's club – the only woman on whom such a status has ever been bestowed.

On another positive front, Mal's eldest daughter, Natasha, achieved two modest A levels, about which both Mal and his wife are immensely proud, for they are the first ever in the family. Natasha has taken time out, before perhaps going to university, to be a holiday rep in the Mediterranean, despite her mother's anxiety about her going so far away. Tony's two daughters have progressed with their education, though the older of the two, Katy, did not go on to university as he had hoped, despite gaining two A levels, and is instead working in an office. Like some of the other children of the more successful Boys, *their* children will have little idea at all about the origins of their grandfathers. For others, the circle is turning in more foreseeable ways and little will appear to have changed.

Bibliography

Ashton, D. and Field, D. (1976), *Young Workers*, London: Hutchinson.

Ashton, D. and Maguire, M. (1983), *The Vanishing Youth Labour Market*, London: Youthaid.

Ashton, D., Maguire, M. and Spilsbury, M. (1990), *Restructuring the Labour Market: The implications for Youth*, London: Macmillan.

Campbell, B. (1993), *Goliath: Britain's Dangerous Places*, London: Methuen.

Carter, K. and Delamont, S. (eds) (1996), *Qualitative Research: The Emotional Dimension*, Aldershot: Ashgate.

Cloward, R. and Ohlin, L. (1961), *Delinquency and Opportunity*, London: Routledge & Kegan Paul.

Evans, K. and Furlong, A. (1997), 'Metaphors of Youth Transitions: Niches, Pathways, Trajectories or Navigations', in J. Bynner, L. Chisholm and A. Furlong (eds), *Youth, Citizenship and Social Change in a European Context*, Aldershot: Ashgate.

Field, J. (2000), *Lifelong Learning and the New Educational Order*, Stoke-on-Trent: Trentham Books.

Furlong, A. and Cartmel, F. (1997), *Young People and Social Change: Individualisation and Risk in Late Modernity*, Buckingham: Open University Press.

Glaser, N. (1956), 'Criminality Theory and Behavioural Images', *American Journal of Sociology*, 61: 433–44.

Helve, H. and Bynner, J. (eds) (1996), *Youth and Life Management: Research Perspectives*, Helsinki: Helsinki University Press.

Herbert, D. and Evans, D. (1973), *Urban Environment and Juvenile Delinquency*, report for the Home Office Research Unit, Department of Geography, Swansea: University of Swansea.

Istance, D., Rees, G. and Williamson, H. (1994), *Young People not in Education, Training or Employment in South Glamorgan*, Cardiff: South Glamorgan Training and Enterprise Council.

Johnston, L., MacDonald, R., Mason, P., Ridley, L. and Webster, C. (2000), *Snakes and Ladders: Young People, Transitions and Social Exclusion*, Bristol: Policy Press.

Lee, G. and Wrench, J. (1981), *Skill Seekers*, Leicester: National Youth Bureau.

MacDonald, R. and Coffield, F. (1991), *Risky Business: Youth and the Enterprise Culture*, London: Routledge.

McRobbie, A. (1980), 'Settling Accounts with Subcultures: A Feminist Critique', *Screen Education*, 34: 37–49.

Manpower Services Commission (1977), *Young People and Work: Report on the Feasibility of a New Programme of Opportunities for Unemployed Young People* (Holland Report), London: Manpower Services Commission.

Mars, G. (1983), *Cheats at Work: An Anthropology of Workplace Crime*, London: Unwin Paperbacks.

Matza, D. (1964), *Delinquency and Drift*, New York: John Wiley.

Social Exclusion Unit (2000), *National Strategy for Neighbourhood Renewal: Report of Policy Action Team 12 – Young People*, London: The Stationery Office.

Sutherland, E. and Cressey, D. (1966), *Principles of Criminology*, Philadelphia, PA: Lippincott.

Sykes, G. and Matza, D. (1957), 'Techniques of Neutralization: A Theory of Delinquency', *American Sociological Review*, 22: 614–70.

Williams, S. (1973, 1977) *The Cardiff Book*, vols 1 and 3, Barry: Stewart Williams.

Williamson, H. (1978), 'Choosing to be a Delinquent', *New Society*, 9 November.

Williamson, H. (1980), 'Why Kids Plead Guilty', *Community Care*, 10 July.

Williamson, H. (1981), 'Juvenile Justice and the Working Class Community', unpublished PhD thesis, University of Wales.

Williamson, H. (1982), 'Client Responses to the Youth Opportunities Programme', in T. Rees and P. Atkinson (eds), *Youth Unemployment and State Intervention*, London: Routledge and Kegan Paul.

Williamson, H. (1997), *Youth and Policy: Context and Consequences*, Aldershot: Ashgate.

Williamson, H. and Williamson, P. (1981), *Five Years*, Leicester: National Youth Bureau.

Willis, P. (1978), *Learning to Labour: How Working Class Kids Get Working Class Jobs*, Farnborough: Saxon House.

Index